Hiking
Sequoia and Kings Canyon National Parks

Laurel Scheidt

FALCONGUIDE®

GUILFORD, CONNECTICUT
HELENA, MONTANA

AN IMPRINT OF THE GLOBE PEQUOT PRESS

A FALCON GUIDE ®

Copyright © 2002 by The Globe Pequot Press

Editing and page composition: Laughingwater Ink
Photo credits: Laurel Scheidt and Scott Scheidt
Map credits: Blue Gecko Graphics

Library of Congress Cataloging-in-Publication Data is available.

ISSN 1545-8121
ISBN 0-7627-1122-1

♻ Text pages printed on recycled paper
Manufactured in the United States of America
First Edition/Third Printing

Contents

Hikes in the Giant Forest

Hikes in the Central High Sierra

Hikes in the Lodgepole and Dorst Areas

Hikes in the Grant Grove Area

Hikes in the Redwood Canyon Area

Hikes in the Cedar Grove and Monarch Divide Areas

Acknowledgments

I would like to give special thanks to Debbie Brenchly, Sierra Crest Sub-District Ranger, and Peter B. Stephens, Wilderness Assistant, of Sequoia and Kings Canyon National Parks; Diana Pietrasanta, Wilderness Manager of the Mount Whitney Ranger Station, Inyo National Forest; Heidi Anderson, Visitor Information Supervisor, and Howard Grice, Forest Service volunteer, of the White Mountain Ranger District, Inyo National Forest; Portia Jelinek, Wilderness Ranger for the Pine Ridge Ranger District, Sierra National Forest; and Frank Gruhot, Hiking Trails Coordinator for the Hume Lake Ranger District, Sequoia National Forest, for their help in reviewing the text for this hiking guide.

Also, many thanks to Frank Scozzari for including my husband and me on his Mount Whitney trip, as well as for sharing his campsite, along with friend Rob, at Roaring River. Thanks to Ted for the hot chocolate and his company at the Big Arroyo, and thanks to my German friends for the tea and for inviting me to sit at the campfire at Bearpaw Meadow. Thanks to the many other friendly people I camped with or met along the trails—your names may escape me, but you haven't been forgotten.

I would like to thank my husband, Scott, for putting up with my long absences during the times he could not accompany me and for his encouragement and support. And thanks to my grandmother, Mary Painter, who opened her Fresno home to me during the first summer of research. She had a warm meal waiting for me after every trek into the mountains, even while she was going through chemotherapy. I only wish she could have lived long enough to see this guide published.

Legend

Interstate		Campground	
US Highway		Picnic Area	
State or Other Principal Road		Peak	9,782 ft.
Forest Route	00 00000	Glacier	
Interstate Highway		Elevation	✕
Paved Road		City	◯ City
Gravel Road		Information	
One Way Road	One Way	Ranger Station/ Ranger Cabin	
Main Trail		Cabin/Building	■
Secondary Trail		Gate	•—•
Cross-country Trail		Point of Interest	
Trail Junction/ Entrance Station	□	View/Overlook	
Trailhead/Parking Area	◯ ⓟ	Pass/Saddle	)(
River/Creek/Waterfall		Tree/Grove	
Bridge		Fallen Tree/Log	
Meadow/Marsh		National Forest/ Park Boundary	
Spring			
Dam	▬	Map Orientation	N
Prospect/Mine			
Cave		Scale	0 0.5 1 Miles
Lakes			

Overview Map

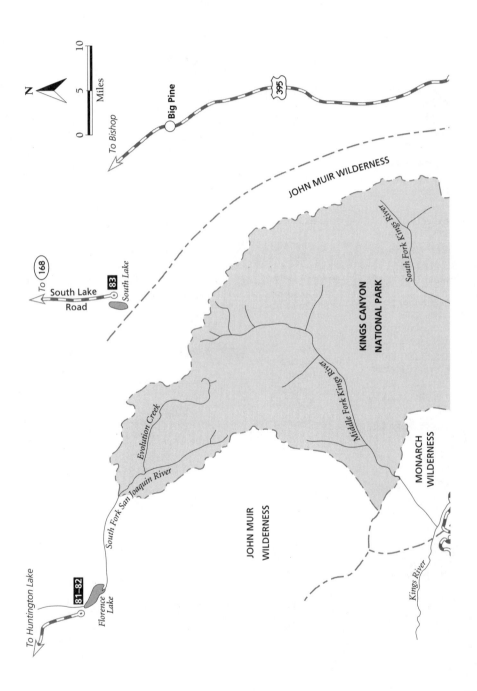

Sequoia and Kings Canyon National Parks

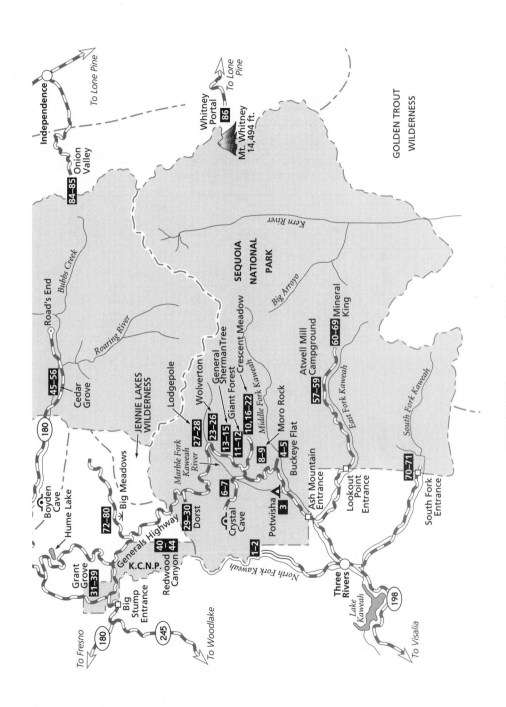

Introduction

Sequoia and Kings Canyon National Parks encompass an area of the Sierra Nevada that is rich in human history, native flora and fauna, and majestic scenery. Whether day hiking or backpacking, each trip holds its own special treasures and memories.

John Muir trekked through the Cedar Grove area and the Giant Forest late in the nineteenth century, preceded by members of the United States Geological Survey. Cabins dating from that era have been maintained or restored throughout the parks for visitors to enjoy. Shepherds and cattlemen forged some of the hiking trails in the years before the parks, and a few trails follow old Native American trading routes. Other trails are on old fire roads that are no longer used for that purpose, and one is actually the old entrance road to Sequoia National Park.

The giant sequoias leave many visitors awestruck at the parks' mid-elevations, while deep glacially carved canyons and austere mountain peaks on the western slopes beckon the explorer. Two forks of the Kings River, four forks of the Kaweah River, and the mighty Kern River all begin in Sequoia and Kings Canyon National Parks. Quiet, shady forests, flower-filled meadows, and cascading waterfalls are along many of the trails. For the hearty backpacker, the drier and more precipitous eastern slope awaits. Here, trails climb over high passes between the craggy peaks on the Sierra Crest.

Mule deer, yellow-bellied marmots, black bears, and the many varieties of squirrel and chipmunk are among the more visible species in the parks, along with an abundance of birds. Coyotes, foxes, bobcats, skunks, and rabbits, as well as many other animals, are a bit more secretive. The most elusive creatures are the mountain lion and the wolverine, the latter only occurring deep in the backcountry.

The main hiking season in Sequoia and Kings Canyon is early summer through fall. Hikes in the lower elevations, such as in the foothills and South Fork areas, are best in the fall and spring. Trails tend to be more crowded on weekends and holidays, and throughout the summer vacation period. The weather can turn at any time, so be prepared! A sunny day can turn into a cold and rainy one without much warning at higher elevations. Bears and mountain lions live in these parks and if you happen to see them, observe them from a safe distance. Rattlesnakes and ticks can be found in the lower elevations; watch your footing in these areas and wear plenty of insect repellent.

Experiencing the backcountry of our national parks can be a very rewarding experience. Tread lightly and enjoy!

PARK HISTORY

Native Americans were the first to discover and inhabit the areas we now know as Sequoia and Kings Canyon National Parks. They were still in the area when it was explored, along with the rest of the Sierra Nevada, by the

California Geological Survey, and were known to the settlers that came up from the San Joaquin Valley, including the cattlemen and shepherds who made the mountains their homes.

One of those settlers was Hale Tharp, who built a homestead and grazed his cattle at Log Meadow, having been led into the Giant Forest by members of the Monachi tribe. Hikers still can visit the historic Tharp's Log (Hike 10), a fire-hollowed sequoia that may have provided shelter for this mountain man.

In the 1870s, John Muir trekked through the area to study the geology and the giant sequoias. During the same decade, the Mineral King area experienced a silver rush, and though very little silver was ever found, the area continued to attract visitors as a resort community.

In the 1880s the loggers came to the area, consumed by the belief that logging the big trees would make them rich. A group of utopian socialists known as the Kaweah Colony laid claim to the Giant Forest, with the intent of logging it. To accommodate this goal, the Colonists began to build a road— by hand—that would lead from the forest to the Three Rivers area. Shortly thereafter, near Grant Grove at Mill Flat Meadow, the Kings River Lumber Company (later known as the Sanger Lumber Company) began work on a mill and reservoir, with plans to log the Converse Basin, which is located outside the present park boundaries. Not long after the mill was completed, construction of a flume began, which eventually stretched 54 miles to the town of Sanger.

George Stewart, the newspaper editor of the *Visalia Delta,* was concerned about the Colonists' logging efforts, and notified the federal government of their plans. In 1890, Sequoia and General Grant National Parks were established, protecting the big trees within both parks and thwarting the Colonists' plans. They had completed their road to the present site of the abandoned Colony Mill Ranger Station and erected a portable sawmill. Logging operations began in spite of the federal protections, and the Colonists were prosecuted for cutting government timber. But once the parks were established they had little hope for success. A few continued to live at Atwell Mill, near Mineral King, before they abandoned the area altogether.

Still, the work of the Kaweah Colonists was incorporated into the parks' landscape. The road they'd built was extended in 1903 to the Giant Forest, and it served as the main entry road into Sequoia National Park until the Generals Highway opened in 1926.

The Sanger Lumber Company had more success. Just after the turn of the twentieth century, the Sanger Lumber Company was purchased by the Hume-Bennett Lumber Company, which went on to create Hume Lake and to build a 17-mile extension of flume to meet Sanger's already existing flume at Millwood. The company logged the Evans Grove area, east of the present boundaries of Kings Canyon National Park.

Another turn-of-the-century notable event occurred when the infamous San Francisco earthquake of 1906 touched off avalanches in the Mineral King Valley, destroying mining operations and leveling the small town of Beulah.

Mount Whitney, seen here from U.S. Highway 395, is both the highest point in the contiguous United States and one of the highlights of Sequoia and Kings Canyon National Parks.

In their earliest years, the parks were patrolled by the U.S. Cavalry. In the early 1900s, Captain Charles Young served as the first park superintendent; at the time, he was the only African-American officer in the U.S. Army. Walter Fry became the first civilian superintendent of the parks in 1914. John Roberts White became superintendent in 1920.

As visitor use increased, the Generals Highway was constructed, opening in 1926. Sequoia National Park was enlarged that year as well—to three times its original size. Construction of the High Sierra Trail, a well-known trans-Sierra route, began shortly thereafter, and the trail reached the top of Mount Whitney in September 1930.

In early 1940, Kings Canyon National Park was established, absorbing General Grant National Park. In 1965, the Big Stump, Tehipite Valley, and Cedar Grove areas were added to the park. Mineral King was the most recent addition to Sequoia National Park; it was added in 1978.

Many park practices have changed over the years—the bears, for instance, are no longer fed at "Bear Hill" for the entertainment of park visitors. Trail quotas and camping regulations have been put in place. Controlled burns of the forest are conducted periodically to reduce fire hazards. The old Giant Forest Lodge has been removed to protect the fragile root systems of the giant sequoias, and some of the park's dirt roads, such as the Kaweah Colonists' old road, are used now only as trails. But in many ways, the lands protected by these national parks remain the same as when the Native Americans roamed here many years ago.

THE GIANT SEQUOIA

The giant sequoia is considered the largest living organism in the world by volume. It can reach 275 feet in height, have a circumference of more than 35 feet, and live two to three thousand years. Only three other species of trees, along with its relative, the coast redwood, grow to a greater height. Only one, the tule cypress, has a greater circumference, and only the bristlecone pine lives longer.

There are about 75 sequoia groves, all located on the western slope of California's Sierra Nevada. Sequoias usually grow in moist, cool locations between 5,000 and 7,000 feet in elevation, which is where you'll find most of the groves in Sequoia National Park.

Sequoias are dependent on fire for reproduction. Fires clear the forest of other conifers that can block sunlight to young sequoias, and clear the duff that carpets the soil of the forest floor. Sequoias retain their cones, and when a fire sweeps through a grove, the heat dries the cones, which then open and release seeds a few days later. Sequoia bark is fire resistant; because of its chemical makeup, the wood also resists decay, usually for more than 100 years.

Unlike the coast redwood, the wood of the sequoia is very brittle. Many of the trees that were logged shattered upon impact; the wood was then used for shingles, railroad ties, fence posts, and grape stakes. Fortunately, logging sequoias was found to be impractical around the turn of the twentieth century, and logging has been discontinued.

TOPOGRAPHIC FEATURES

Mount Whitney, at 14,494 feet, is the highest point in the contiguous United States. It is located on the Sierra Crest in Sequoia National Park. Other peaks topping 14,000 feet also rise along the crest, which forms the eastern border of both Sequoia and Kings Canyon National Parks; these include 14,375-foot Mount Williamson, the second highest peak in the lower forty-eight, which is located just outside the park and north of Mount Whitney. The Palisades, with North Palisade cresting at 14,242 feet, is far to the north in Kings Canyon National Park.

On most of the day hikes in this guide, the Sierra Crest is blocked from view by the Great Western Divide, a formidable range rising to more than 13,000 feet. The Kaweah Peaks rise over this divide near its midsection. The mighty Kern River is located between the Great Western Divide and the Sierra Crest. The Kaweah River, divided into four forks, flows down to the San Joaquin Valley on the west side of the Great Western Divide.

The Silliman Crest, The Tablelands, a short portion of the Great Western Divide, and the Kings-Kern Divide separate Kings Canyon National Park from Sequoia National Park. The Monarch Divide and the Cirque Crest separate two of the three forks of the Kings River that are located in Kings Canyon National Park. Northern Kings Canyon is bordered by Kettle Ridge and the Le Conte Divide in the west, and the Glacier Divide in the north. The Goddard Divide separates the headwaters of the South Fork of the San Joaquin River from the drainage of the Middle Fork of the Kings River.

The giant sequoia is considered the largest living organism on the planet by volume, and it grows to a height of 275 feet.

Planning Your Trip

GETTING TO SEQUOIA AND KINGS CANYON

Sequoia and Kings Canyon National Parks are located in south-central California, in the Sierra Nevada. There are three entrance stations: the Big Stump entrance, just south of Grant Grove on California Highway 180; the Ash Mountain entrance, just north of the town of Three Rivers on California Highway 198; and the Lookout Point entrance on Mineral King Road. Expect to pay a fee at entrance stations; trailheads that begin on other roads leading to the park boundary or national forest areas (excluding portions of the Hume Lake Ranger District) have no fee. The majority of the roads in the park are two-laned and paved, with speed limits of 35 to 45 miles per hour. The exceptions are Crescent Meadow Road (narrow), Mineral King Road (narrow and winding, with dirt sections), and South Fork Drive (dirt inside the park). Forest Service roads can range from paved two-lane roads to rutted dirt logging roads, but all are passable with any two-wheel-drive vehicle.

If you are coming from out of state, the city of Fresno has a small airport with connecting flights to San Francisco and Los Angeles, and a few direct flights from other cities. Both Fresno and the smaller city of Visalia are west of the parks, in the San Joaquin Valley, and have many choices for food and lodging. From Fresno, Kings Canyon National Park can be reached by driving east on CA 180. Sequoia National Park can be reached by turning south onto the Generals Highway beyond the Big Stump entrance to Kings Canyon. From Visalia, Sequoia National Park can be reached by driving east on CA 198 through the town of Three Rivers, which also has food and lodging available. Kings Canyon can be reached by following the Generals Highway, which is the continuation of CA 198, north to Grant Grove and beyond.

Lodging is also available inside the parks at Cedar Grove, Grant Grove, the newly constructed Wuksachi Village, and the privately owned Silver City Resort near Mineral King. In the Sequoia National Forest, the Stony Creek Lodge and the privately owned Montecito Sequoia Lodge are along the Generals Highway, between Kings Canyon and Sequoia in the Sequoia National Forest. The privately owned Kings Canyon Lodge is located on CA 180, between Grant Grove and Cedar Grove, also in the Sequoia National Forest.

Access to the parks from the eastern side of the Sierra Nevada can be made from the towns of Bishop, Big Pine, Independence, and Lone Pine. All of these communities have food and lodging.

The Sequoia Bark, the park's free newspaper, contains details on campgrounds, food, lodging, showers, and laundry facilities. To receive a copy, write or call:

Visitor Information
Sequoia & Kings Canyon National Parks
Three Rivers, CA 93271
(559) 565-3341
www.nps.gov/seki/

GETTING A BACKCOUNTRY PERMIT

For overnight trips into the backcountry, you will need a wilderness permit. For more information, you should call the park at (559) 565-3341 to request the "Backcountry Basics" trip planner. This contains the latest backcountry regulations, locations for picking up permits for each trailhead, fishing regulations, backcountry bear box locations, and other useful information.

Keep in mind that most trailheads are subject to quotas. Popular trailheads may have full quotas during the height of the backpacking season, in which case you won't be able to start your backcountry trek from that trailhead. If you don't make reservations in advance, come with an alternate plan, just in case the quota for the trailhead you wish to start from is full.

Reservations are available for trips starting between May 21 and September 21; otherwise all permits are issued on a first-come, first-served basis. Advance reservations must be made at least 21 days prior to departure and are taken between March 1 and August 31. Reservations are $10 for each permit and are recommended for large groups and for trips that include holiday weekends. Permits also can be picked up the day of the hike at the visitor center or ranger station closest to the trailhead you wish to start from, and are free.

Free permits for hikes beginning on Forest Service lands usually can be picked up from the ranger station closest to the trailhead, with some exceptions. There is a $3 charge for each reserved permit for trailheads in the Sierra National Forest. The Sequoia National Forest does not take reservations. The Inyo National Forest charges $5 per person, and reservations must be made at least two days in advance of your trip. See Appendix A for addresses and phone or fax numbers for each of these forests.

Climbing Mount Whitney requires a special permit, even for day hikes, and must be applied for in advance (reservations are awarded through a lottery held on February 15 of each year). The fee is $15 per person, and this fee is applicable from any trailhead if you enter the Mount Whitney Zone at some point during your trip.

EMERGENCY MEDICAL SERVICES (PERSONAL RESPONSIBILITY)

Visiting natural areas always imposes risks—wild animals, rockslides, falling trees, and sudden changes in weather have the potential for danger. YOU are responsible for your own safety. This means you should take heed of the warnings on bulletin boards, be aware of what is around you, and not exceed your own limits. Dial 911 for any medical emergency.

Using This Guidebook

HOW THIS GUIDE IS ORGANIZED

Hikes that begin in and travel through specific areas of Sequoia and Kings Canyon National Parks are grouped together. The areas are arranged in order of their popularity and accessibility. Some hikes that begin near specific trailheads may be covered in separate chapters. For example, in the case of hikes beginning off the Big Meadows Road, one chapter includes hikes that stay within wilderness area boundaries, and the second covers hikes that travel through a wilderness area into the park.

TYPES OF HIKES

The suggested hikes have been put into three classifications, which are defined below.

Out-and-back: You will be traveling to a specific destination, then retracing your steps back to the trailhead.

Loop: The trail starts and finishes at the same trailhead, with no (or very little) retracing of your steps.

Semi-loop: The route starts and finishes at the same trailhead, and you will retrace your steps along a portion of the trail.

RATINGS

To help you plan your hike, the trails are rated for difficulty. The ratings serve only as a general guide. Bear in mind not just how strenuous a trail is, but how long the hike is as well. Remember, what might be easy to one person could be hard for another. Rating definitions are defined below:

Very easy: These trails are suitable for any hiker, including children and the elderly, with minimal or a very short section of elevation gain.

Easy: Also suitable for any hiker, including children and the elderly, these trails don't have serious elevation gain or places where the trail becomes faint.

Moderate: These routes are suitable for hikers with an average fitness level. The hike may have short sections of faint trail, extended mileage, or increased elevation gain, usually more than 1,000 feet.

Difficult: These trails are suitable for hikers with an above-average fitness level. The hike may have some sections of faint trail, extended mileage, or considerable elevation gain, usually more than 2,500 feet.

DISTANCES

Distances in this guide have been measured from U.S. Geological Survey and park maps. Every effort has been made to be as accurate as possible, but mileages could be slightly off.

MAPS

All hikers should carry a map of the trail they are hiking with them to avoid getting lost. A basic overview map of Sequoia and Kings Canyon by National Geographic/Trails Illustrated (which I have found a few discrepancies on), and inexpensive maps for Giant Forest, Lodgepole, Grant Grove, Cedar Grove, and Mineral King, are available at the parks' visitor centers. For hikes in the foothills, Redwood Canyon, and South Fork areas, USGS quad maps may be purchased; these are also available at visitor centers. The Forest Service sells two separate topographic maps for adjacent wilderness areas: one covers the Jennie Lakes and Monarch Wilderness Areas, and the second covers the John Muir and Sequoia and Kings Canyon Wilderness Areas. These Forest Service maps are available at map stores, sporting goods stores, and Forest Service offices. For those hikers with computers, TOPO! Sequoia Kings Canyon and Surrounding Wilderness Areas covers the entire area and is sold at map stores, sporting goods stores, and online at www.topo.com.

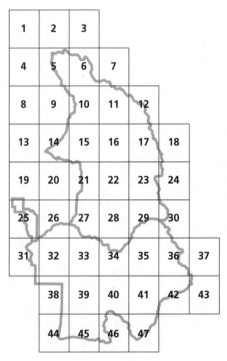

USGS Topographic Maps

1. Florence Lake
2. Mt. Hilgard
3. Mt. Tom
4. Ward Mountain
5. Mt. Henry
6. Mt. Darwin
7. Mt. Thompson
8. Courtright Reservoir
9. Blackcap Mountain
10. Mt. Goddard
11. North Palisades
12. Split Mountain
13. Rough Spur
14. Tehipite Dome
15. Slide Bluffs
16. Marion Peak
17. Mt. Pinchot
18. Aberdeen
19. Hume
20. Wren Peak
21. Cedar Grove
22. The Sphinx
23. Mt. Clarence King
24. Kearsarge Peak
25. General Grant Grove
26. Muir Grove
27. Mt. Silliman
28. Sphinx Lakes
29. Mt. Brewer
30. Mt. Williamson
31. Shadequarter Mountain
32. Giant Forest
33. Lodgepole
34. Triple Divide Peak
35. Mt. Kaweah
36. Mt. Whitney
37. Mt. Langley
38. Case Mountain
39. Silver City
40. Mineral King
41. Chagoopa Falls
42. Johnson Peak
43. Cirque Peak
44. Dennison Peak
45. Moses Mountain
46. Quinn Peak
47. Kern Lake

ELEVATION CHARTS

Elevation charts accompany most of the hikes. These charts do not give a detailed picture of elevation gain and loss, but they do give you a general idea of the ups and downs of the route. If a hike does not have a chart, it is either very short or has minimal elevation gain or loss.

SHARING

Most hikers would like to have the trails all to themselves, but this usually isn't the case. Not only do you share the routes with other hikers, but with horseback riders as well. If you meet horses on the trail, remember that proper trail etiquette requires you to step off the trail on the downhill side and wait quietly until the horses have passed. Stay in plain view of the horses—they may think you are a wild animal and bolt if you are behind a rock or tree or if you startle them.

BACKCOUNTRY REGULATIONS

Backcountry regulations help preserve the wilderness and protect hikers. These regulations will be given to you when you pick up a wilderness permit:

- Pets, weapons, wheeled vehicles, and motorized equipment are prohibited.

- Shortcutting trails is prohibited. Stay on trails to reduce erosion and preserve vegetation. Do not build cairns or other trail markers.

Yellow-bellied marmots live among the rocks in the higher reaches of Sequoia and Kings Canyon National Parks.

- To protect bighorn sheep, all cross-country travel is prohibited above 11,000 feet east of the John Muir/Pacific Crest Trail between Sawmill Pass and Dragon Pass.

- Camp at least 100 feet from water where terrain permits.

- Camp on bare ground, never on vegetation or in meadows. Choose a site screened from trails and other campers if possible. Avoid sites near dead standing trees or overhanging dead limbs.

- Do not construct rock walls, trenches, new fire rings, bough beds, etc.

- Bury human waste 6 inches deep and at least 100 feet from trails, camps, and all water sources.

- Purify all water from natural sources by boiling or by using a filter that eliminates bacteria and the parasite that causes giardiasis.

- Never wash anything directly in a water source—that includes clothes, dishes, or yourself. Carry water 100 feet from the source before washing. Since biodegradable soap pollutes, use and dispose of it away from water sources.

- Pack out all trash.

Campfires

- Use only existing fire rings. Do not build new rings or add rocks to existing fire rings.

- Use only dead wood found on the ground. Do not chop live vegetation or remove branches from standing trees.

- Never leave fires unattended.

- Do not attempt to burn aluminum foil in campfires; it does not burn or break down. Pack it out.

- Plastic emits toxic fumes when burned. Pack out plastic items.

- Put out a fire one half-hour before leaving a campsite by dousing it with water and stirring the ashes. Do not use dirt to put out fires.

Wood fires are PERMITTED in Kings Canyon National Park below 10,000 feet except in Granite Basin and Redwood Canyon.

Wood fires are PERMITTED in Sequoia National Park in the Kaweah Drainage below 9,000 feet. Wood fires are prohibited in the following areas of the park:

- Hamilton Lakes Basin.

- Mineral King Valley above the ranger station.

- Pinto Lake.

Wood fires are PERMITTED in the Kern River drainage below 11,200 feet, but are prohibited at:

- Little Claire Lake within 1,200 feet of the lake.

- Little Five Lakes above 10,400 feet.

- Lower Soldier Lake within 1,200 feet of the lake.

- Milestone Basin and Kern headwaters (north of Milestone Basin junction) above 10,400 feet.

- Miter Basin above 10,800 feet.

- New Army Pass Trail above 10,800 feet. Fires are permitted at the junction of New Army Pass Trail and Rock Creek.

- Nine Lake Basin and Big Arroyo drainage above 10,000 feet.

- Tyndall Creek frog ponds within 1,200 feet of the ponds.

- Tyndall Creek crossing of the John Muir/Pacific Crest Trail within 1,200 feet of the crossing.

- Wallace and Wright Creek above 10,800 feet. Fires are permitted on Wallace Creek up to Waterfall Meadow at 10,860 feet.

Specific Camping Restrictions

- **Emerald Lake, Pear Lake:** Camp in designated sites only.

- **Bearpaw Meadow:** Camp in designated sites only. If none are available, you will have to move on.

- **Hamilton Lakes:** There is a two-night camp limit.

- **Timberline Lake:** Closed to all camping.

- **Eagle Lake:** There is no camping between the trail and shoreline of the lake.

- **Mosquito Lake 1:** Closed to all camping.

- **Hockett Meadow:** There is no camping between the trail and Whitman Creek.

- **Little Claire Lake:** No camping is permitted within 100 feet of the lake.

- **Paradise Valley:** Use designated sites only. There is a two-night stay limit within the valley.

- **Rae Lakes:** There is a two-night limit per lake.

- **Kearsarge Lakes, Charlotte Lake:** There is a two-night camp limit.

- **Bullfrog Lake:** Closed to all camping.

FOOD STORAGE AND BEARS

When bears have access to human food and garbage, they can become destructive or aggressive, and may be killed as a result. It is your responsibility to prevent bears from obtaining your food. Park-approved, bear-proof food storage containers are required in some backcountry areas. See Appendix A for more information.

Please follow these regulations:

- Food and related items (coolers, etc.) left in vehicles at trailheads attract bears, which are very destructive when they try to get into a vehicle. Food must be kept in the metal storage boxes where provided. If boxes are not available, ask a ranger about other alternatives.

- In the backcountry, food must be stored properly at all times. Store anything with a strong odor (soap, sunscreen, toothpaste, garbage) the same as you would food.

- Lightweight, bear-proof canisters provide the greatest flexibility in planning for a trip. Canisters are available for sale or rent at Cedar Grove, Grant Grove, Lodgepole, Ash Mountain, and Mineral King, and outdoor equipment stores.

- Some popular campsites have metal food storage boxes; ask a park ranger for a list of these camps.

- If food storage boxes are not available, you must post a 24-hour guard or use the counterbalance method of hanging food. Hanging food is sometimes unsuccessful; you should camp near your food—but not right next to it—to better defend it.

- If a bear gets your food or camp gear, you must pack out all debris.

Some recommendations to avoid bear problems:

- Avoid bringing odorous foods and personal care items.

- Plan to camp, eat, and store food before dark. Leave packs on the ground overnight, empty of food and scented items, with pockets open.

- Do not let bears approach you. If you encounter a bear, yell, clap, or make loud noises. Throw things at it from a safe distance to scare it. Be bold, but use good judgment.

- Report injuries, property damage, or unusual encounters to a ranger.

All members of your party are responsible for knowing and following these regulations. Violations can result in fines up to $500 and/or six months' imprisonment.

FOOD STORAGE REGULATIONS

All parties traveling within the restricted areas described below must have park-approved bear-resistant food storage containers with the capacity to store all garbage, scented, and food items. This regulation applies regardless of party size, whether the party is traveling on trails or cross-country, and includes those with stock or receiving stock support. The areas subject to these restrictions include:

- The Dusy Basin area, which includes all camping areas from Bishop Pass to the junction of the Pacific Crest and John Muir Trails in Le Conte Canyon, as well as all cross-country areas in Dusy Basin and Palisades Basin.

- The Rae Lakes Loop vicinity: This area includes all of the Rae Lakes Loop; south along the Pacific Crest/John Muir Trail to Forester Pass; the Bubbs Creek drainage and all other drainages feeding Bubbs Creek east of and including East Creek, east to the park boundary and south to the Kings-Kern Divide.

- The Inyo National Forest.

Zero Impact

Going into a wild area is like visiting a famous museum. You obviously do no want to leave your mark on an art treasure in the museum. If everybody going through the museum left one little mark, the piece of art would be quickly destroyed—and of what value is a big building full of trashed art? The same goes for pristine wildlands. If we all left just one little mark on the landscape, the backcountry would soon be spoiled.

A wilderness can accommodate human use as long as everybody behaves. But a few thoughtless or uninformed visitors can ruin it for everybody who follows. All backcountry users have a responsibility to know and follow the rules of zero impact camping.

Nowadays most wilderness users want to walk softly, but some aren't aware that they have poor manners. Often their actions are dictated by the outdated habits of a past generation of campers that cut green boughs for evening shelters, built campfires with fire rings, and dug trenches around tents. In the 1950s, these "camping rules" may have been acceptable. These days, wild places are becoming rare, the number of users is mushrooming, and more and more camping areas show unsightly signs of heavy use.

Consequently, a new code of ethics now enables us to cope with the unending waves of people who want a perfect backcountry experience. Today, we all must leave no clues that we were there. Enjoy the wild, but leave no trace of your visit.

THREE FALCON PRINCIPLES OF ZERO IMPACT

- Leave with everything you brought.

- Leave no sign of your visit.

- Leave the landscape as you found it.

- Most of us know better than to litter—in or out of the backcountry. Be sure you leave nothing, regardless of how small it is, along the trail or at your campsite. This means you should pack out everything, including orange peels, flip tops, cigarette butts, and gum wrappers. Also, pick up any trash that others leave behind.

- Follow the main trail. Avoid cutting switchbacks and walking on vegetation beside the trail.

- Don't pick up "souvenirs," such as rocks, antlers, or wildflowers. The next person wants to see them too, and collecting such souvenirs violates many regulations.

- Avoid making loud noises on the trail (unless you are in bear country) or in camp. Be courteous—remember, sound travels easily in the backcountry, especially across water.

- Carry a lightweight trowel to bury human waste 6 to 8 inches deep at least 300 feet from any water source. Pack out used toilet paper. Keep any human waste (including dishwater, soaps, and toothpaste) at least 300 feet from any water source.

- Go without a campfire. Carry a stove for cooking and flashlight, candle lantern, or headlamp for light. For emergencies, learn how to build a no-trace fire.

- Camp in designated sites when available. Otherwise, camp and cook on durable surfaces such as bedrock, sand or gravel bars, or bare ground.

- Finally, and perhaps most importantly, strictly follow the pack-in/pack-out rule. If you carry something into the backcountry, consume it or carry it out.

Leave no trace—and put your ear to the ground and listen carefully. Thousands of people coming behind you are thanking you for your courtesy and good sense.

Details on these guidelines and recommendations of zero impact principles for specific outdoor activities can be found in the FalconGuide *Leave No Trace*. Visit your local bookstore for a copy.

Make It a Safe Trip

BEING PREPARED

The Boy Scouts of America have been guided for decades by what is perhaps the single best piece of safety advice—be prepared! For starters, this means carrying survival and first-aid materials, proper clothing, compass, and topographic map—and knowing how to use them.

Perhaps the second-best piece of safety advice is to tell somebody where you're going and when you plan to return. Pilots must file flight plans before every trip, and anybody venturing into the wilderness should do the same. File your "flight plan" with a friend or relative before taking off. If you end up being overdue, they can inform park officials by calling (559) 565-3341; the line is open 24 hours.

Close behind being prepared and filing a flight plan is physical conditioning. Being fit not only makes wilderness travel more fun, it makes it safer. To whet your appetite for more knowledge of wilderness safety and preparedness, here are a few more tips:

- Check the weather forecast. Be careful not to get caught at high altitude in a bad storm or along a stream in a flash flood. Watch cloud formations closely, so you don't get stranded on a ridgeline during a lightning storm. Avoid traveling during prolonged periods of cold weather.

- Avoid traveling alone in the wilderness.

- Keep your party together.

- Study basic survival and first aid before leaving home.

- Don't eat wild plants unless you have positively identified them.

- Before you leave the trailhead, find out as much as you can about the route, especially the potential hazards.

- Don't exhaust yourself or other members of your party by traveling too far or too fast. Let the slowest person set the pace.

- Don't wait until you're confused to look at your maps. Follow them as you go along, from the moment you start moving up the trail, so you have a continual fix on your location.

- If you get lost, don't panic. Sit down and relax for a few minutes while you carefully check your topo and take a reading with your compass. Confidently plan your next move. It's often smart to retrace your steps until you find familiar ground, even if you think it might lengthen your trip. Lots of people get temporarily lost in the wilderness and survive—usually by calmly and rationally dealing with the situation.

- Stay clear of all wild animals.

- Take a first-aid kit that includes, at a minimum, the following items: a sewing needle, a snake-bite kit, aspirin, antibacterial ointment, two antiseptic swabs, two butterfly bandages, adhesive tape, four adhesive strips, four gauze pads, two triangular bandages, codeine tablets, two inflatable splints, moleskin or Second Skin for blisters, one roll of 3-inch gauze, a CPR shield, rubber gloves, and lightweight first-aid instructions.

- Take a survival kit that includes, at minimum, the following items: a compass, a whistle, matches in a waterproof container, a cigarette lighter, a candle, a signal mirror, a flashlight, fire starter, aluminum foil, water purification tablets, a space blanket, and flares.

Last but not least, don't forget that the best defense against unexpected hazards is knowledge. Read up on the latest in wilderness safety information in the FalconGuide *Wild Country Companion*.

SEASONS AND WEATHER

Mountains are prone to sudden thunderstorms. If you get caught in a lightning storm, take special precautions. Remember:

- Lightning can travel far ahead of the storm, so be sure to take cover before the storm hits.

- Don't try to make it back to your vehicle. It isn't worth the risk. Seek shelter instead, even if it's only a short way back to the trailhead. Lightning storms usually don't last long, and from a safe vantage point, you might enjoy the sights and sounds.

- Be especially careful not to get caught on a mountaintop or exposed ridge; under large, solitary trees; in the open; or near standing water.

- Seek shelter away from anything that might attract lightning, such as metal tent poles, graphite fishing rods, or pack frames.

- Crouch down and keep both feet firmly on the ground.

- If you have a pack (without a metal frame) or sleeping pad with you, put your feet on it for extra insulation against shock.

- Don't huddle together. Instead, stay 50 feet apart, so if somebody gets hit by lightning, others in the party can give first aid.

- If you're in a tent, stay there, in your sleeping bag with your feet on your sleeping pad.

HYPOTHERMIA—THE SILENT KILLER

Be aware of the danger of hypothermia—a condition in which the body's internal temperature drops below normal. It can lead to mental and physical collapse and death.

Brilliant red snowplant thrives in the duff on the forest floor.

Hypothermia is caused by exposure to cold and is aggravated by wetness, wind, and exhaustion. The moment you begin to lose heat faster than your body produces it, you're suffering from exposure. Your body starts involuntary exercise, such as shivering, to stay warm, and makes involuntary adjustments to preserve normal temperature in vital organs, restricting blood flow in the extremities. Both responses drain your energy reserves.

The only way to stop the drain is to reduce the degree of exposure.

With full-blown hypothermia, as energy reserves are exhausted, cold reaches the brain, depriving you of good judgment and reasoning power. You won't be aware that this is happening. You lose control of your hands. Your internal temperature slides downward. Without treatment, this slide leads to stupor, collapse, and death.

To defend against hypothermia, stay dry. When clothes get wet, they lose about 90 percent of their insulating value. Wool loses relatively less heat; cotton, down, and some synthetics lose more. Choose rain clothes that cover the head, neck, body, and legs and provide good protection against wind-driven rain. Most hypothermia cases develop in air temperatures between 30 and 50 degrees Fahrenheit, but hypothermia can develop in warmer temperatures.

If your party is exposed to wind, cold, and wet, think hypothermia. Watch yourself and others for these symptoms: uncontrollable fits of shivering; vague, slow, slurred speech; memory lapses; incoherence; immobile, fumbling hands; frequent stumbling or lurching gait; drowsiness (to sleep is to die); apparent exhaustion; and inability to get up after a rest.

When a member of your party has hypothermia, he or she may deny any problem. Believe the symptoms, not the victim. Even mild symptoms demand treatment, which is defined below.

- Get the victim out of the wind and rain.

- Strip off all wet clothes.

- If the victim is only mildly impaired, give him or her warm drinks. Then get the victim in warm clothes and a warm sleeping bag. Place well-wrapped water bottles filled with heated water close to the victim.

- If the victim is badly impaired, attempt to keep him or her awake. Put the victim in a sleeping bag with another person—both naked. If you have a double bag, put two warm people in with the victim.

ALTITUDE SICKNESS

Because of reduced air pressure at high altitudes, less oxygen is available in the atmosphere, and a person's lungs are not able to take in as much oxygen as they can at sea level. Lack of oxygen can cause side effects as mild as a headache or as severe as death. Ascending to high altitudes slowly and camping at middle elevations, allowing the body to acclimate before reaching higher elevations, is the best prevention against altitude sickness. Also, staying hydrated, eating well, and getting plenty of rest can reduce the chance of getting altitude sickness. But nothing can guarantee you will not develop this affliction.

The symptoms of mild altitude sickness are headache, nausea, restlessness, and insomnia. Many people will experience at least one of these symptoms at high altitudes. Acute mountain sickness can occur when an ascent is made too quickly. Symptoms include those of mild altitude sickness, along with loss of appetite, dizziness, fatigue, drowsiness, shortness of breath, irregular breathing, anxiety attacks, hallucinations, and possibly a blue tint to the lips and tongue. Not all symptoms may be present.

To treat altitude sickness and acute mountain sickness, eat food high in carbohydrates, drink plenty of liquids, and take aspirin or acetaminophen if a headache is present. Taking a few deep breaths and walking around without a heavy pack can also help. If symptoms persist to the point of misery, descend to a lower elevation.

The most severe forms of altitude sickness are high altitude pulmonary edema syndrome or HAPES, a condition where the lungs fill with fluid, and high altitude cerebral edema syndrome or HACES, swelling of the brain. The symptoms of HAPES include those already mentioned for altitude and acute mountain sicknesses, and a severe and persistent cough (possibly frothy), rapid pulse, rapid breathing, confusion, delirium, irrational behavior, and gurgling sounds in the chest. If a person loses consciousness, he or she may die within a few hours. The symptom that distinguishes HACES from HAPES is loss of coordination. If no action is taken, permanent brain damage or death can result. If any of the symptoms for HAPES or HACES are present, the affected person should descend immediately, and if the symptoms are severe, the victim should be taken to a hospital.

DRINKING WATER AND GIARDIASIS

Giardiasis (also known as giardia) is caused by an intestinal parasite, *Giardia lamblia,* which can be found in mountain lakes and streams. The symptoms of giardiasis include nausea, abdominal cramps, flatulence, lethargy, diarrhea, and weight loss, and usually occur 6 to 15 days after consuming impure water. To prevent giardiasis, boil water before drinking or use a water filter, which can also remove additional bacteria and protozoa. Should you contract giardiasis, see your doctor, as symptoms can last for months if untreated.

HIGH WATER

River and creek crossings can be dangerous at any time of year. Although many trails in the park cross rivers with the aid of bridges, some do not. If you reach an unbridged crossing, look for a natural bridge, such as a fallen log or rocks. Be careful, they can be slippery even if they are dry. If you must wade, cross where the water is wide and shallow. Make sure the crossing is not above rapids or a waterfall, in case you are sucked into the current. If you are wearing a large backpack, unbuckle the waist strap. Using a long stick or trekking poles can help your stability, and it's a good idea to carry extra shoes for river crossings (lightweight tennis shoes work well). If you are traveling with a group, cross together, holding onto each other. A rope can be strung across a stream as an aid, but never tie yourself into the rope, as you can become entangled and drown. The best time to cross a river or creek is in the early morning, when the water level is at its lowest.

POISON OAK

Poison oak is a shrub common to foothill regions up to 5,000 feet. In the spring, the leaves are green and very shiny, in groups of three. In the fall the leaves are red, and white berries are present. If you come in contact with any part of the plant, you should wash your skin and clothes with warm, soapy water as quickly as possible. If a rash develops, many over-the-counter medications are available.

TICKS

Ticks are most often encountered on foothill trails. They usually perch at the ends of grasses and twigs, waiting for an animal to brush by and pick them up. A person may or may not feel them bite, and they can carry Lyme disease. If a tick attaches itself to you, remove it carefully with tweezers, as it can embed its head into the skin. If a reddish circle appears around the bite a few days later, seek medical attention. The best prevention against ticks is to wear an insect repellent with deet, and light-colored clothing that can be easily checked for the parasites. A new vaccine for Lyme disease is now also available through your doctor.

MOSQUITOES AND BITING FLIES

Mosquitoes are at their worst in late June and early July. A good insect repellent with deet will usually remedy the situation. Biting flies are most numerous during the hottest part of the summer, and are usually found on trails with heavy horse traffic. Most mosquito repellents will repel biting flies, but in extreme cases a headnet may be needed.

RATTLESNAKES

Rattlesnakes are most often found in the lower elevations, but can occasionally be encountered as high as 10,000 feet. Snakes usually retreat if they sense something large approaching, and most bites occur when someone teases or tries to handle a snake. The best way to prevent a run-in with a rattlesnake is to watch where you step, especially in rocky areas and when crossing over fallen logs. If you are bitten, seek medical attention immediately, because tissue damage can result if the bite is not treated quickly.

BE BEAR AWARE

Black bears inhabit Sequoia and Kings Canyon National Parks, and they have become quite adept at raiding park visitors' food supplies. Bears will not hesitate to break into a car to get at food, and they can cause extensive damage. Some bears become very aggressive and destructive and then, unfortunately, must be killed. Carelessness with your food could mean the eventual death of a bear.

A foremost consideration for visitors to the parks is how to keep food stored in their cars safe from bears. Ice chests and bags of food should never be left in plain sight in an unattended vehicle. Food items and coolers, as well as anything with an odor, should be sealed, put on the floor of the car, and covered. If your vehicle has a trunk, food should be locked inside.

Many campgrounds have bear-resistant food storage boxes. All food, ice chests, and toiletries must be stored inside, with the box properly latched at all times. The campsite should be kept clean—do not leave any food out. All refuse should be put in bear-resistant garbage containers as soon as possible. Violations can result in a fine of up to $500.

If a bear does get your food, you are responsible for cleanup and disposal of anything left behind, and for reporting the incident to the nearest ranger.

Some backcountry campsites have bear boxes for food storage, but the best way to protect your food is to buy or rent a bear canister. The canisters can be rented at park visitor centers and markets. Counterbalancing food bags in trees is no longer recommended, as the bears have found ways to attain food hung in trees. All garbage should be packed out inside the bear canister.

If a bear enters your campsite, make noise, shout, and wave your arms. If this doesn't scare the bear away, toss small rocks in its direction, but try not to actually hit the animal. Black bear attacks on humans are rare, but you should always keep a safe distance from any bear, especially if you come across a mother bear with her cubs.

Unlike bears and mountain lions, the tiny, shy pika isn't likely to inflict any harm on a hiker, even if provoked.

The first step of any hike in bear country is an attitude adjustment. Being prepared for bears means not only having the right equipment, such as pepper spray, but also having the right information. While attacks are rare, bears don't like to be surprised, and a female can be very defensive when she has cubs.

The greatest danger of a bear encounter is present if you handle your food improperly. If a bear eats your food, and destroys your equipment in doing it, your trip is ruined. If you are deep in the wilderness, your life may be at risk as a result. Moreover, letting a bear get human food rapidly conditions it to seek human food in the future. The slogan "a fed bear is a dead bear" is often true. Think of following proper bear etiquette as protecting the bears as much as protecting yourself.

Camping in Bear Country
The presence of food, cooking, and garbage can attract a bear into an overnight camp. Remember, you are in bear country at night, when bears are usually most active.

A few basic practices greatly minimize the chance of a bad encounter. To be as safe as possible, store everything that has any food smell. Zip-locked bags are perfect for reducing food smell, and they help keep food from spilling on your pack, clothing, or other gear. Before going to bed, change into other clothes for sleeping and store clothes with food smells with food and garbage in bearproof containers. If you take the soiled clothes into the tent, you haven't separated your sleeping area from food smells and may attract bears to your tent. Make every effort to keep food odors off your pack.

Finalize your food storage plans before it gets dark. Not only is it difficult to store food after darkness falls, but it's easier to forget some juicy morsel on the ground. Store food in airtight, sturdy, waterproof bags to prevent odors from circulating throughout the forest. You can purchase dry bags at most outdoor specialty stores, but you can get by with a trash compactor bag. Don't use regular garbage bags because they can break too easily.

Avoid smelly foods and consciously reduce the number of dishes you use. (You should pack out all food scraps.) By consuming everything on your plate as well as paying careful attention to storage, you will make your backpacking culinary experience not only more enjoyable and hassle-free but also more bear-proof.

Read the FalconGuide *Bear Aware* for complete information on camping in bear country.

MOUNTAIN LIONS

It is unlikely that you will see a mountain lion, or cougar, but they do inhabit these parks. Though many people consider themselves lucky indeed to see a mountain lion in the wild, the big cats—nature's perfect predator—are potentially dangerous. Attacks on humans are extremely rare, but it's wise to educate yourself before heading into mountain lion habitat.

Guidelines for Traveling in Mountain Lion Country

To stay as safe as possible when hiking in mountain lion country, follow this advice.

1. Travel with a friend or group and stay together.

2. Don't let small children wander away by themselves.

3. Don't let pets run unleashed.

4. Avoid hiking at dawn and dusk—the times mountain lions are most active.

5. Know how to behave if you encounter a mountain lion.

What to Do If You Encounter a Mountain Lion

In the vast majority of mountain lion encounters, these animals exhibit avoidance, indifference, or curiosity that doesn't result in human injury. They see you much more often than you see them. It is natural to be alarmed if you have an encounter of any kind. However, try to keep your cool and consider the following:

- Recognize threatening mountain lion behavior. A few cues may help you gauge the risk of attack. If a mountain lion is more than 50 yards away and directs its attention to you, it may be only curious. This situation represents only a slight risk for adults but a more serious risk for unaccompanied children. At this point, you should move away, while keeping the animal in your peripheral vision. Also, look for rocks, sticks, or something to use as a weapon, just in case.

- If a mountain lion is crouched and staring at you less than 50 yards away, it may be assessing the chances of a successful attack. If this behavior continues, the risk of attack may be high.

- Do not approach a mountain lion. Give the animal the opportunity to move on. Slowly back away, but maintain eye contact if close. Mountain lions are not known to attack humans to defend their young or a kill, but they have been reported to "charge" in rare instances and may want to stay in the area. It's best to choose another route or time to hike through the area.

- Do not run from a mountain lion. Running may stimulate the mountain lion's predatory response.

- Make noise. If you encounter a mountain lion, be vocal; talk or yell loudly and regularly. Try not to panic. Shout to make others in the area aware of the situation.

- Maintain eye contact. Eye contact presents a challenge to the mountain lion, showing you are aware of its presence. Eye contact also helps you know where it is. However, if the behavior of the mountain lion is not threatening (if the animal is, for example, grooming itself or periodically looking away), maintain visual contact through your peripheral vision and move away.

- Appear larger than you are. Raise your arms above your head and make steady waving motions. Raise your jacket or another object above your head. Do not bend over, since this will make you appear smaller and more "prey-like."

- If you are with small children, pick them up. Bring children close to you, maintain eye contact with the mountain lion, and pull the children up without bending over. If you are with other children or adults, band together.

- Defend yourself and others. If attacked, fight back. Try to remain standing. Do not feign death. Pick up a branch or rock; pull out a knife, pepper spray, or other deterrent. Individuals have fended off mountain lions with rocks, tree limbs, and even cameras. Keep in mind this is a last effort, and defending pets is not recommended.

- Respect any warning signs posted by agencies.

- Teach others in your group how to behave in case of a mountain lion encounter.

- Report encounters. Record your location and the details of any encounter and notify the nearest landowner or land management agency. The land management agency (federal, state, or county) may want to visit the site and, if appropriate, post education or warning signs. Fish and wildlife agencies should also be notified because they record and track such encounters.

- If physical injury occurs, it is important to leave the area and not disturb the site of attack. Mountain lions that have attacked people must be killed, and an undisturbed site is critical for effectively locating the dangerous mountain lion.

See the FalconGuide *Mountain Lion Alert* for more details and tips for safe outdoor recreation in mountain lion country.

Whether approaching an exposed summit—like this at Lookout Peak—or wandering through a sequoia grove, hikers should proceed with caution and knowledge.

Sequoia and Kings Canyon National Parks Trail Finder

	EASY	MODERATE	DIFFICULT
Hikes along Streams	27 Tokopah Falls 49 Roaring River Falls to Zumwalt Meadow 50 Road's End to the Bailey Bridge 60 Cold Springs Nature Trail 64 Black Wolf Falls	3 Marble Falls 4 Paradise Creek 5 Middle Fork Trail 38 North Boundary and Lone Pine Trails 42 Redwood Canyon 47 Don Cecil Trail 55 Paradise Valley 70 Ladybug Camp and Whisky Log Camp	19 Big Arroyo 51 Junction Meadow 52 Vidette Meadow 53 Upper Bubbs Creek 54 Copper Creek Trail 56 Rae Lakes Loop 63 Monarch Lakes 65 Franklin Lakes 66 Farewell Gap 67 White Chief Bowl 68 Eagle Lake 77 Roaring River 81 Goddard Canyon 82 Evolution Valley
Hikes to Mountaintops	8 Moro Rock and Hanging Rock 29 Little Baldy 43 Buena Vista Peak	44 Big Baldy Ridge	24 Alta Peak 57 Paradise Peak 75 Mitchell Peak 76 Lookout Peak 86 Mount Whitney
Hikes with Great Views	8 Moro Rock and Hanging Rock 29 Little Baldy 43 Buena Vista Peak 60 Cold Springs Nature Trail 72 Weaver Lake	16 High Sierra Trail to Bearpaw Meadow 23 Lakes Trail 39 Park Ridge Trail 44 Big Baldy Ridge 61 Timber Gap 69 Mosquito Lakes 73 Jennie Lake 74 Deer Meadow	17 Hamilton Lakes 18 Nine Lakes Basin 21 Pinto Lake 22 Little Five Lakes 24 Alta Peak 25 Alta Meadow 53 Upper Bubbs Creek 56 Rae Lakes Loop 57 Paradise Peak 62 Crystal Lakes 63 Monarch Lakes 65 Franklin Lakes 66 Farewell Gap 67 White Chief Bowl 68 Eagle Lake 75 Mitchell Peak 76 Lookout Peak 77 Roaring River 80 Ranger and Beville Lakes 81 Goddard Canyon 82 Evolution Valley 83 Dusy Basin 84 Onion Valley to Kearsarge Lakes 86 Mount Whitney

	EASY	MODERATE	DIFFICULT
Hikes in the Lower Elevations		1 Lower Colony Mill Trail 2 North Fork Trail 3 Marble Falls 4 Paradise Creek 5 Middle Fork Trail	
Really Flat Trails	11 Round Meadow Trail 27 Tokopah Falls 49 Roaring River Falls to Zumwalt Meadow 64 Black Wolf Falls		
Hikes to Waterfalls	27 Tokopah Falls 32 Hitchcock Meadow 49 Roaring River Falls to Zumwalt Meadow 64 Black Wolf Falls	3 Marble Falls 4 Paradise Creek 5 Middle Fork Trail 33 South Boundary Trail 36 Sunset Trail 55 Paradise Valley	81 Goddard Canyon
Hikes to Meadows	10 Crescent and Log Meadows 11 Round Meadow Trail 12 Huckleberry Trail 15 Circle Meadow 26 Long Meadow Trail 32 Hitchcock Meadow 49 Roaring River Falls to Zumwalt Meadow	16 High Sierra Trail to Bearpaw Meadow 20 Redwood Meadow 55 Paradise Valley 58 Atwell-Hockett Trail to Hockett Meadows 74 Deer Meadow	25 Alta Meadow 51 Junction Meadow 52 Vidette Meadow 56 Rae Lakes Loop 67 White Chief Bowl 82 Evolution Valley
Hikes in Sequoia Groves	10 Crescent and Log Meadows 11 Round Meadow Trail 12 Huckleberry Trail 13 Congress Trail 15 Circle Meadow 30 Muir Grove 31 Big Stump Loop 35 General Grant Loop 37 North Grove and Dead Giant Loops	14 Trail of the Sequoias 20 Redwood Meadow 38 North Boundary and Lone Pine Trails 40 Hart Tree Trail 41 Sugarbowl Trail 42 Redwood Canyon 70 Ladybug Camp and Whisky Log Camp	57 Paradise Peak 58 Atwell-Hockett Trail to Hockett Meadows 71 Garfield Grove
Hikes to or over Passes		61 Timber Gap 66 Farewell Gap 73 Jennie Lake	18 Nine Lake Basin 22 Little Five Lakes 56 Rae Lakes Loop 75 Mitchell Peak 83 Dusy Basin 84 Onion Valley to Kearsarge Lakes 85 Charlotte Lake 86 Mount Whitney

	EASY	MODERATE	DIFFICULT
Best Backpacking Trips		16 High Sierra Trail to Bearpaw Meadow 23 Lakes Trail 28 Twin Lakes Trail 70 Ladybug Camp and Whisky Log Camp 73 Jennie Lake 78 Seville Lake	17 Hamilton Lakes 22 Little Five Lakes 24 Alta Peak 25 Alta Meadow 51 Junction Meadow 55 Paradise Valley 56 Rae Lakes Loop 58 Atwell-Hockett Trail to Hockett Meadows 62 Crystal Lakes 63 Monarch Lakes 65 Franklin Lakes 67 White Chief Bowl 68 Eagle Lake 80 Ranger and Beville Lakes 81 Goddard Canyon 82 Evolution Valley 83 Dusy Basin 84 Onion Valley to Kearsarge Lakes 85 Charlotte Lake 86 Mount Whitney
Trails to Avoid if You Don't Want to Share with Horses	2 North Fork Trail 26 Long Meadow Trail 72 Weaver Lake	16 High Sierra Trail to Bearpaw Meadow 38 North Boundary and Lone Pine Trails 61 Timber Gap	51 Junction Meadow 52 Vidette Meadow 55 Paradise Valley 56 Rae Lakes Loop 66 Farewell Gap 67 White Chief Bowl 75 Mitchell Peak 77 Roaring River 81 Goddard Canyon 82 Evolution Valley 84 Onion Valley to Kearsarge Lakes
Trails to Avoid if You Don't Like to Ford Creeks		4 Paradise Creek 5 Middle Fork Trail 20 Redwood Meadow 40 Hart Tree Trail 42 Redwood Canyon 70 Ladybug Camp and Whisky Log Camp	17 Hamilton Lakes 18 Nine Lakes Basin 19 Big Arroyo 21 Pinto Lake 22 Little Five Lakes 45 Deer Cove Trail to Grizzly Lakes 46 Lewis Creek Trail 56 Rae Lakes Loop 58 Atwell-Hockett Trail to Hockett Meadows 59 Evelyn Lake and Cahoon Rock 65 Franklin Lakes 66 Farewell Gap 77 Roaring River 86 Mount Whitney

	EASY	MODERATE	DIFFICULT
Hikes to Backcountry Lakes	72 Weaver Lake	23 Lakes Trail 28 Twin Lakes Trail 69 Mosquito Lakes 73 Jennie Lake 78 Seville Lake	17 Hamilton Lakes 18 Nine Lakes Basin 21 Pinto Lake 22 Little Five Lakes 54 Copper Creek Trail 56 Rae Lakes Loop 59 Evelyn Lake and Cahoon Rock 62 Crystal Lakes 63 Monarch Lakes 65 Franklin Lakes 68 Eagle Lake 79 Lost Lake 80 Ranger and Beville Lakes 83 Dusy Basin 84 Onion Valley to Kearsarge Lakes 85 Charlotte Lake
Hikes in the High Country			17 Hamilton Lakes 18 Nine Lake Basin 19 Big Arroyo 21 Pinto Lake 22 Little Five Lakes 53 Upper Bubbs Creek 54 Copper Creek Trail 56 Rae Lakes Loop 62 Crystal Lakes 63 Monarch Lakes 65 Franklin Lakes 66 Farewell Gap 67 White Chief Bowl 68 Eagle Lake 82 Evolution Valley 83 Dusy Basin 84 Onion Valley to Kearsarge Lakes 85 Charlotte Lake 86 Mount Whitney
Hikes to Avoid if You Don't Want to See Many People	7 Sunset Rock 8 Moro Rock and Hanging Rock 10 Crescent and Log Meadows 11 Round Meadow Trail 13 Congress Trail 27 Tokopah Falls 30 Muir Grove 31 Big Stump Loop 35 General Grant Loop 49 Roaring River Falls to Zumwalt Meadow		86 Mount Whitney

Author's Favorite Hikes

For Photography	22 Little Five Lakes
	24 Alta Peak
	25 Alta Meadow
	48 Hotel Creek Trail
	53 Upper Bubbs Creek
	62 Crystal Lakes
	63 Monarch Lakes
	66 Farewell Gap
	67 White Chief Bowl
	75 Mitchell Peak
	80 Ranger and Beville Lakes
	81 Goddard Canyon
	82 Evolution Valley
	83 Dusy Basin
	84 Onion Valley to Kearsarge Lakes
	86 Mount Whitney
For High Altitude Scenery	17 Hamilton Lakes
	18 Nine Lake Basin
	22 Little Five Lakes
	23 Lakes Trail
	24 Alta Peak
	25 Alta Meadow
	53 Upper Bubbs Creek
	56 Rae Lakes Loop
	62 Crystal Lakes
	63 Monarch Lakes
	65 Franklin Lakes
	66 Farewell Gap
	67 White Chief Bowl
	80 Ranger and Beville Lakes
	82 Evolution Valley
	83 Dusy Basin
	84 Onion Valley to Kearsarge Lakes
	85 Charlotte Lake
	86 Mount Whitney

For Wildlife	5 Middle Fork Trail
	6 Upper Colony Mill Trail
	7 Sunset Rock
	10 Crescent and Log Meadows
	12 Huckleberry Trail
	14 Trail of the Sequoias
	16 High Sierra Trail to Bearpaw Meadow
	17 Hamilton Lakes
	20 Redwood Meadow
	25 Alta Meadow
	27 Tokopah Falls
	31 Big Stump Loop
	51 Junction Meadow
	52 Vidette Meadow
	67 White Chief Bowl
	68 Eagle Lake
	69 Mosquito Lakes
	77 Roaring River
	86 Mount Whitney
For Wildflowers	1 Lower Colony Mill Trail
	2 North Fork Trail
	3 Marble Falls
	10 Crescent and Log Meadows
	11 Round Meadow Trail
	15 Circle Meadow
	16 High Sierra Trail to Bearpaw Meadow
	18 Nine Lake Basin
	25 Alta Meadow
	26 Long Meadow Trail
	60 Cold Springs Nature Trail
	81 Goddard Canyon
For Fall Color	6 Upper Colony Mill Trail
	42 Redwood Canyon
	55 Paradise Valley
	56 Rae Lakes Loop
	60 Cold Springs Nature Trail
	83 Dusy Basin
For Giant Sequoias	11 Round Meadow Trail
	12 Huckleberry Trail
	14 Trail of the Sequoias
	37 North Grove and Dead Giant Loops
	71 Garfield Grove

For an Easy Day Hike	6 Upper Colony Mill Trail
	27 Tokopah Falls
	29 Little Baldy
	37 North Grove and Dead Giant Loops
	60 Cold Springs Nature Trail
	72 Weaver Lake
For a Moderate Day Hike	39 Park Ridge Trail
	40 Hart Tree Trail
	41 Sugarbowl Trail
	42 Redwood Canyon
	44 Big Baldy Ridge
	61 Timber Gap
	69 Mosquito Lakes
	73 Jennie Lake
For a Long, Hard Day Hike	23 Lakes Trail
	24 Alta Peak
	25 Alta Meadow
	47 Don Cecil Trail
	63 Monarch Lakes
	65 Franklin Lakes
	66 Farewell Gap
	67 White Chief Bowl
	75 Mitchell Peak
For a First Night in the Wilderness	16 High Sierra Trail to Bearpaw Meadow
	55 Paradise Valley
	70 Ladybug Camp and Whisky Log Camp
	78 Seville Lake
For a Moderate Overnighter	23 Lakes Trail
	62 Crystal Lakes
	63 Monarch Lakes
	73 Jennie Lake
	78 Seville Lake

For a True Wilderness Experience

Hikes in the Foothills

The first two hikes in this chapter begin at the end of North Fork Drive, north of the town of Three Rivers. The next three are located north of the Ash Mountain Visitor Center, along the Generals Highway. Marble Falls begins at the Potwisha Campground, and Paradise Creek and the Middle Fork Trail begin farther east at the Hospital Rock picnic area.

1 Lower Colony Mill Trail

Highlights:	This route was forged by the Kaweah Colonists, a utopian socialist group intent on filing several claims to land in the Giant Forest. Built mainly with hand tools, this road led to a site near the old Colony Mill Ranger Station, where a portable sawmill was erected. In 1890, the establishment of Sequoia National Park thwarted the Colonists' plans. Thirteen years later, the route was extended to the Giant Forest by the U.S. Cavalry and served as the first road into the park until 1926, when the Generals Highway opened. It is now used as a hiking trail.
Type of hike:	Out-and-back, day hike.
Total distance:	7 miles.
Difficulty:	Moderate.
Best months:	October through May.
Maps:	USGS Shadequarter Mountain and Giant Forest, or TOPO! Sequoia Kings Canyon CD-ROM.
Permits:	None.
Special considerations:	Ticks are numerous on this trail, so wear plenty of insect repellent and check your clothing often.
Parking and facilities:	No facilities are located at this trailhead. Park to the side of the right road fork, and do not block the roadway. The trail begins by following the right road fork uphill to the east.

Finding the trailhead: From central Three Rivers follow North Fork Drive past a few BLM recreational sites. The road becomes dirt before you reach a fork with an "End" sign at approximately 10.2 miles.

Key points:

- 0.0   Trailhead.
- 0.5   Pass the park boundary.
- 1.6   Pass the spring.
- 2.9   Cross Maple Creek.
- 3.5   Reach the view of Big Baldy.

The hike: As you begin this trek, private property is on either side of you, so stay on the road. A steel cable may be strung across the road; it is permissible to go over or around it. After traveling through a shady canopy of oaks you reach another obstacle just before the park boundary. The owner of the property to the

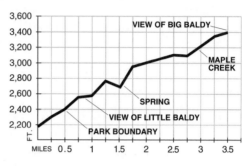

west of the park has unlawfully placed a chainlink gate across the road, blocking public access. Legally you can go over, under, or around this ob-

Lower Colony Mill Trail

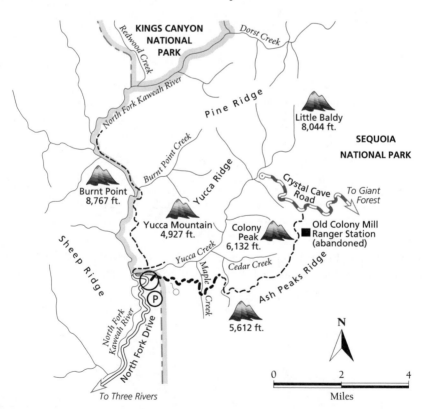

struction. At 0.5 mile you reach another gate with a pedestrian bypass, and enter Sequoia National Park.

The old road heads east, high above Yucca Creek, through buckeye and areas of poison oak. Bears frequent this trail, leaving their scat for you to dodge. You'll have a view down to the large, grassy expanse known as Yucca Flat, which was the site of a native village and an old homestead. After rounding a couple of small ridges, views of Little Baldy and Colony Peak open to the northeast. The wide path then curves into a drainage and reaches a small spring at 1.6 miles. An old concrete water tank is located to the right of this spring.

Beyond the spring, you round another ridge and travel through sunny areas thick with chamise and some manzanita. Look for tiny black ticks at the tips of tall stalks of grass, just waiting to get a free ride and a meal.

As you pass seasonal creeklets, the route enters the shade of oaks and alders, and wild ginger grows along the trail in the dappled light. At 2.9 miles you reach Maple Creek, shaded by maples and alders. Pass through another grove of maples; then bay laurels line the path, giving it a spicy scent. At 3.5 miles and the turnaround point, you have a good view of Big Baldy to the north, peeking out over the shoulder of Yucca Mountain. From here, backtrack to your car (7 miles).

Options: It is possible to hike all the way to the old Colony Mill Ranger Station (8 miles) and Crystal Cave Road (9.9 miles). This would give you an elevation gain of approximately 3,600 feet. An easier option is the Upper Colony Mill Trail (Hike 6).

---

2 North Fork Trail

Highlights:	This trek brings you to expansive Yucca Flat, then traverses the lower flanks of Yucca Mountain to views of the North Fork of the Kaweah and shady Burnt Point Creek.
Type of hike:	Out-and-back, day hike.
Total distance:	7.9 miles.
Difficulty:	Moderate.
Best months:	November through April.
Maps:	USGS Shadequarter Mountain and Giant Forest, or TOPO! Sequoia Kings Canyon CD-ROM.
Permits:	None.
Special considerations:	Ticks are found in the shadier portions of this trail, so wear plenty of insect repellent and check your clothing often.
Parking and facilities:	There are no facilities. There are two areas for parking, one on the right, and another downhill to the left. The trail begins at the bridge across Yucca Creek, visible from the upper parking area.

Finding the trailhead: From central Three Rivers follow North Fork Drive past a few BLM recreational sites. The pavement gives way to dirt; you reach a fork in the road with an "End" sign at approximately 10.2 miles. Take the left fork past the "End" sign, and continue for another 0.7 mile to the parking area.

Key points:
0.0   Trailhead.
0.3   Reach the Yucca Flat Trail.
0.6   Arrive at Yucca Flat.
0.9   Cross the first creek.
1.4   Pass a tiny creek.
2.5   Reach the third creek.
3.9   Pass the next creek.
4.2   Reach Burnt Point Creek.

The hike: The trail begins at a new footbridge across Yucca Creek, then joins what was an old dirt road on the other side. Pass a park sign just south of a cement slab foundation from when this area was the Grunigen Ranch.

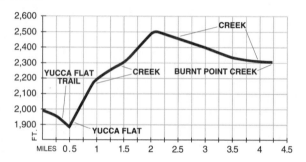

The route passes over a small brook running through a culvert and reaches the Yucca Flat Trail at 0.3 mile. Take the right (east) branch and follow this side trail along Yucca Creek, soon passing a small, double waterfall. A footpath leads up to the left (north), to the western edge of Yucca Flat; this ends at two large pines, while the side trail continues on to the center of the flat at 0.6 mile. A short rock wall lines the southern edge of this grassy expanse as the narrowing trail leads back toward the creek.

After you have enjoyed the flat, return to the main North Fork Trail, make a right, and begin a steady climb to the north. At 1 mile, a barely discernible roadbed leads to a pair of small cement structures built into the hillside on the left (west), just across a tiny creek at 0.9 mile. Continue to climb, passing through the remnants of an old gate. Fiddlenecks, red maids, baby blue-eyes, popcorn flowers, and many others bloom along the trail in the spring. The route passes over a couple of small brooks and levels out a bit. To the south you can see Ash Peaks Ridge and a portion of the Lower Colony Mill Trail (Hike 1).

The path crosses over a small ridge and begins a slight descent. At 1.4 miles the old roadbed passes by a tiny creek. To the west, across the North Fork of the Kaweah River, the view includes Sheep Ridge and Pattee Rocks. Burnt Point is the high mountain to the northwest. After passing through another gate, you reach a shady creek at 2.5 miles, complete with calling frogs in springtime. The trail swings back into the sunlight, gains a view to

North Fork Trail

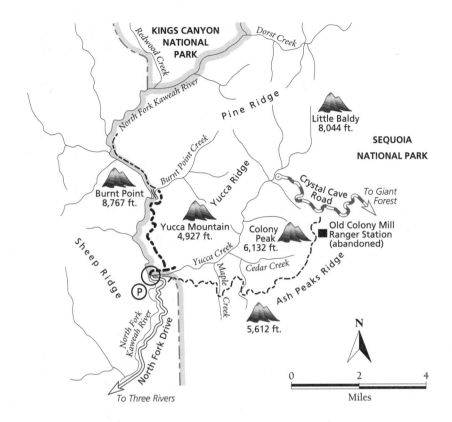

the north-northeast of the Pine Ridge Grove of sequoias, and passes another small creek surrounded by yucca plants at 3.9 miles.

The river soon becomes audible, and as the trail bends to the northeast, pools and cascades on the North Fork of the Kaweah, as well as a small waterfall on the lower portion of Burnt Point Creek, become visible through the vegetation. Views up the canyon increase as you near the creek, then are blocked as you enter the shade of tall sycamores enclosing Burnt Point Creek at 4.2 miles. This is a nice spot for a picnic lunch before heading back to your car (8.4 miles).

Option: The trail continues for about 3.5 more miles, climbing slightly for the first two, then more moderately the last mile and a half. The trail turns right (southeast) to climb toward Hidden Springs, and becomes brushy and impassable. Volunteers from the Backcountry Horse Club are working to clear this segment of the trail, and hope to clear another old section of trail leading from Hidden Springs to Crystal Cave Road, near the upper portion of the Colony Mill Trail. This would enable horseback riders and hikers to travel an enormous loop, perfect for early season trekking.

3 Marble Falls

Highlights:	This hike traverses the steep eastern wall of Deep Canyon, high above the Marble Fork of the Kaweah River, to the dramatic spectacle of Marble Falls.
Type of hike:	Out-and-back, day hike.
Total distance:	6.2 miles.
Difficulty:	Moderate.
Best months:	October through May.
Maps:	USGS Giant Forest or TOPO! Sequoia Kings Canyon CD-ROM.
Permits:	None.
Special considerations:	Ticks are found in the shadier portions of this trail. Wear plenty of insect repellent and check your clothing often. Poison oak is abundant the whole length of this trip; be careful not to touch or brush up against it. The trail is generally too hot to be hiked in the summer.
Parking and facilities:	Restrooms are located in Potwisha Campground. Two small parking areas are on the west side of the dirt road. The trail begins at the north end of the second parking area.

Finding the trailhead: From the Ash Mountain entrance station, drive 3.6 miles northeast on the Generals Highway, past the Ash Mountain Visitor Center and Tunnel Rock (now closed to traffic), to Potwisha Campground. Go left (north), follow the main road through the campground to a dirt road leading north at campsite 16, and turn right (north). The small parking area is just ahead at 3.9 miles.

Key points:
- 0.0 Trailhead.
- 0.6 Reach the first unnamed creek.
- 1.0 Pass the second creek.
- 1.4 Cross the third creek.
- 2.7 Pass the last creek.
- 3.1 Arrive at the falls.

The hike: This excursion begins by following the chained-off portion of the dirt road north, passing a side trail leading down to a river gauging station. Cross a wooden bridge spanning a flume operated by the Southern California Edison power company. The route follows the flume before arriving at the signed Marble Falls Trail, on which you make a right (southeast) turn. Com-

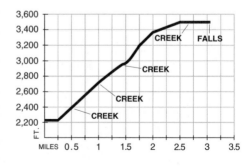

40

Marble Falls

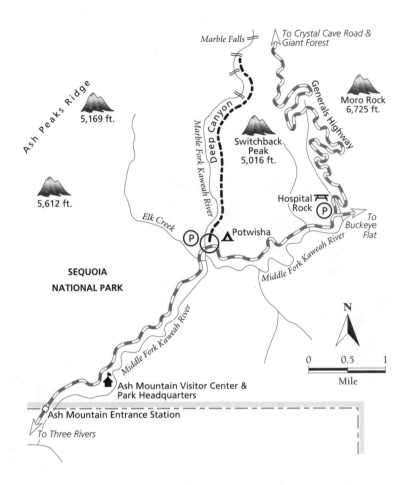

mon madia, Chinese houses, pretty faces, brodiaea, and pink globe lilies skirt the path, along with many other wildflowers in the spring.

The path rises up a few steep switchbacks, then turns north and passes through a shady woodland of cottonwoods, redbuds, and dogwoods, before reaching the first unnamed creek at 0.6 mile. Soon the route enters an open, sunny slope amidst chamise, yucca, and yerba santa. Rufous-sided towhees and other birds chirp and trill from within the thick brush. Continue to two more unnamed creeks at 1 mile and 1.4 miles. The footpath becomes narrow in some areas, and the roar of the Marble Fork can be heard far below. Sycamores and California bay laurels line the path in a few shady groves.

A turn to the northeast gives you views down to the tumultuous river below. Begin a slight descent past marble outcroppings and reach the last unnamed creek, tumbling down marble slabs, at 2.7 miles. Immediately across the creek the path switchbacks steeply to the right (the trail to the left is a dead end).

You will start to have views of the falls as a side trail drops down to a viewpoint on your left (west). The pathway descends, passing a double-plumed fall, and enters a grove of California nutmeg (which look very much like a fir tree). The dwindling footpath leads around an outcropping, crosses a narrow ledge above the swiftly flowing river, and deposits you on an expanse of white marble at the foot of a churning cascade at 3.1 miles.

During the spring runoff, it is impossible to hear anything but the thunderous whitewater. Exercise caution in this area—the marble can be very slippery and fractures easily. The actual "Marble Falls" is a little farther up the canyon, but inaccessible.

When you are ready to return to your vehicle, retrace your steps to the trailhead at 6.2 miles.

The Marble Fork of the Kaweah River cascades along the trail.

4 Paradise Creek

Highlights: Beginning at the site of an old Monachi village, this voyage offers a superb wildflower show in the spring, and also rewards you with two small waterfalls and many beautiful cascades.

Type of hike: Out-and-back, day hike.

Total distance: 5.8 miles.

Difficulty: Moderate.

Best months: October through May.

Maps: USGS Giant Forest or TOPO! Sequoia Kings Canyon CD-ROM.

Permits: None.

Special considerations: Ticks are found on this trail; wear plenty of insect repellent and check your clothing often. Poison oak also is abundant the whole length of this trip; be careful not to touch or brush up against it.

Parking and facilities: Restrooms, water, and a pay phone are available at Hospital Rock, as well as picnic tables and grills. The hike begins at the crosswalk located at the northeast end of the parking area.

Finding the trailhead: From the Ash Mountain entrance station, drive 5.9 miles northeast on the Generals Highway, past the Ash Mountain Visitor Center, Tunnel Rock (now closed to traffic), and Potwisha Campground, to the Hospital Rock Picnic Area. Park at the picnic area—parking at Buckeye Flat Campground (where the trail starts) is permitted only for campers.

Key points:
- 0.0 Begin at the Hospital Rock parking area.
- 0.6 Reach the trailhead.
- 0.8 Cross the Middle Fork bridge.
- 1.3 Reach a seasonal creek.
- 1.8 Make the first Paradise Creek crossing.
- 1.9 Make the second crossing.
- 2.9 Reach the waterfall.

The hike: Start this excursion by crossing the Generals Highway in the crosswalk provided. You will find some Monachi bedrock mortars and an interpretive sign on the south side of the road to Buckeye Flat Campground. Hospital Rock is on the north side of this road, along with a stone stairway that leads up to a small viewing platform across from the native pictographs painted on its side.

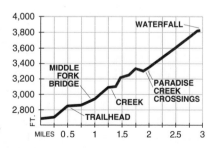

Paradise Creek • Middle Fork Trail

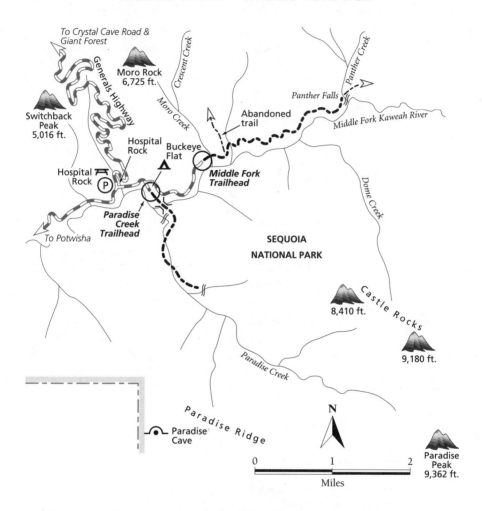

After inspecting the pictographs, follow the paved road east, passing a large hollow under Hospital Rock, which was used by the Monachis as a shelter for the sick and injured. Hale Tharp, who homesteaded the area of Crescent and Log Meadows (Hike 10), named the rock after visiting the Monachi village here.

After the road passes over a pleasant little brook, you exit the shady oaks to views of the turbulent Middle Fork of the Kaweah below. In spring, bush monkey flower, yerba santa, popcorn flowers, mariposa lilies, and lupine brighten the grassy areas between the oaks, bay laurels, buckeyes, redbuds, and tall stalks of yucca.

The Castle Rocks come into view and immediately after a sharp turn, a dirt road branches left (east), leading to the Middle Fork Trail (Hike 5). Continue on the paved road, drop down into the campground, and reach the signed Paradise Creek Trail, across from campsite 28, at 0.6 mile.

The path travels through the shade of oaks and redbuds as a track leading up from campsite 25 joins your course. Below you and on the right (southwest) three rock dams appear, which were once part of the park's old fish hatchery.

You will reach the new bridge spanning the Middle Fork at 0.8 mile. In the winter of 1997 the bridge was washed out when a freak tropical storm brought a warm and early rain, melted the Sierra's snow, and caused flooding in many areas in the southern mountains.

Just across the bridge, the main trail turns left (southeast), while a side path leads to the right and forks. Take a side trip by following the spur path: The trail that goes straight leads to a small, pretty waterfall and a swimming hole on Paradise Creek. The fork leading to your right brings you to the rocky bluffs of the Middle Fork between the bridge and the confluence of the creek and river. These are both pleasant areas for a picnic lunch before or after your hike.

Continuing on the main trail, you wind through huge manzanitas and pass another footpath leading to the river. A couple more side trails lead off to the creek, then the river, as the path switchbacks through a dry, rocky zone above the before-mentioned waterfall.

The route crosses a small, seasonal creek in a shady nook at 1.3 miles, then travels through pines and cedars, with a ground cover of bear clover. An unusual view of Moro Rock opens up to the north, and beyond, you enter a beautiful flower garden filled in spring with rosy globe lilies, common madia, Chinese houses, mustang clover, California poppies, Indian pinks, prairie stars, and fiesta flowers.

Picturesque cascades appear below on Paradise Creek, and at 1.8 miles you reach the first crossing of this creek, which may require a wade in early season. Be prepared! You must cross or wade the creek once more at 1.9 miles, at times amidst bleeding hearts. The shady path, now decked with wild ginger, nears the alder- and dogwood-lined creek—another nice area to stop and relax.

The trail begins to curve to the east, climbing into the canyon of a tributary. The route becomes more and more narrow and overgrown as you traverse high above the tiny creeklet. This is prime tick habitat: Check your clothing often!

At 2.9 miles you arrive at a diminutive waterfall, trickling down a large granite slab. From this point the pathway becomes very narrow and increasingly harder to follow as it heads toward Paradise Canyon, where it eventually fades out. The trail used to continue up the canyon, over Paradise Ridge, past the Oriole Grove of sequoias, and over Conifer Ridge to Mineral King Road, but this section has not been maintained for many years.

After reaching the journey's end, backtrack to the parking area at 5.8 miles.

5 Middle Fork Trail

Highlights: This path takes you to a shady campsite beside a tranquil pool with a pretty cascade.

See Map on Page 44

Type of hike: Out-and-back, day hike.

Total distance: 9 miles.

Difficulty: Moderate.

Best months: October through May.

Maps: USGS Giant Forest and Lodgepole, or TOPO! Sequoia Kings Canyon CD-ROM.

Permits: None.

Special considerations: Ticks can be found on this trail; wear plenty of insect repellent and check your clothing often. Be alert for poison oak—do not touch or brush up against it! Also, this trail can be quite hot, so get an early start or save it for a cool and cloudy day.

Parking and facilities: Restrooms, water, and a pay phone are available at Hospital Rock, as well as picnic tables and grills. The hike begins at the crosswalk located at the northeast end of the parking area.

Finding the trailhead: From the Ash Mountain entrance station, drive 5.9 miles northeast on the Generals Highway, past the Ash Mountain Visitor Center, Tunnel Rock (now closed to traffic), and Potwisha Campground, to the Hospital Rock Picnic Area. Park at the picnic area.

Note: When it is open, you can drive 0.5 miles on the paved Buckeye Flat Road to the Buckeye Flat Campground. Go left (east) onto a dirt road just before you reach the camp, and follow this road for 1.3 miles to a small parking area. This will cut the hike down to 5.4 miles.

Key points:
- 0.0   Begin at the parking area.
- 0.5   Reach the dirt road.
- 1.3   Arrive at the trailhead.
- 1.8   Cross Moro Creek.
- 2.3   Cross a second creek.
- 4.5   Arrive at Panther Creek and Falls.

The hike: Start your journey by crossing the Generals Highway using the crosswalk, and visit some Monachi bedrock mortars and an interpretive sign on the south

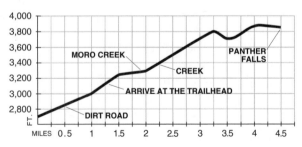

The small, delicate mariposa lily is one of many wildflowers that bloom in the late spring and summer throughout both Sequoia and Kings Canyon National Parks.

side of the road to Buckeye Flat Campground. On the north side of this road is Hospital Rock, along with a stone stairway that leads up to a small viewing platform across from the pictographs painted on the rock's side.

After inspecting the pictographs, follow the paved road east, passing a large hollow under Hospital Rock that was used by the Monachis as a shelter for the sick and injured. Hale Tharp, who homesteaded the area of Crescent and Log Meadows (Hike 10), named the rock after visiting the native village here.

After the road passes over a pleasant little brook, you exit the shady oaks to gain views of the turbulent Middle Fork of the Kaweah below. In spring, bush monkey flower, yerba santa, popcorn flowers, mariposa lilies, and lupine brighten the grassy areas between the oaks, bay laurels, buckeyes, redbuds, and tall stalks of yucca.

The Castle Rocks come into view, and at 0.5 mile, immediately after a sharp turn, you reach an unnamed dirt road. Make a left (east) turn on this road. The paved road, which drops down into Buckeye Flat Campground, leads to the Paradise Creek Trail (Hike 4).

The dirt road winds through oaks dotting the grassy hillsides, passing above the bridge over the Middle Fork on the Paradise Creek Trail. Chamise and manzanita line the trail, and you have views of Alta Peak (Hike 24), Mount Stewart, the Castle Rocks, and the Middle Fork of the Kaweah River below. At 1.3 miles, you reach the trailhead at a small, seasonal parking area where a corral used to be located.

The trail leads downhill just past a mileage sign, and quickly switchbacks down to a precarious rock hop of willow- and alder-lined Moro Creek at 1.8

miles, just below a surging cascade. After passing through the ruins of a drift fence and climbing a switchback, the path contours around a small ridge and passes a no-longer discernible junction with an abandoned trail. This side trail appears on several maps of the area, and portions of it are visible on the return trip.

The main trail dips across a small brook on stones at 2.3 miles. After switch-backing up on the other side of the brook, you may be able to spot parts of the abandoned trail on the ridge behind you, as well as Moro Rock to the northwest. Once used by Monachis to travel to the Giant Forest area, the defunct route is now overgrown due to lack of maintenance and damage caused by the Buckeye Fire of 1988.

The trail now climbs, sometimes quite steeply, through chamise and man-zanita, dipping into shady side canyons to cross seasonal creeks, one sporting a tiny campsite. The mystical Castle Rocks watch over your progress from across the Middle Fork Canyon. A descent, a climb, and a couple of switch-backs occur before the path drops down closer to the river, above a nearly vertical wooded slope. A very steep and slippery descent leads down to peaceful Panther Creek at 4.5 miles, where a rock hop leads to a campsite on a creekside bluff. A lacy cascade spills into a glassy pool above the crossing. Panther Falls is just beyond the rim of a lower pool and can be safely viewed by hiking a short distance farther up the trail. If you descend to the lower pool, use extreme caution.

After lingering for a while, return to the parking area at 9 miles.

Options: The Middle Fork Trail can be used as an alternate to the High Sierra Trail to reach Bearpaw Meadow and Redwood Meadow. From the parking area, it is 9.7 miles to Bearpaw Meadow, with almost 4,000 feet of elevation gain. Redwood Meadow is 8.6 miles from the parking area, with a little more than 2,000 feet of elevation gain.

Hikes in the Giant Forest

The first two hikes in this chapter begin on the Crystal Cave Road, and are listed from west to east. The following three hikes start on the Crescent Meadow Road, and again are listed from west to east. The Round Meadow and Huckleberry hikes are located along the Generals Highway, just north of the Giant Forest Museum. The last three hikes begin near the General Sherman Tree.

6 Upper Colony Mill Trail

Highlights:	This trek follows the old dirt road that served as the entrance to Sequoia National Park and the Giant Forest before the completion of the Generals Highway in 1926.
Type of hike:	Semi-loop, day hike.
Total distance:	5.8 miles.
Difficulty:	Easy.
Best months:	May through June, October through early November.
Maps:	USGS Giant Forest, or TOPO! Sequoia Kings Canyon CD-ROM.
Permits:	None.
Special considerations:	The gate across Crystal Cave Road just past the Marble Fork Bridge is closed every night at 5 P.M. Be out of the area before this time or you may be locked in.
Parking and facilities:	No facilities are available at this trailhead. Restrooms and water are available 2.3 miles farther west down the road at the Crystal Cave parking area when the cave is open for tours (from 11 A.M. to 4 P.M. daily between the months of May and September; subject to change). The trail begins at the west end of the parking area, just beyond the large logs blocking the old dirt road.

Finding the trailhead: Drive either 13.8 miles north on the Generals Highway from the Ash Mountain entrance station, or 4.2 miles south from the Sherman Tree area, to Crystal Cave Road. Turn west onto the road and drive about 4.1 miles, past the Marble Fork bridge, to the Colony Mill parking area. The small parking turnout is located on the south side of the road, and the dirt road (trail) is blocked off by logs.

Key points:

- 0.0 Trailhead.
- 1.4 Reach a trail fork.
- 2.4 Arrive at the ranger cabin.
- 2.5 Reach another trail fork.
- 2.9 Reach Panorama Point.
- 3.3 Return to the trail fork.
- 3.8 Reach the last trail fork.

The hike: The old road/trail leads west for a short distance, then curves south, dropping slightly through dogwoods and a shady mixed forest. Wild iris

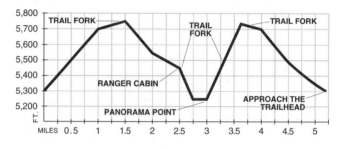

sometimes springs up in the middle of the trail. The wide path curves toward the southeast, climbing gently below Colony Peak, and passes your return route at the trail fork at 1.4 miles—an overgrown road to the right (southwest). Go left (southeast). After crossing over a small ridge, the trail descends to Admiration Point. Below you is Marble Falls, though it may not be visible due to the brush growing wildly on the hillside below. To the east stands the Great Western Divide, with Moro Rock in the foreground.

The Upper Colony Mill Trail leads past the rundown Colony Mill Ranger Station at the old entrance to Sequoia National Park.

50

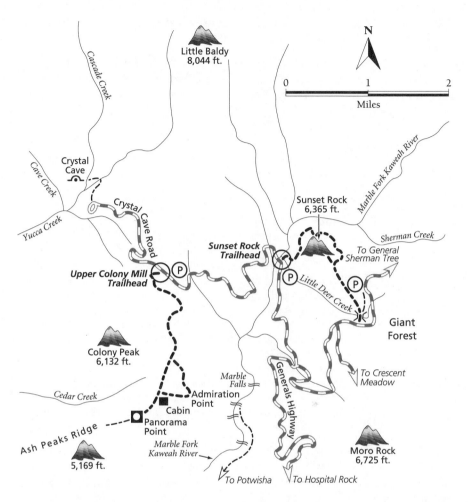

The trail leads west, through chamise, manzanita, and wildflowers in early summer. At 2.4 miles you arrive at the old entrance station to Sequoia National Park, marked by the dilapidated Colony Mill Ranger Station, obviously no longer in use. The infamous mill constructed by the Kaweah Colonists was located nearby; see the Lower Colony Mill Trail (Hike 1) for more information. Continue on down the trail, past toppled outhouses, to the junction with your return route at 2.5 miles; stay left (southwest).

At 2.9 miles you reach Panorama Point, where you can enjoy views to the east. Two trails used to lead off from this point: one led to the highest point on Ash Peaks Ridge, where a fire lookout was once located; the other traveled downhill to the Generals Highway by way of Elk Creek. Both of these abandoned trails are now too overgrown to be followed. The Colony Mill trail continues another 7 miles to North Fork Drive.

Retrace your steps to the junction with your return trail, now 3.3 miles into the hike. Follow the overgrown route up (left/northeast) over the ridge to rejoin the main trail. You may see mountain quail and their chicks in this lightly traveled area. Upon reaching the main trail at 3.8 miles, turn left (north) and return to the parking area at 5.8 miles.

Options: You can continue this hike all the way to the beginning of Colony Mill Road, a total of 9.9 miles one-way. This would give you an elevation gain of approximately 3,600 feet on the return trip. An easier option is to follow the Lower Colony Mill Trail (Hike 1).

7 Sunset Rock

Highlights:	This seldom-traveled path takes you past the roaring Marble Fork of the Kaweah, through a peaceful forest, and to great views from Sunset Rock.
Type of hike:	Out-and-back, day hike.
Total distance:	6.4 miles.
Difficulty:	Moderate.
Best months:	May through June, October through early November.
Maps:	USGS Giant Forest, or TOPO! Sequoia Kings Canyon CD-ROM.
Permits:	None.
Parking and facilities:	There are no facilities at this trailhead. The trail begins on the north side of the road, next to the east end of the bridge spanning the Marble Fork of the Kaweah River.

See Map on Page 51

Finding the trailhead: Drive either 13.8 miles north on the Generals Highway from the Ash Mountain entrance station or 4.2 miles south from the Sherman Tree area to Crystal Cave Road. Turn onto the road and head west for approximately 1.6 miles to the Marble Fork bridge. The parking area is located on the west side of the bridge, down a very short entry road.

Key points:
- 0.0 Trailhead.
- 1.4 Enjoy a view of Little Baldy.
- 2.0 Cross a creek.
- 2.4 Reach Sunset Rock.
- 3.1 Cross the bridge over Little Deer Creek.
- 3.2 Arrive at the Giant Forest Museum.

The hike: This trek begins by following the slender path north, past a trail sign that gives mileages to various destinations, along the turbulent Marble Fork of the Kaweah. The trail begins an ascent of many switchbacks, first through the shade of oaks, cedars, firs, and dogwoods, then, at about 0.6

mile, across a more exposed slope of overgrown bear clover (also known as mountain misery, which may be a more fitting name here). The trail reenters the shade in sugar pines and continues up a few more switchbacks. At about 1.4 miles you will gain a view of

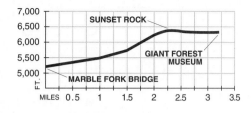

Little Baldy (Hike 29) to the northwest, and of Mount Silliman, through the trees and to the northeast.

After a couple more switchbacks, the route crosses a tiny, moss-lined brook at 2 miles. You may be treated to the melodic song of the hermit thrush in this lightly traveled area. One more switchback and a long up-hill bring you to Sunset Rock at 2.4 miles. Views to the west include the Ash Peaks Ridge and Colony Peak. To the northwest is Little Baldy, and Mount Silliman can be spotted from the far end of the rock to the north-east, still partially obscured by trees.

From Sunset Rock, take the paved trail leading south toward the site of the Giant Forest Museum, scheduled to be completed in 2002. A slight de-scent brings you to a cheerful meadow known as Eli's Paradise, in which you cross a small footbridge. Sequoias begin to appear and the path climbs a small rise before dipping down to Little Deer Creek at 3.1 miles. A short uphill on the other side of the bridge spanning this creek deposits you at the Generals Highway, across from the old store being remodeled to house the museum at 3.2 miles.

When you are ready, return the way you came.

Option: The Round Meadow Trail (Hike 11) can be combined with this trip, and is reached by taking the trail that heads east from the bridge spanning Little Deer Creek for 0.3 mile. This side trip adds 1.2 miles and negligible elevation gain to your hike.

8 Moro Rock and Hanging Rock

Highlights:	This hike takes you to excellent views from the summit of 6,725-foot Moro Rock and to mysterious Hanging Rock.
Type of hike:	Out-and-back, day hike.
Total distance:	1.2 miles.
Difficulty:	Easy.
Best months:	June through October.
Maps:	USGS Giant Forest; Sequoia National Park Giant Forest; or TOPO! Sequoia Kings Canyon CD-ROM.
Permits:	None.
Special considerations:	A risk of being struck by lightning exists on the summit of Moro Rock. If dark clouds are nearby, or if hail, rain, thunder, or static electricity are in the air, descend immediately.
Parking and facilities:	A drinking fountain and restrooms are located at the trailhead. The trail begins at the southeast end of the parking area, near the drinking fountain and the Sugar Pine Trail.

Finding the trailhead: Drive either 15.9 miles north on the Generals Highway from the Ash Mountain entrance station, or 2.1 miles south from the Sherman Tree area, to Crescent Meadow Road. Turn east, follow the narrow, winding road to the Moro Rock turnoff, and make a right (south) turn. The small Moro Rock parking area is 1.6 miles from the highway.

Key points:
- 0.0 Trailhead.
- 0.2 Reach the Moro Rock summit.
- 0.4 Return to the trailhead.
- 0.7 Arrive at the Hanging Rock Trail.
- 0.8 Reach Hanging Rock.

The hike: The trail ascends several sets of concrete steps and a ramp to an interpretive sign identifying peaks on the Great Western Divide, which is your view to the east. Wind through granite blocks for a view to the west, and more stairs. Cars appear in miniature on the Generals Highway twisting up the ridge far below.

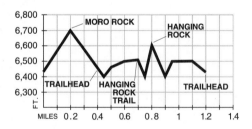

The route heads to the east side of the rock again, climbs a few more staircases and ramps, then crosses to the west side and rises up another series of steps and a ramp to the summit at 0.2 mile.

Moro Rock and Hanging Rock

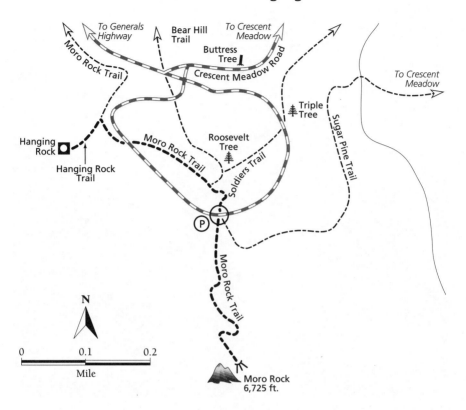

Guardrails enclose the narrow, level area of Moro Rock, and interpretive signs identify landmarks. To the north Mount Silliman and Alta Peak are visible, and to the east is the Great Western Divide with the Castle Rocks in the foreground. To the west you can see the Middle Fork of the Kaweah River winding down the canyon toward the town of Three Rivers and the hazy San Joaquin Valley.

After enjoying the view, return to the trailhead. Cross the parking area to its northeast end and pick up the Soldiers Trail at 0.4 mile. Follow the rock steps up to the trail, which heads west. When you arrive at the junction, take the fork to the left (west) leading to Hanging Rock, leaving the Soldiers Trail behind.

The path parallels the road as it passes through the forest, and crosses the pavement to another junction at 0.7 mile. Take the left (west) fork again and trek through tall bracken fern. Two short side trails lead to small overlooks with nice views of Moro Rock, while the main trail heads steeply uphill through the trees, reaching Hanging Rock at 0.8 mile.

This large, oblong boulder sits precariously on a granite slope, looking as if it could go tumbling down into the canyon at any minute. If you are brave enough to look over the edge of the incline, you can see the Generals Highway switchbacking directly below you. Once you have taken in this spectacle, retrace your route to the parking area at 1.2 miles.

Options: Moro Rock and Hanging Rock can be done as separate hikes for shorter trips, or they can be combined with the Sugar Pine Trail (Hike 9) for a longer one.

The Castle Rocks as seen from the viewpoint on Moro Rock.

9 Sugar Pine Trail

Highlights: This trek through a sugar pine forest takes you past bedrock mortars used by Native Americans to a couple of nice overlooks above the Middle Fork of the Kaweah River. Bird watchers may see many species along the trail.

Type of hike: Semi-loop, day hike.

Total distance: 3.1 miles.

Difficulty: Moderate.

Best months: June through October.

Maps: USGS Giant Forest and Lodgepole; Sequoia National Park Giant Forest; or TOPO! Sequoia Kings Canyon CD-ROM.

Permits: None.

Special considerations: Because it is on a dry south-facing slope, this trail is best done in early or late season.

Parking and facilities: A drinking fountain and restrooms are located at the trailhead. The trail begins at the southeast end of the parking area, near the drinking fountain and the Moro Rock Trail.

Finding the trailhead: Drive 15.9 miles north on the Generals Highway from the Ash Mountain entrance station, or 2.1 miles south from the Sherman Tree area, to Crescent Meadow Road. Turn east, follow the narrow, winding road to the Moro Rock turnoff, and make a right (south) turn. The small Moro Rock parking area is 1.6 miles from the highway.

Key points:

- 0.0 Trailhead.
- 1.0 Reach a trail junction.
- 1.2 Arrive at Bobcat Point.
- 1.4 Reach the Kaweah Vista.
- 1.5 Reach the junction with the High Sierra Trail.
- 2.1 Pass a trail junction.

The hike: The trail heads steeply downhill from the trailhead, then levels out in a dry, shrubby area before reentering the woods. You will see very large pine cones— some may even be a foot long— from the sugar pines for which this trail is named. Pass former overlooks that are no longer in use because the trees have grown and now block the views. The pathway dips to an area lush with dogwoods, thimbleberries, and ferns, then crosses a small tributary of Crescent Creek. A brief climb takes you through an

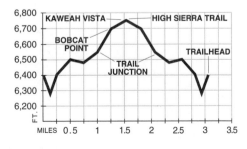

Sugar Pine Trail

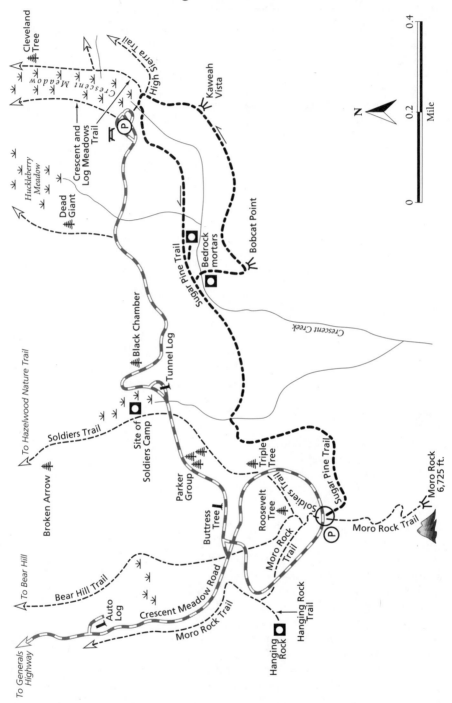

open, fire-scarred zone, then into a dense and shady forest. Brown creepers, hermit thrushes, red-breasted nuthatches, western bluebirds, western tanagers, white-headed woodpeckers, and many kinds of warblers frequent this area, so you may see several species at once.

You will hear rushing water and come to a trail fork at 1 mile. Make a right (south) turn, and head toward Bobcat Point (the left-hand trail is your return route). Jump across Crescent Creek as it flows over granite slabs near a few bedrock mortars. After a short but earnest climb, you reach Bobcat Point at 1.2 miles, with a spectacular view of the Castle Rocks across the canyon. You can also see Moro Rock to the west, as well as the people on top!

Resume your ascent up the ridge with vistas across the canyon to the right (south) and the profuse greenery of Crescent Creek below you on the left (north). At 1.4 miles, you arrive at Kaweah Vista, which gives you a breathtaking vista up the Middle Fork Canyon to the Great Western Divide.

The route turns northeast, rises a bit more, then descends along a granite knoll to join the High Sierra Trail briefly at 1.5 miles. Turn left (northwest) and follow the wide path a few yards to the pavement of the Crescent Meadow Trail. Continue left (northwest) at the junction and continue to Crescent Creek. Make a left (west) turn onto the small footpath following the creek's south bank.

As the trail passes through bracken fern, you cross the creek on a wooden footbridge. Join a trail coming from the Crescent Meadow parking area and turn left (southwest). After the ferns and flowers beside the creek, you pass through a burned area carpeted with mustang clover in summer. Cross a tributary stream from Huckleberry Meadow and meet a side trail that leads to more bedrock mortars.

At 2.1 miles, you arrive at the junction with the trail to Bobcat Point, on which you traveled earlier. Retrace your steps back to the parking area at 3.1 miles.

Options: This hike can be combined with Moro Rock and Hanging Rock (Hike 8), or with Crescent and Log Meadows (Hike 10), for a longer trip.

10 Crescent and Log Meadows

Highlights: This partially paved hike takes you past one of John Muir's favorite meadows and to a real "log cabin." Wildlife frequents these meadows and deer and bear sightings are common.

Type of hike: Loop, day hike.

Total distance: 1.7 miles.

Difficulty: Easy.

Best months: June through October.

Maps: USGS Giant Forest and Lodgepole; Sequoia National Park Giant Forest; or TOPO! Sequoia Kings Canyon CD-ROM.

Permits: None.

Parking and facilities: Restrooms, water, and a picnic area are available at this trailhead. The trail begins at the southeast end of the parking area, just south of the restrooms.

Finding the trailhead: Drive either 15.9 miles north on the Generals Highway from the Ash Mountain entrance station, or 2.1 miles south from the Sherman Tree area, to Crescent Meadow Road. Turn east and follow the narrow, winding road for 2.5 miles, past the Moro Rock turnoff, to the Crescent Meadow parking area at the road's end.

Key points:
- 0.0 Trailhead.
- 0.3 Pass the trail junction to the Cleveland Tree; stay right.
- 0.8 Reach Tharp's Log.
- 1.2 Pass the Chimney Tree.

The hike: As you begin this jaunt, heading counterclockwise around the loop, the paved path you are on coincides with the beginning of the High Sierra Trail. After crossing Crescent Creek on two wooden footbridges, you take the

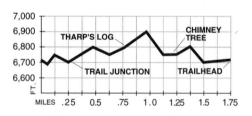

fork to the left (northeast), leaving the celebrated trans-Sierra route. A large sign at the end of Crescent Meadow proclaims it the "Gem of the Sierra," a quote from John Muir. Wildflowers bloom amidst the green and yellow grasses: shooting stars and leopard lilies in early season, lavender-colored lupines in the middle of summer, and the bright spears of meadow goldenrods near the summer's end.

The trail travels north along the southeast end of the meadow and reaches a dirt track at 0.3 mile that leads to the Cleveland and Chimney Trees. Continue on the paved path through the forest, passing another dirt trail departing to the right, which loops around the east side of Log Meadow. Stay left, walking along the west side of Log Meadow; if the trail is not crowd-

Crescent and Log Meadows

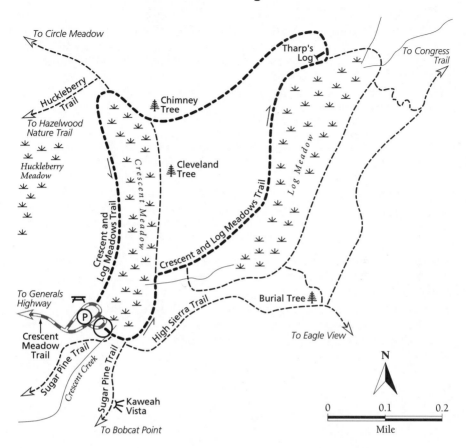

To Circle Meadow

Tharp's Log

To Congress Trail

Huckleberry Trail

To Hazelwood Nature Trail

Chimney Tree

Huckleberry Meadow

Crescent and Log Meadows Trail

Cleveland Tree

Crescent Meadow

Log Meadow

Crescent and Log Meadows Trail

To Generals Highway

Burial Tree

High Sierra Trail

Crescent Meadow Trail

To Eagle View

P

Sugar Pine Trail

Crescent Creek

Sugar Pine Trail

Kaweah Vista

N

To Bobcat Point

| 0 | 0.1 | 0.2 |

Mile

ed, you may spot a bear or a doe with her young. Yellow-rumped and orange-crowned warblers often flit about in the trees above the trail.

Farther along you lose the pavement, and reach Tharp's Log at 0.8 mile. Hale Tharp homesteaded the Log Meadow area and may have used this fire-hollowed sequoia, which was converted into a cabin, as a shelter while he grazed his cattle, long before the national park was established. A split rail corral, now overgrown with snowbrush, is barely visible behind a log bench.

From Tharp's Log, the unpaved footpath ascends the low ridge separating the two meadows, climbing over a very large log with steps carved into it. The trail then descends and you come to the Chimney Tree and a junction with the Cleveland Tree trail at 1.2 miles. Proceed west, around the northern tip of Crescent Meadow, before turning south. The dirt path skirts the sunlit meadow before arriving at the picnic area and the trailhead at 1.7 miles.

Options: This hike can be combined with the Sugar Pine Trail (Hike 9), which can also be used as a route to Moro Rock and Hanging Rock (Hike 8), for an even longer trip.

11 Round Meadow Trail

Highlights:	This trail, designed to be accessible to the handicapped, takes you around verdant Round Meadow and past the former site of the Giant Forest Lodge.
Type of hike:	Loop, day hike.
Total distance:	0.6 mile.
Difficulty:	Very easy.
Best months:	May through November.
Maps:	USGS Giant Forest; Sequoia National Park Giant Forest; or TOPO! Sequoia Kings Canyon CD-ROM.
Permits:	None.
Parking and facilities:	Only portable toilets are available at this large parking area. The trail is just a short distance up the road that heads north from the parking area and on your right (east).

Finding the trailhead: Drive 16.2 miles north on the Generals Highway from the Ash Mountain entrance station, or 1.8 miles south from the Sherman Tree area, to the short side road leading 0.1 mile to the Round Meadow parking area. The parking lot is on the north side of the road just west and across the highway from the Hazelwood Nature Trail parking area, and next to the former site of the Giant Forest Lodge, which has been removed to protect the giant sequoias.

Key points:
- 0.0   Trailhead.
- 0.3   Pass unnamed trail to General Sherman Tree area.
- 0.6   Complete loop.

The hike: Begin by following the road leading out of the parking area to the north, on the left side of the meadow, to the beginning of the trail. The nearly level path follows Little Deer Creek before the watercourse swings away toward the far end of the meadow. Interpretive signs identify the trees and plants along the way. The view across the sequoia-enveloped meadow is awe-inspiring to say the least.

The route travels upon a raised, wooden trail platform, edged with horsetails and meadow grasses. Tiny chipmunks scurry amongst the trees while blackbirds, robins, and other feathered creatures flutter about in the sun-filled meadow. Many wildflowers bloom here in summer as well.

At the halfway point, an unnamed trail branches left, eventually leading to the General Sherman Tree area. Continue over Little Deer Creek and pass an enormous boulder before reaching the former site of the Giant Forest Lodge. A landmark in the Giant Forest for many years, the lodge and its cabins were removed in 1999 to protect the fragile root systems of the giant sequoias. Accommodations were built north of Lodgepole at Wuksachi Village to replace the ones lost by the elimination of the old lodge.

Round Meadow Trail

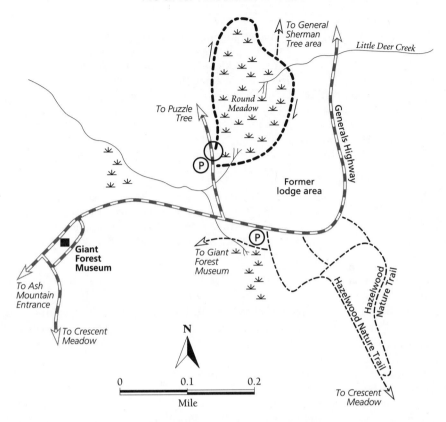

The route passes over another wood platform before bringing you back to the parking area at 0.6 mile.

Options: This short jaunt can be done in conjunction with Sunset Rock (Hike 7) or the Huckleberry Trail (Hike 12).

12 Huckleberry Trail

Highlights:	If you are hoping to see a bear, this loop should give you plenty of opportunities. The historic Squatter's Cabin, Huckleberry Meadow, and the Washington Tree are also along the way.
Type of hike:	Loop, day hike.
Total distance:	4.2 miles.
Difficulty:	Moderate.
Best months:	June through October.
Maps:	USGS Giant Forest; Sequoia National Park Giant Forest; or TOPO! Sequoia Kings Canyon CD-ROM.
Permits:	None.
Parking and facilities:	There are no facilities at this trailhead. The trail begins at the southeast end of the parking area. There is also overflow parking at a large turnout just east on the highway, with a spur trail leading south to the Hazelwood Nature Trail.

Finding the trailhead: Drive 16.3 miles north from the Ash Mountain entrance station on the Generals Highway, or 1.7 miles south from the Sherman Tree area, to the Hazelwood Nature Trail parking area. The parking area is located on the south side of the road, across from the former site of the Giant Forest Lodge, which has been removed to protect the giant sequoias.

Key points:
- 0.0 Trailhead.
- 0.3 Reach the three-way junction.
- 0.6 Pass the Alta and Huckleberry Trails junction.
- 1.6 Arrive at Squatter's Cabin.
- 1.8 Pass the Crescent Meadow junction.
- 2.1 Pass the trail to the General Sherman Tree area.
- 2.4 Pass another trail to the General Sherman Tree area.
- 2.7 Reach the Washington Tree.
- 2.9 Reach the Alta Trail junction.
- 3.0 Pass the trail to the former lodge.
- 3.6 Return to the Alta and Huckleberry Trails junction.
- 3.9 Pass the three-way junction.

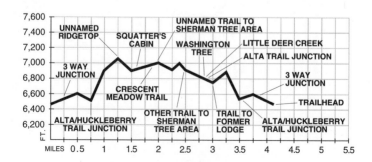

Huckleberry Trail

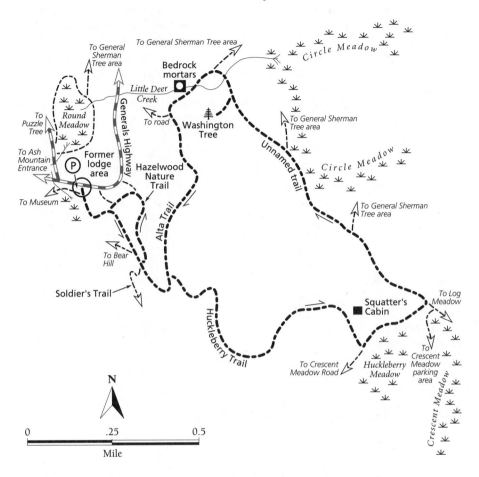

The hike: You begin by following the verdant Hazelwood Nature Trail east, passing interpretive signs along the way. In 0.3 mile, you reach a three-way trail junction with a directional sign. Take the middle fork—the Alta Trail. After passing the Soldier's Trail and a blocked side trail, a short climb brings you to another fork at 0.6 mile. Take the Huckleberry Trail to the right (east), and begin the steady climb to the top of the ridge.

An abandoned trail, which led to the Soldier's Trail, branches off to the right, barely discernible due to blowdowns. Just below the ridge crest, you enter an open, fire-scarred sector. Descending through the quiet forest on the other side, you may see many different birds or deer along the way. At 1.6 miles you come to Squatter's Cabin, an abandoned homestead, and flower-filled Huckleberry Meadow, a good place to spot a bear.

Following walking through a brief wooded section, you reach the next trail junction at 1.8 miles. A very short side trip to the right (east) would take you to the northern tip of Crescent Meadow, John Muir's "gem of the Sierra," which you can see on the right. The route follows the fork to the left (northwest), on an unnamed trail climbing toward Circle Meadow.

Golden-mantled ground squirrels scurry about the area as you continue left (northwest) at the next junction at 2.1 miles; this other unnamed trail leads to the General Sherman Tree, which is a portion of the Trail of the Sequoias. Pass a path that skirts Circle Meadow on your right (east); this path does not appear on maps. Stay left (northwest), traveling along a small section of the pleasant meadow.

Again, remain to the left at the following unnamed trail, which leads to the Bear's Bathtub and the General Sherman Tree area at 2.4 miles, entering another good bear-viewing area. You can see the crowns of giant sequoias to the west, and at 2.7 miles, you arrive at a side trail to the left (southwest), which leads to the base of the massive Washington Tree. This tree ranks as the second largest living organism behind the General Sherman Tree.

Retrace your steps back to the main trail, and cross Little Deer Creek on a large log at 2.8 miles. Rejoin the Alta Trail on the other side at 2.9 miles; turn left (southwest).

In less than one-tenth of a mile you step across the same refreshing creek and pass Native American bedrock mortars on your right. Continue following the Alta Trail to your left (south) at the next junction at 3 miles; the intersecting trail leads to the Rimrock Trail, the Generals Highway, and the former Giant Forest Lodge area.

Traveling through chinquapin, you arrive back at the junction with the Huckleberry Trail at 3.6 miles. Take the fork to your right (south, then north) and return to the three-way junction, rejoining the Hazelwood Nature Trail at 3.9 miles. From here, follow the remainder of the nature trail to your right (northeast) to return to the parking area at 4.2 miles.

Option: This loop can be done in either direction.

13 Congress Trail

Highlights:	This paved interpretive trail takes you to the General Sherman Tree, the largest living thing on earth, as well as many other impressive "Giants."
Type of hike:	Loop, day hike.
Total distance:	1.9 miles.
Difficulty:	Easy.
Best months:	June through October.
Maps:	USGS Giant Forest; Sequoia National Park Giant Forest; or TOPO! Sequoia Kings Canyon CD-ROM.
Permits:	None.
Special considerations:	In 2001, the National Park Service began work on the Congress Trail, repaving and making minor changes to clarify trail junctions and make route-finding easier. Upon completion, there may be slight variations to the hike described here.
Parking and facilities:	Restrooms and water are available at the parking area. The trail begins at the General Sherman Tree, north of the parking area. Interpretive brochures can be purchased near the General Sherman Tree or at one of the park visitor centers.

Finding the trailhead: Drive either 18.3 miles north on the Generals Highway from the Ash Mountain entrance station, or 2.2 miles south from Lodgepole, to the General Sherman Tree parking area. The parking area is on the east side of the road. Overflow parking is available on the west side of the highway.

Key points:
- 0.0 Trailhead.
- 0.6 Reach the cutoff trail.
- 0.9 Arrive at a four-way junction.
- 1.4 Reach the second four-way junction.
- 1.7 Pass the cutoff trail.

The hike: The best way to begin this journey is to visit the General Sherman Tree. Named for William Tecumseh Sherman, a Union general in the Civil War, this giant sequoia is the largest living organism on the face of the earth. It is almost 275 feet tall,

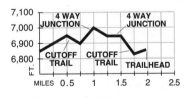

about 36.5 feet wide at its base, and weighs approximately 1,385 tons. After taking in this awesome sight, begin following the paved path along the east side of the entrance road to the parking area. Passing young sequoias, you soon reach the signed Congress Trail, which gets its name from the titles of some of the trees along the path.

Congress Trail

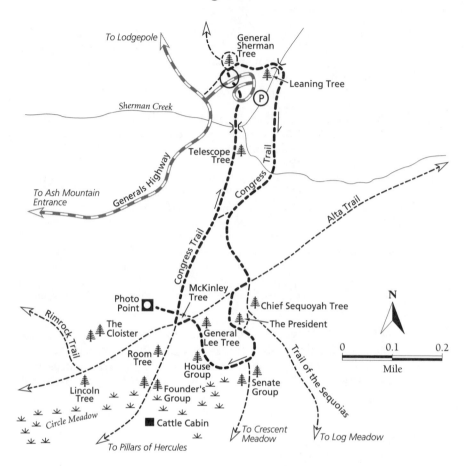

A very short downhill stretch brings you to a small bridge on Sherman Creek and the Leaning Tree, then the trail begins a gradual climb. Traveling through the big trees, past many numbered stops described in the interpretive pamphlet, you meet a cutoff trail at 0.6 mile.

Continue on to the four-way junction of the Trail of the Sequoias (Hike 14) and the Alta Trail at 0.9 mile. Follow the pavement to your right (southwest) and continue to the fourth largest sequoia, known as The President. The Chief Sequoyah Tree, named in honor of a Cherokee Indian who developed a phonetic alphabet for his tribe, is just up the side trail to the right (east) of The President.

The paved path arrives next at a group of large sequoias dubbed The Senate. The footpath leading through the center of these behemoths is the culmination of the Trail of the Sequoias. A little farther down the trail, after you have passed a portion of Circle Meadow, you will reach a group of sequoias known as The House, named to honor the House of Representatives. Beyond the House group, you come upon the General Lee Tree.

At 1.4 miles, you reach another four-way junction near the McKinley Tree. The trail to the left (south) and the Alta Trail ahead are covered in the Circle Meadow trail description (Hike 15). Make a right, and proceed on the paved path heading north.

On your left (west) a spur path leads to a photo point of the McKinley Tree, named for President McKinley after his assassination. Beyond, the trail begins to descend and passes more interpretive stops as you approach the cutoff trail at 1.7 miles. Farther north, you advance through a tunnel in an enormous sequoia that fell across the trail in 1965. The pathway then crosses gurgling Sherman Creek on a footbridge and ascends to attain the parking area at 1.9 miles.

Options: This hike can be combined with the Trail of the Sequoias (Hike 14), Circle Meadow (Hike 15), or both for a much longer day hike.

14 Trail of the Sequoias

Highlights:	This hike is a long extension of the Congress Trail, traveling all the way to the Crescent Meadow area and back, with a good chance for bear sightings.
Type of hike:	Loop, day hike.
Total distance:	6.2 miles.
Difficulty:	Moderate.
Best months:	June through October.
Maps:	USGS Giant Forest and Lodgepole; Sequoia National Park Giant Forest; or TOPO! Sequoia Kings Canyon CD-ROM.
Permits:	None.
Special considerations:	In 2001, the National Park Service began work on the Congress Trail, repaving and making minor changes to clarify trail junctions and make route-finding easier. Upon completion, there may be slight variations to the hike described here.
Parking and facilities:	Restrooms and water are available at the parking area. The trail begins at the General Sherman Tree, north of the parking area.

Finding the trailhead: Drive either 18.3 miles north on the Generals Highway from the Ash Mountain entrance station, or 2.2 miles south from Lodgepole, to the General Sherman Tree parking area. The parking area is on the east side of the road. Overflow parking is available on the west side of the highway.

Key points:
- 0.0 Trailhead.
- 0.9 Reach a four-way junction.
- 1.0 Pass the side trail.
- 2.2 Reach the Crescent Creek crossing.
- 2.9 Cross a tributary creek.
- 3.1 Reach the Burial Tree trail junction.
- 3.3 Pass the Log Meadow trail junction.
- 3.4 Pass Tharp's Log.
- 3.5 Reach the second Crescent Meadow Trail junction on the west side of Log Meadow.
- 3.8 Reach the Chimney Tree and Cleveland Tree trail junction.
- 4.0 Reach the Huckleberry Trail junction.
- 4.4 Leave the Huckleberry Trail.
- 4.5 Pass the trail to Circle Meadow.
- 5.4 Arrive at the Congress Trail junction.

The hike: Begin this ramble by following the Congress Trail (Hike 13) for 0.9 mile to the four-way junction with the Alta Trail. Continue straight ahead, taking the signed Trail of the Sequoias uphill to the Chief Sequoyah Tree, named in honor of a Cherokee Indian who developed a phonetic alphabet for

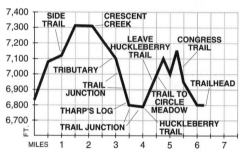

his tribe, at 1 mile. To your right (southwest) is a side trail leading down to the tree known as The President. Proceed up the ridge, passing through tunnels in two fallen sequoias along the way. After topping the rise, the trail descends slightly to a step crossing of fledgling Crescent Creek at 2.2 miles.

The trail ascends a bit more among numerous sequoias before dropping to cross a tributary stream at 2.9 miles. At 3.1 miles you meet a junction with a trail leading to the Burial Tree. Take the trail downhill to your right (west), and meet yet another path at 3.3 miles that leads around the east side of Log Meadow.

Make a right (northwest) turn again and cross both the tributary and Crescent Creek on footbridges before reaching Tharp's Log at 3.4 miles. Hale Tharp homesteaded the Log Meadow area and may have used this fire-hollowed sequoia-turned-cabin as a shelter while he grazed his cattle, long before the national park was established.

Bears frequent the Log and Crescent Meadow area; if you see one, observe it from a safe distance. Beyond Tharp's Log, at 3.5 miles, the trail passes an intersection with the Crescent Meadow Trail, which leads along the west side of Log Meadow. The trail then travels over a small ridge, climbing a very large log with steps carved into it in the process.

The route comes to the Chimney Tree at the northern end of Crescent Meadow at 3.8 miles. Here, you also meet a trail leading south to the Cleve-

Trail of the Sequoias

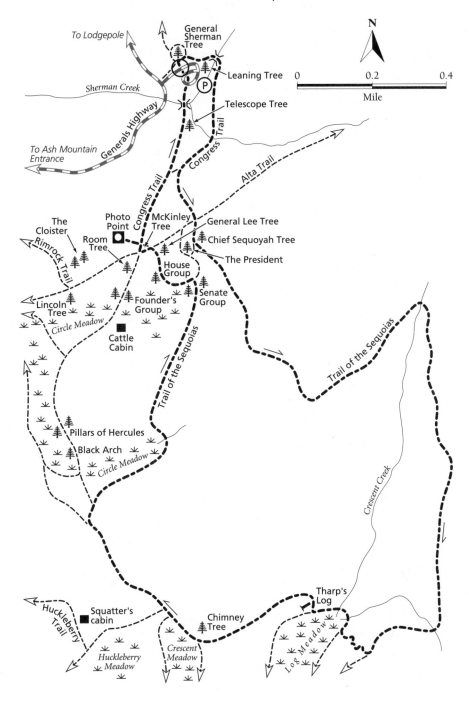

land Tree. Proceed west, past the Crescent Meadow Trail junction; in just a few more feet, at 4 miles, you meet the Huckleberry Trail (Hike 12). Turn right (uphill and to the northwest) on the unnamed trail that is a portion of the Huckleberry Trail. Stay to the right at the next junction at 4.4 miles, leaving the Huckleberry Trail and nearing Circle Meadow.

After traveling through a burned area, make another right (north) turn at the junction with the trail to Circle Meadow at 4.5 miles. The route skirts the southern finger of Circle Meadow, heading steeply uphill. The trail dips to cross the creek feeding this clearing, and passes a long view back down the meadow, which is filled with colorful wildflowers in summer. After crossing a small ridge, the trail approaches the northern finger of Circle Meadow and enters the group of sequoias known as The Senate before meeting the Congress Trail at 5.4 miles. This time, make a left (west) turn and follow the remainder of the Congress Trail to the parking area at 6.2 miles.

Option: For an even longer hike, this trip can be combined with Circle Meadow (Hike 15).

---

15 Circle Meadow

Highlights:	This trek around sequoia-rimmed Circle Meadow is a peaceful extension of the Congress Trail. The trail is away from the crowds and tours some less-visited named trees.
Type of hike:	Loop, day hike.
Total distance:	3.9 miles.
Difficulty:	Easy.
Best months:	June through October.
Maps:	USGS Giant Forest; Sequoia National Park Giant Forest; or TOPO! Sequoia Kings Canyon CD-ROM.
Permits:	None.
Special considerations:	In 2001, the National Park Service began work on the Congress Trail, repaving and making minor changes intended to clarify trail junctions and make route-finding easier. Upon completion, there may be slight variations to the hike described here.
Parking and facilities:	Restrooms and water are available at the parking area. The trail begins at the General Sherman Tree, north of the parking area.

Finding the trailhead: Drive either 18.3 miles north on the Generals Highway from the Ash Mountain entrance station, or 2.2 miles south from Lodgepole, to the General Sherman Tree parking area. The parking area is on the east side of the road. Overflow parking is available on the west side of the highway.

Key points:
- 0.0   Trailhead.
- 1.4   Stay southbound at the junction.
- 1.7   Reach the trail that connects to the Alta Trail.
- 2.1   Take the trail that connects to the Huckleberry Trail.
- 2.4   Take the northbound trail.
- 2.8   Pass the Alta Trail spur trail.
- 2.9   Reach the Alta Trail junction.
- 3.2   Pass the Rimrock Trail junction.
- 3.3   Reach the Congress Trail junction.

The hike: Begin this excursion by following the Congress Trail (Hike 13) for 1.4 miles to the four-way junction at the McKinley Tree. At this intersection, which is

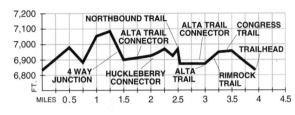

about halfway around the Congress Trail loop, you stand on the Alta Trail facing southwest. The Alta Trail stretches ahead of you as well as behind. Make a left and follow the southbound trail toward Circle Meadow. You first come to the Room Tree, a large, fire-hollowed sequoia that you can enter. Beyond, you reach the Founder's Group, dedicated to the individuals who helped establish Sequoia National Park.

After crossing the northern branch of Circle Meadow, which is actually shaped more like the letter "C," you arrive at Cattle Cabin. This structure was built by ranchers who grazed cattle in the Giant Forest in the days before the park was established.

At 1.7 miles you pass a spur to the Alta Trail; continue straight ahead and begin a gentle incline. Lupines and a myriad of colorful wildflowers bloom beside the path in summer. Just before the southern branch of Circle Meadow, the trail passes between the Pillars of Hercules and through the fire-gutted Black Arch. Cross the meadow and its small creek by balancing on logs to attain a junction not shown on maps at 2.1 miles. Take the trail to your right (west), skirting the meadow, and then join part of the Huckleberry Trail (Hike 12).

At 2.4 miles, you stay right at the succeeding junction and head north. The path follows along the west side of Circle Meadow, where various small forest creatures congregate. The trail reaches the Bear's Bathtub; here two sequoias have fused together at their bases and water collects in the cavity between them. Legend has it that a guide surprised a bear bathing in the water many, many years ago.

The trail continues north and meets the connecting trail once again before stepping across Little Deer Creek at 2.8 miles. Arrive at the Alta Trail at 2.9 miles and turn right (northeast).

At 3.2 miles you meet a junction with the Rimrock Trail, right across from the immense Lincoln Tree, which ranks as the fifth largest sequoia. A group

Circle Meadow

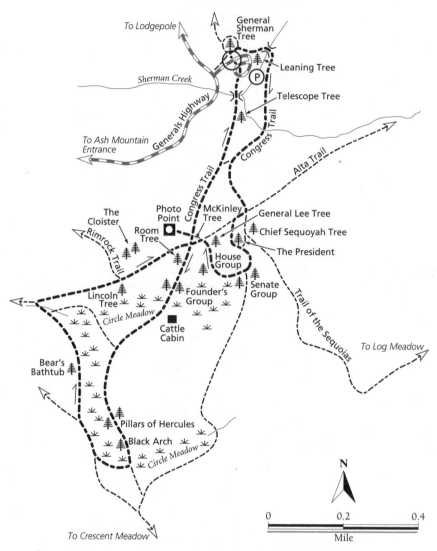

of sequoias on the north side of the trail is known as The Cloister. At 3.3 miles, you arrive back at the McKinley Tree; make a left and follow the remainder of the Congress Trail north to the parking area (3.9 miles).

Option: This hike can also be done in conjunction with the Trail of the Sequoias (Hike 14), for a very long day hike.

Hikes in the Central High Sierra

These hikes all begin at Crescent Meadow, but leave the Giant Forest to travel through the central High Sierra. All of the treks follow the High Sierra Trail, though the last three leave this trans-Sierra route at Bearpaw Meadow and travel into the wilderness to the southeast.

16 High Sierra Trail to Bearpaw Meadow

Highlights:	This trip takes you along the High Sierra Trail, up the scenic Middle Fork Canyon, to a large campground across from the Bearpaw Meadow High Sierra Camp.
Type of hike:	Out-and-back, backpack.
Total distance:	22 miles.
Difficulty:	Moderate.
Best months:	June through October.
Maps:	USGS Giant Forest, Lodgepole, and Triple Divide Peak; USFS John Muir Wilderness and Sequoia–Kings Canyon Wilderness; or TOPO! Sequoia Kings Canyon CD-ROM.
Permits:	Obtain a permit at the Lodgepole Visitor Center.
Special considerations:	This trail is also used by horseback riders. Please remember proper trail etiquette by stepping off the trail on the downhill side and waiting quietly until the horses have passed. Stay in plain view of the horses; they may think you are a wild animal and bolt if you are hidden behind a rock or tree.
Parking and facilities:	Restrooms, water, and a picnic area are all available at this trailhead. The trail begins at the southeast end of the parking area, just south of the restrooms.

Finding the trailhead: Drive 15.9 miles north from the Ash Mountain entrance station on the Generals Highway, or 2.1 miles south from the General Sherman Tree area, to Crescent Meadow Road. Turn east and follow the narrow, winding road for 2.5 miles, past the Moro Rock turnoff, to the Crescent Meadow parking area at the road's end.

Key points:
- 0.0   Trailhead.
- 0.5   Reach the four-way junction.
- 0.7   Reach Eagle View.
- 2.5   Pass the Wolverton Cutoff.
- 5.5   Cross Mehrten Creek.
- 6.3   Reach Seven Mile Trail.
- 9.3   Cross Buck Creek.
- 11.0   Reach the Bearpaw Meadow campsites.

The hike: You begin by following a very short portion of the paved Crescent Meadow Trail. After you pass the second footbridge and a part of the Sugar Pine Trail (Hike 9) on your right (west), you come to the signed High Sierra Trail. Follow this path uphill, through shady woods, passing another segment of the Sugar Pine Trail.

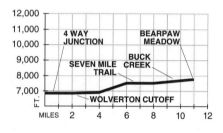

At 0.5 mile, reach a four-way junction and take the path to your right (southeast). After passing an informational sign about the Buckeye Fire of 1988, which burned much of the forest below the trail, you reach signed Eagle View (0.7 mile), which gives you views east to the Great Western Divide, across the canyon to the Castle Rocks, and west to Moro Rock and Three Rivers.

The trail dips and rises through oaks and bear clover, reaching the Wolverton Cutoff at 2.5 miles. Views to the north are of Alta Peak. The path crosses several small branches of Panther Creek, lined with wildflowers in summer. The route ascends and descends Seven Mile Hill, covered with a shady forest before arriving at Mehrten Creek at 5.5 miles. Campsites and a bear box are located a short distance uphill from the trail.

The trail passes through exposed granite immediately beyond the creek and rounds a curve to views of Little Blue and Sugarbowl Domes. The Seven Mile Trail intersects your path at 6.3 miles as you begin winding into side canyons, easily crossing the small creeks within them.

Pass some campsites and a bear box to the right (south) of the trail and rock-hop Ninemile Creek, which may require a wade in early season. After another up and down you reach Buck Canyon, and switchback down past a campsite to cross its creek on a new wooden bridge at 9.3 miles. Remnants of the old trail can be seen across the canyon leading toward the area where the old bridge washed out.

The path switchbacks up the other side of the canyon, passing the abandoned section of trail mentioned before, and climbs steadily to the south. Climb a few more switchbacks before arriving at the Redwood Meadow Trail, which leads to the Bearpaw Meadow campsites. Make a right (south) turn and follow this trail to the camping area at 11 miles. The campground is on the west side of Bearpaw Meadow and has piped water, but it must be boiled or filtered before consumption. Deer, bear, and many birds frequent this verdant location. After your stay, retrace your steps to your car at 22 miles.

High Sierra Trail to Bearpaw Meadow

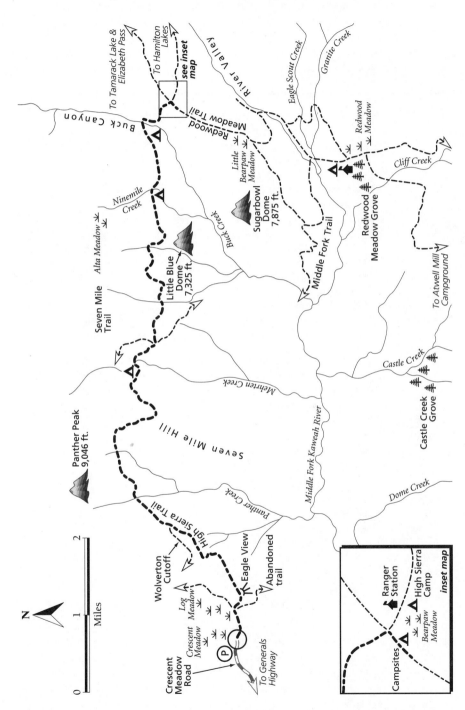

Options: See the route descriptions for Hamilton Lakes (Hike 17), Nine Lakes Basin (Hike 18), and Big Arroyo (Hike 19) for additions to this hike, or travel the loop described at the end of Big Arroyo for a long backpacking adventure.

17 Hamilton Lakes

Highlights:	From the Bearpaw Meadow High Sierra Camp, the High Sierra Trail leads past Valhalla to campsites with picturesque views at the lower of the clear Hamilton Lakes.
Type of hike:	Out-and-back, backpack.
Total distance:	30.8 miles.
Difficulty:	Difficult.
Best months:	July through mid-October.
Maps:	USGS Giant Forest, Lodgepole, and Triple Divide Peak; USFS John Muir Wilderness and Sequoia–Kings Canyon Wilderness; or TOPO! Sequoia Kings Canyon CD-ROM.
Permits:	Obtain a permit at the Lodgepole Visitor Center.
Parking and facilities:	Restrooms, water, and a picnic area are all available at this trailhead. The trail begins at the southeast end of the parking area, just south of the restrooms.

Finding the trailhead: Drive either 15.9 miles north from the Ash Mountain entrance station on the Generals Highway, or 2.1 miles south from the General Sherman Tree area, to Crescent Meadow Road. Turn east and follow the narrow, winding road for 2.5 miles, past the Moro Rock turnoff, to the Crescent Meadow parking area at the road's end.

Key points:
- 0.0   Trailhead.
- 0.5   Reach the four-way junction.
- 0.7   Reach Eagle View.
- 2.5   Pass the Wolverton Cutoff.
- 5.5   Cross Mehrten Creek.
- 6.3   Pass the Seven Mile Trail.
- 9.3   Cross Buck Creek.
- 11.0   Reach the Bearpaw Meadow campsites.
- 12.0   Take the footbridge across Lone Pine Creek.
- 15.4   Reach the lower Hamilton Lake.

The hike: Follow the High Sierra Trail to Bearpaw Meadow (Hike 16), arriving at the junction just before the campground at 11 miles. From this junction, the trail passes the Bearpaw Meadow High Sierra Camp (advance reservations are required) and the backcountry ranger station. The path then dips and rises through gardens of colorful wildflowers high on the canyon wall before crossing a rocky ledge that curves into Lone Pine Creek Canyon.

The route switchbacks down to a new bridge over Lone Pine Creek at 12 miles, avoiding a portion of abandoned trail that leads to a partially washed-out culvert bridge upstream. Nearly vertical granite walls enclose

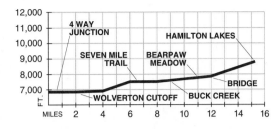

the creek below the footbridge, and the trail winds steeply uphill on the other side to meet the other end of the abandoned path, which also leads to a campsite near the old culvert.

Continue on the main trail to its junction with the rugged Elizabeth Pass Trail, taking the fork that leads straight ahead (east). The path climbs up many switchbacks, then descends through oaks as you near the falls on Hamilton Creek. After another ascent on a couple of switchbacks, you rock-hop the creek just above its billowing falls. More switchbacks bring you to a small, willow-lined lake, where you travel along a dynamited ledge. Valhalla (also known as Angels Wing) towers above as another climb brings you to the first and largest Hamilton Lake.

The route passes an overflow camping area and a trail leading to the pit toilet before reaching campsites and bear boxes at the west end of the deep blue lake at 15.4 miles. Views to the east include Mount Stewart, Kaweah Gap, and Eagle Scout Peak. To the west, Valhalla is the spectacle, catching a warm glow at sunset.

When you are ready to return, retrace your steps to Crescent Meadow, for a grand total of 30.8 miles.

Options: See the route descriptions for Nine Lake Basin (Hike 18) and Big Arroyo (Hike 19) for additions to this hike, or travel the loop described at the end of Big Arroyo for a long backpacking adventure.

Valhalla towers above the trail to Hamilton Lakes.

Hamilton Lakes • Nine Lake Basin • Big Arroyo

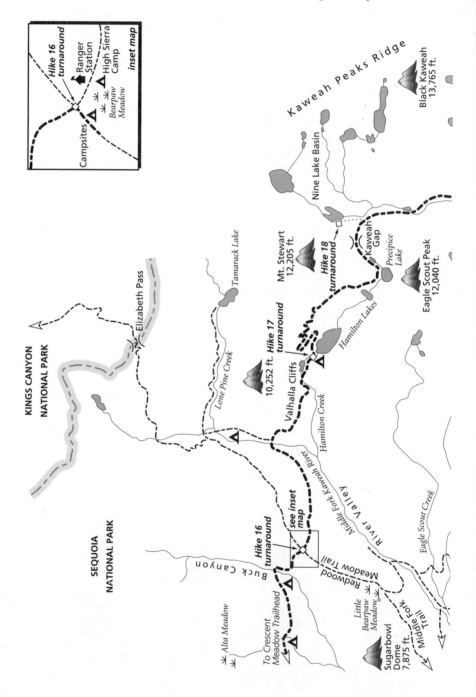

inset map

Hike 16 turnaround

Ranger Station

High Sierra Camp

Bearpaw Meadow

Campsites

Kaweah Peaks Ridge

Black Kaweah 13,765 ft.

Nine Lake Basin

Tamarack Lake

Mt. Stewart 12,205 ft.

Hike 18 turnaround

Kaweah Gap

Precipice Lake

Eagle Scout Peak 12,040 ft.

Elizabeth Pass

KINGS CANYON NATIONAL PARK

10,252 ft. Hike 17 turnaround

Valhalla Cliffs

Hamilton Lakes

Lone Pine Creek

Hamilton Creek

Eagle Scout Creek

Middle Fork Kaweah River

River Valley

SEQUOIA NATIONAL PARK

Hike 16 turnaround

see inset map

Buck Canyon

Redwood Meadow Trail

Alta Meadow

To Crescent Meadow Trailhead

Little Bearpaw Meadow

Sugarbowl Dome 7,875 ft.

Middle Fork Trail

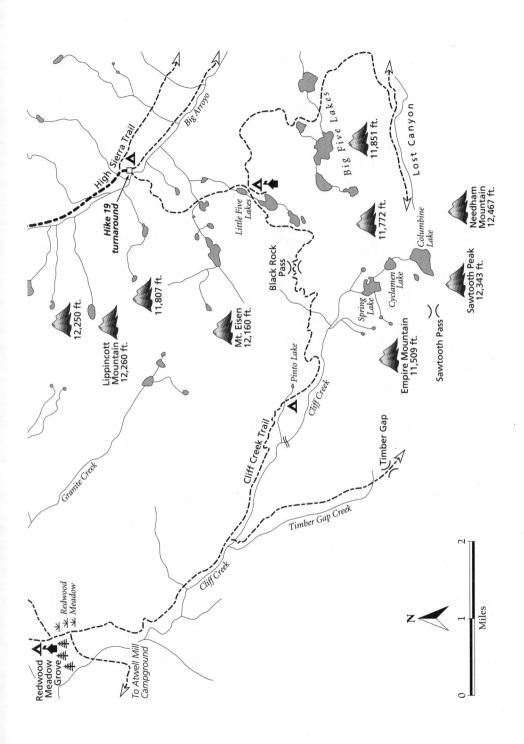

18 Nine Lake Basin

Highlights: From lower Hamilton Lake, travel through fields of alpine flowers to Kaweah Gap, then drop down to a high basin of striking lakes.

See Map on Page 80

Type of hike: Out-and-back, backpack.
Total distance: 38 miles.
Difficulty: Difficult.
Best months: July through mid-October.
Maps: USGS Giant Forest, Lodgepole, and Triple Divide Peak; USFS John Muir Wilderness and Sequoia–Kings Canyon Wilderness; or TOPO! Sequoia Kings Canyon CD-ROM.
Permits: Permits may be obtained at the Lodgepole Visitor Center.
Parking and facilities: Restrooms, water, and a picnic area are all available at this trailhead. The trail begins at the southeast end of the parking area, just south of the restrooms.

Finding the trailhead: Drive either 15.9 miles north from the Ash Mountain entrance station on the Generals Highway, or 2.1 miles south from the General Sherman Tree area, to Crescent Meadow Road. Turn east and follow the narrow, winding road for 2.5 miles, past the Moro Rock turnoff, to the Crescent Meadow parking area at the road's end.

Key points:

0.0	Trailhead.
0.5	Reach the four-way junction.
0.7	Enjoy Eagle View.
2.5	Pass the Wolverton Cutoff.
5.5	Cross Mehrten Creek.
6.3	Pass Seven Mile Trail.
9.3	Cross Buck Creek.
11.0	Reach the Bearpaw Meadow campsites.
15.4	Arrive at the Hamilton Lakes.
17.3	Cross Kaweah Gap.
19.0	Reach the lowest lake in Nine Lake Basin.

The hike: Follow the High Sierra Trail to Bearpaw Meadow (Hike 16) and the junction at 11 miles. Then, follow the trail to Hamilton Lakes (Hike 17), arriving at the lower Hamilton Lake at 15.4 miles.

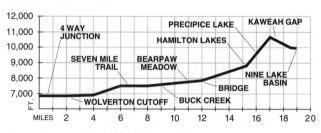

82

From the lake, rock-hop the outlet and ascend a granite slab to the first of several long switchbacks leading through chinquapin, ceanothus, and manzanita. Views down to the sapphire lake are superb as you climb higher and higher. After the switchbacks, the route contours around ridges, climbing less steeply than before. At one point, the path enters a steep side canyon on a dynamited shelf and passes through a short tunnel blasted through the granite. Evidence of a bridge that once spanned this chasm has been left behind.

As the route travels below Mount Stewart, you advance through a gorgeous alpine flower garden interspersed with small cascades. You may hear the barks of pikas and whistles of marmots along the way. Easier switchbacks lead through granite talus, dotted with grasses and flowers in summer, to above the upper Hamilton Lake. The rockbound body of water takes on a stunning azure hue as you rise up more switchbacks to Precipice Lake. Midnight blue in color, this lake has a sheer granite cliff as a backdrop, with Eagle Scout Peak looming above.

The trail switchbacks again leading above Precipice Lake, and continues through a rocky moonscape before passing grassy meadows and small tarns. High ridges on either side of the trail protect you from buffeting winds as you continue to rise toward Kaweah Gap.

One last switchback and you attain the pleasant gap at 17.3 miles, along with an up-close view of Black Kaweah. The lowest lake of the Nine Lake Basin, at 19 miles, is visible below to the north, as well as the canyon of the Big Arroyo to the south. The trail switchbacks down to the valley floor just south of the basin. To reach the lakes you must travel cross-country, leaving the main trail and heading north just before it nears the beginnings of the Big Arroyo. The lakes are all above the treeline and trail-less, so you must make your own primitive campsite on whatever flat, bare ground you can find.

The basin is surrounded by Mount Stewart and Lion Rock on its west side, and Triple Divide Peak to the north. Lawson Peak, the Kaweah Queen, and Black Kaweah border the basin on its east side. To the south is the canyon of the Big Arroyo, with Eagle Scout Peak near Kaweah Gap to the southwest.

When you are ready to return to civilization, retrace the trail to the parking area at 38 miles.

Options: See the route description for Big Arroyo (Hike 19) for an addition to this hike, or travel the loop described at the end of Big Arroyo for a long backpacking adventure.

19 Big Arroyo

See Map on Page 80

Highlights: From the barren Nine Lake Basin, this trip takes you down part of the Big Arroyo to creekside campsites.

Type of hike: Out-and-back, backpack.

Total distance: 44 miles.

Difficulty: Difficult.

Best months: July through mid-October.

Maps: USGS Giant Forest, Lodgepole, and Triple Divide Peak; USFS John Muir Wilderness and Sequoia–Kings Canyon Wilderness; or TOPO! Sequoia Kings Canyon CD-ROM.

Permits: Obtain a permit at the Lodgepole Visitor Center before your trek.

Parking and facilities: Restrooms, water, and a picnic area are all available at this trailhead. The trail begins at the southeast end of the parking area, just south of the restrooms.

Finding the trailhead: Drive either 15.9 miles north from the Ash Mountain entrance station on the Generals Highway, or 2.1 miles south from the General Sherman Tree area, to Crescent Meadow Road. Turn east and follow the narrow, winding road for 2.5 miles, past the Moro Rock turnoff, to the Crescent Meadow parking area at the road's end.

Key points:

0.0	Trailhead.
0.5	Reach the four-way junction.
0.7	Enjoy Eagle View.
2.5	Pass the Wolverton Cutoff.
5.5	Cross Mehrten Creek.
6.3	Intersect the Seven Mile Trail.
9.3	Cross Buck Creek.
11.0	Reach the Bearpaw Meadow campsites.
15.4	Pass the Hamilton Lakes.
17.3	Cross Kaweah Gap.
19.0	Reach the lowest lake in Nine Lake Basin.
20.5	Make the Big Arroyo crossing.
22.0	Reach the Big Arroyo campsites.

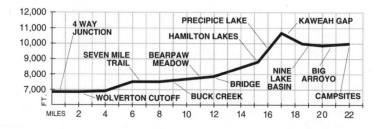

From the lake, rock-hop the outlet and ascend a granite slab to the first of several long switchbacks leading through chinquapin, ceanothus, and manzanita. Views down to the sapphire lake are superb as you climb higher and higher. After the switchbacks, the route contours around ridges, climbing less steeply than before. At one point, the path enters a steep side canyon on a dynamited shelf and passes through a short tunnel blasted through the granite. Evidence of a bridge that once spanned this chasm has been left behind.

As the route travels below Mount Stewart, you advance through a gorgeous alpine flower garden interspersed with small cascades. You may hear the barks of pikas and whistles of marmots along the way. Easier switchbacks lead through granite talus, dotted with grasses and flowers in summer, to above the upper Hamilton Lake. The rockbound body of water takes on a stunning azure hue as you rise up more switchbacks to Precipice Lake. Midnight blue in color, this lake has a sheer granite cliff as a backdrop, with Eagle Scout Peak looming above.

The trail switchbacks again leading above Precipice Lake, and continues through a rocky moonscape before passing grassy meadows and small tarns. High ridges on either side of the trail protect you from buffeting winds as you continue to rise toward Kaweah Gap.

One last switchback and you attain the pleasant gap at 17.3 miles, along with an up-close view of Black Kaweah. The lowest lake of the Nine Lake Basin, at 19 miles, is visible below to the north, as well as the canyon of the Big Arroyo to the south. The trail switchbacks down to the valley floor just south of the basin. To reach the lakes you must travel cross-country, leaving the main trail and heading north just before it nears the beginnings of the Big Arroyo. The lakes are all above the treeline and trail-less, so you must make your own primitive campsite on whatever flat, bare ground you can find.

The basin is surrounded by Mount Stewart and Lion Rock on its west side, and Triple Divide Peak to the north. Lawson Peak, the Kaweah Queen, and Black Kaweah border the basin on its east side. To the south is the canyon of the Big Arroyo, with Eagle Scout Peak near Kaweah Gap to the southwest.

When you are ready to return to civilization, retrace the trail to the parking area at 38 miles.

Options: See the route description for Big Arroyo (Hike 19) for an addition to this hike, or travel the loop described at the end of Big Arroyo for a long backpacking adventure.

19 Big Arroyo

Highlights:	From the barren Nine Lake Basin, this trip takes you down part of the Big Arroyo to creekside campsites.
Type of hike:	Out-and-back, backpack.
Total distance:	44 miles.
Difficulty:	Difficult.
Best months:	July through mid-October.
Maps:	USGS Giant Forest, Lodgepole, and Triple Divide Peak; USFS John Muir Wilderness and Sequoia–Kings Canyon Wilderness; or TOPO! Sequoia Kings Canyon CD-ROM.
Permits:	Obtain a permit at the Lodgepole Visitor Center before your trek.
Parking and facilities:	Restrooms, water, and a picnic area are all available at this trailhead. The trail begins at the southeast end of the parking area, just south of the restrooms.

See Map on Page 80

Finding the trailhead: Drive either 15.9 miles north from the Ash Mountain entrance station on the Generals Highway, or 2.1 miles south from the General Sherman Tree area, to Crescent Meadow Road. Turn east and follow the narrow, winding road for 2.5 miles, past the Moro Rock turnoff, to the Crescent Meadow parking area at the road's end.

Key points:

0.0	Trailhead.
0.5	Reach the four-way junction.
0.7	Enjoy Eagle View.
2.5	Pass the Wolverton Cutoff.
5.5	Cross Mehrten Creek.
6.3	Intersect the Seven Mile Trail.
9.3	Cross Buck Creek.
11.0	Reach the Bearpaw Meadow campsites.
15.4	Pass the Hamilton Lakes.
17.3	Cross Kaweah Gap.
19.0	Reach the lowest lake in Nine Lake Basin.
20.5	Make the Big Arroyo crossing.
22.0	Reach the Big Arroyo campsites.

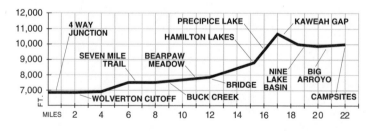

The hike: Follow the High Sierra Trail to Bearpaw Meadow (Hike 16) and the junction near the campsites at 11 miles. Continue to the Hamilton Lakes (Hike 17), then to Nine Lake Basin (Hike 18). After visiting the lakes, return to the main trail and head south along the west side of Big Arroyo Creek, passing a windswept campsite on your right. The path travels through grassy, open areas and stunted foxtail pines, then enters a more heavily forested area. At 20.5 miles you rock-hop the creek; this may require a wade early in the season.

The trail continues through the woods on the east side of the Big Arroyo, reaching a trail junction where the High Sierra Trail proceeds to the east just north of the camping area. Turn right and head south, past a trail crew cabin, to a bear box and campsites surrounding the Moraine Lake/Little Five Lakes trail junction at 22 miles. When you are ready to leave, return the way you came (44 miles), or use the options described below.

Options: Hikes 16 through 19 can be combined with hikes 20 through 22 for an extended semi-loop backpacking trip.

To link the routes, hike uphill from the Big Arroyo for 3.3 miles on a steep path to Little Five Lakes: The trail crosses the Big Arroyo (creek-sized here) on stones just south of the junction with the Moraine Lake Trail. The path steadily switchbacks up the slope under thin forest cover, then dips to an unnamed lake, which is not part of the Little Five Lakes—don't be fooled!

The route continues to climb to the lowest of the Little Five Lakes, and travels closely along its south shore. After another brief uphill, you reach the four-way junction at the east end of the second lake, next to the bear box. Campsites are located all along the trail leading past the bear box; the trail eventually takes you to the backcountry ranger station (this section of trail is not shown on maps).

From Little Five Lakes, follow the routes described in the next three hikes—Little Five Lakes (Hike 22), Pinto Lake (Hike 21), and Redwood Meadow (Hike 20)—in reverse. Then retrace your steps from Bearpaw Meadow (Hike 16) to the parking area. This trip totals 49.6 miles. Be sure to pick up a good topographic map or maps before setting out on this extended trip.

20 Redwood Meadow

Highlights:	This trip takes you from Bearpaw Meadow to an attractive meadow and the secluded Redwood Meadow grove of sequoias.
Type of hike:	Out-and-back, backpack.
Total distance:	29.4 miles.
Difficulty:	Moderate.
Best months:	June through October.
Maps:	USGS Giant Forest and Lodgepole; USFS John Muir Wilderness and Sequoia–Kings Canyon Wilderness; or TOPO! Sequoia Kings Canyon CD-ROM.
Permits:	Acquire a permit at the Lodgepole Visitor Center.
Special considerations:	This trail is used by horseback riders. Please remember proper trail etiquette by stepping off the trail on the downhill side and waiting quietly until the horses have passed. Stay in plain view of the horses— they may think you are a wild animal and bolt if you are hidden behind a rock or tree.
Parking and facilities:	Restrooms, water, and a picnic area are all available at this trailhead. The trail begins at the southeast end of the parking area, just south of the restrooms.

Finding the trailhead: Drive either 15.9 miles north from the Ash Mountain entrance station on the Generals Highway, or 2.1 miles south from the General Sherman Tree area, to Crescent Meadow Road. Turn east and follow the narrow, winding road for 2.5 miles, past the Moro Rock turnoff, to the Crescent Meadow parking area at the road's end.

Key points:
- 0.0 Trailhead.
- 0.5 Reach the four-way junction.
- 0.7 Reach Eagle View.
- 2.5 Pass the Wolverton Cutoff.
- 5.5 Cross Mehrten Creek.
- 6.3 Pass Seven Mile Trail.
- 9.3 Cross Buck Creek.
- 11.0 Reach the Bearpaw Meadow campsites.
- 12.5 Make the Kaweah River crossing.
- 14.7 Reach the Redwood Meadow campsites.

The hike: Follow the High Sierra Trail to Bearpaw Meadow (Hike 16), reaching the campsites just beyond the trail junction at 11 miles. From here, the path winds down through the forest under a canopy of firs before passing Little Bearpaw Meadow and a spur trail leading right (west) to the Middle Fork Trail.

The route drops down many switchbacks lined with manzanita and oaks to a crossing of the Middle Fork of the Kaweah River at 12.5 miles. Usually a wide rock hop, this crossing may need to be waded early in the summer.

On the south side of the river, the trail winds down River Valley, passing another trail connecting to the Middle Fork Trail on the right (west), and comes to a bridged crossing of Eagle Scout Creek. The

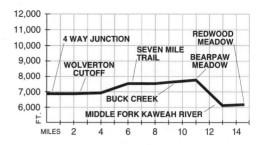

ascent and descent of a small ridge brings you to a step-stone crossing of Granite Creek. A short rise and a long downhill take you past yet another spur trail leading west to the Middle Fork Trail.

You arrive at the small Redwood Meadow camping area, which is surrounded by giant sequoias, at 14.7 miles. An outhouse is located to the north of the campsites and there is a water spigot, which was not working at the time of this writing (the park sometimes removes spigots when the water source becomes contaminated). The backcountry ranger station is a bit farther down the trail, along with a signed arch for Redwood Meadow and, of course, more sequoias.

After you have enjoyed your outing, return the way you came (29.4 miles).

Option: This route, along with those described in previous and subsequent hikes, can be combined for a long backpacking loop. See the description following Little Five Lakes (Hike 22) for details.

Foxglove is another of the lovely wildflowers you will find blooming in the backcountry of Sequoia and Kings Canyon National Parks.

Redwood Meadow • Pinto Lake • Little Five Lakes

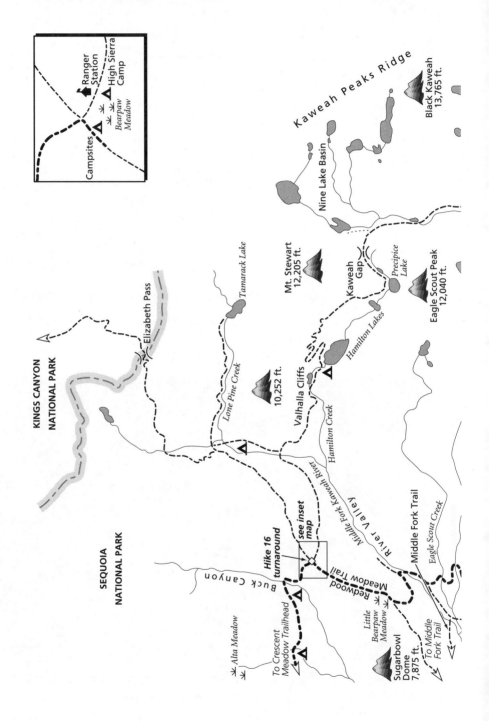

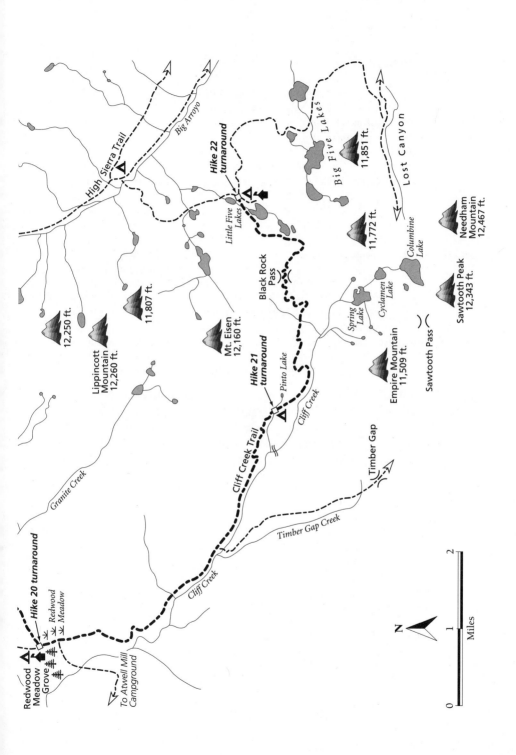

Redwood Meadow

Hike 20 turnaround

Redwood Meadow

Redwood Meadow Grove

To Atwell Mill Campground

Granite Creek

Cliff Creek

Cliff Creek

Timber Gap Creek

Cliff Creek Trail

Timber Gap

Cliff Creek

Hike 21 turnaround

Pinto Lake

12,250 ft.

Lippincott Mountain 12,260 ft.

11,807 ft.

Mt. Eisen 12,160 ft.

Black Rock Pass

Little Five Lakes

Hike 22 turnaround

High Sierra Trail

Big Arroyo

Big Five Lakes

11,851 ft.

Lost Canyon

11,772 ft.

Columbine Lake

Cyclamen Lake

Spring Lake

Empire Mountain 11,509 ft.

Sawtooth Pass

Sawtooth Peak 12,343 ft.

Needham Mountain 12,467 ft.

N

0   1   2

Miles

21 Pinto Lake

Highlights: From Redwood Meadow, this challenging route takes you to campsites near a small but lovely body of water.

See Map on Page 88

Type of hike: Out-and-back, backpack.
Total distance: 40.6 miles.
Difficulty: Difficult.
Best months: June through October.
Maps: USGS Giant Forest, Lodgepole, and Triple Divide Peak; USFS John Muir Wilderness and Sequoia–Kings Canyon Wilderness; or TOPO! Sequoia Kings Canyon CD-ROM.
Permits: Obtain a permit at the Lodgepole Visitor Center.
Special considerations: This trail is used by horseback riders. Please remember proper trail etiquette by stepping off the trail on the downhill side and waiting quietly until the horses have passed. Stay in plain view of the horses—they may think you are a wild animal and bolt if you are hidden behind a rock or tree.
Parking and facilities: Restrooms, water, and a picnic area are all available at this trailhead. The trail begins at the southeast end of the parking area, just south of the restrooms.

Finding the trailhead: Drive either 15.9 miles north from the Ash Mountain entrance station on the Generals Highway, or 2.1 miles south from the General Sherman Tree area, to Crescent Meadow Road. Turn east and follow the narrow, winding road for 2.5 miles, past the Moro Rock turnoff, to the Crescent Meadow parking area at the road's end.

Key points:
0.0   Trailhead.
0.5   Reach the four-way junction.
0.7   Visit Eagle View.
2.5   Pass the Wolverton Cutoff.
5.5   Cross Mehrten Creek.
6.3   Pass Seven Mile Trail.
9.3   Cross Buck Creek.
11.0   Arrive at the Bearpaw Meadow campsites.
12.5   Make the Kaweah River crossing.
14.7   Reach the Redwood Meadow campsites.
17.9   Arrive at the Timber Gap Trail junction.
20.3   Reach Pinto Lake.

The hike: Follow the High Sierra Trail to Bearpaw Meadow (Hike 16), arriving at the campsites just beyond the junction at 11 miles.

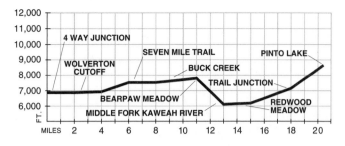

Next, follow the trail to Redwood Meadow (Hike 20) to the campsites at 14.7 miles.

From the small camping area, the trail heads south past the arched entrance to Redwood Meadow, which is across from the backcountry ranger station; the trail from Atwell Grove intersects your path on the right (west). Continue straight ahead (south) and begin to climb through sequoias and bear clover. This long stretch of trail dips to cross seasonal creeks under thick forest cover and passes through manzanita in drier areas. As you near the Timber Gap Trail junction, campsites appear to the left (northeast); a bear box and another campsite are at the junction at 17.9 miles.

Make a left (southeast) turn, and begin climbing on the rough and indirect Cliff Creek Trail, passing through the semi-shade of overgrown foliage. Enter a boulder-strewn floodplain below the spray of Cliff Falls, then ascend steeply on several switchbacks of crushed rock along the cascades of Pinto Lake's outlet. The path crosses the outlet and zigzags up a rocky ridge to bear boxes in full sun and a camping area in a grove of pines at 20.3 miles. Side trails lead to the tiny, but picturesque lake.

After your stay, retrace your steps to the trailhead (40.6 miles).

Option: This route, along with those described in previous and subsequent hikes, can be combined for a long backpacking loop. See the description following Little Five Lakes (Hike 22) for details.

22 Little Five Lakes

Highlights:	Leading on from Pinto Lake, this trek climbs to Black Rock Pass and expansive views, then drops to campsites at one of the ravishing Little Five Lakes.

See Map on Page 88

Type of hike: Out-and-back, backpack.
Total distance: 49.2 miles.
Difficulty: Difficult.
Best months: July through October.
Maps: USGS Giant Forest, Lodgepole, and Triple Divide Peak; USFS John Muir Wilderness and Sequoia–Kings Canyon Wilderness; or TOPO! Sequoia Kings Canyon CD-ROM.

Permits:	Obtain a permit at the Lodgepole Visitor Center.
Special considerations:	This trail is used by horseback riders. Please remember proper trail etiquette by stepping off the trail on the downhill side and waiting quietly until the horses have passed. Stay in plain view of the horses—they may think you are a wild animal and bolt if you are hidden behind a rock or tree.
Parking and facilities:	Restrooms, water, and a picnic area are all available at this trailhead. The trail begins at the southeast end of the parking area, just south of the restrooms.

Finding the trailhead: Drive either 15.9 miles north from the Ash Mountain entrance station on the Generals Highway, or 2.1 miles south from the General Sherman Tree area, to Crescent Meadow Road. Turn east and follow the narrow, winding road for 2.5 miles, past the Moro Rock turnoff, to the Crescent Meadow parking area at the road's end.

Key points:

0.0	Trailhead.
0.5	Reach the four-way junction.
0.7	Enjoy Eagle View.
2.5	Pass the Wolverton Cutoff.
5.5	Cross Mehrten Creek.
6.3	Pass the Seven Mile Trail.
9.3	Cross Buck Creek.
11.0	Reach the Bearpaw Meadow campsites.
12.5	Make the Kaweah River crossing.
14.7	Arrive at the Redwood Meadow campsites.
17.9	Pass the Timber Gap Trail junction.
20.3	Reach Pinto Lake.
22.8	Cross Black Rock Pass.
24.6	Arrive at the Little Five Lakes campsites.

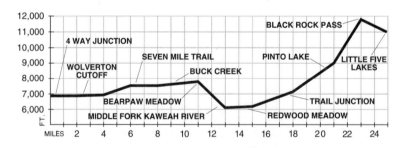

The hike: First, follow the High Sierra Trail to Bearpaw Meadow (Hike 16), to the campsites just past the junction at 11 miles, then follow the trail to Redwood Meadow (Hike 20) to the campsites at 14.7 miles. And finally, follow the route to Pinto Lake (Hike 21) to the campsites at 20.3 miles.

From the Pinto Lake campsites, the trail passes through a large meadow, then begins the arduous task of ascending many rocky switchbacks. Colorful wildflowers cheer you as you climb, exiting the treeline as you near Black

Rock Pass. Several long, nicely graded switchbacks lead you up, giving inspiring vistas south of Spring and Cyclamen Lakes, with Needham Mountain and Sawtooth Peak looming above.

At 22.8 miles you attain Black Rock Pass and unparalleled views. To the east are the mighty Kaweahs: Black Kaweah, Red Kaweah, Second Kaweah, and Mount Kaweah. Mount Whitney peeks up over Red Spur, and to its right, the Sierra Crest south to Mount Langley is visible. To the west you can see down the Cliff Creek drainage to the lower Middle Fork and on to Moro Rock.

After taking in the view, descend switchbacks of multicolored crushed rock, passing above the highest of the Little Five Lakes. Dropping through areas of granite, the path switchbacks downward to the north shore of the largest lake. Following the shoreline, the route intersects a signed four-way junction at a bear box. Campsites (24.6 miles) are located along the trail to the backcountry ranger station to your right (south), and there is a beautiful view northeast of the Kaweahs from the meadowed east shore of the lake.

When you must tear yourself away, return to the parking area as you came—a grand total of 49.2 miles.

Options: Hikes 20 through 22 can be combined with hikes 16 through 19 for an extended semi-loop backpacking trip. Link the routes by hiking from Little Five Lakes for 3.3 miles on a steep downhill to the Big Arroyo. From the four-way junction, the trail heads downhill, travels closely along the shore of the lowest of the Little Five Lakes, then passes an unnamed lake that is not part of the chain. The path steadily switchbacks down to a rock-hop of the Big Arroyo (creek-sized here), and reaches a bear box and campsites surrounding the Moraine Lake/Little Five Lakes Trail junction, just south of a trail crew cabin.

Follow the routes to Big Arroyo (Hike 19), Nine Lake Basin (Hike 18), and Hamilton Lakes (Hike 17) in reverse. Then retrace your steps from Bearpaw Meadow (Hike 16), in reverse, to the parking area. The route covers 49.6 miles.

Black Kaweah, Red Kaweah, and Second Kaweah loom above Little Five Lakes.

Hikes in the Lodgepole and Dorst Areas

The first four hikes in this section begin at Wolverton. The next two hikes—Tokopah Falls and Twin Lakes—start at the Lodgepole Campground. The Little Baldy hike begins along the Generals Highway north of Lodgepole; the Muir Grove hike also is off the Generals Highway, beginning at the Dorst Campground.

23 Lakes Trail

Highlights:	This jaunt culminates at exquisite Pear Lake, the last lake on the Lakes Trail. In the shadow of Alta Peak, this austere glacial bowl is a marvelous destination.
Type of hike:	Out-and-back, backpack or a long day hike.
Total distance:	12 miles.
Difficulty:	Moderate.
Best months:	Mid-June through October.
Maps:	USGS Lodgepole, Sequoia National Park Lodgepole and Wolverton, or TOPO! Sequoia Kings Canyon CD-ROM.
Permits:	If you plan to stay overnight, obtain a permit at the Lodgepole Visitor Center.
Parking and facilities:	Restrooms and water are available at the south side of the parking area. The trail begins on the north side of the parking lot.

Finding the trailhead: Drive 1.6 miles south from Lodgepole on the Generals Highway, or 0.5 mile north from the General Sherman Tree parking area, to Wolverton Road. Follow the road 1.5 miles to the parking area at its end.

Key points:
- 0.0 Trailhead.
- 0.1 Pass the Lodgepole Trail junction.
- 1.8 Reach the Panther Gap Trail junction.
- 2.0 Arrive at the Watchtower/Hump Trail junction.
- 4.1 Reach Heather Lake.
- 5.0 Pass Emerald Lake.
- 5.5 Meet the trail to the ranger station.
- 6.0 Arrive at Pear Lake.

The hike: The trip starts by ascending concrete steps, heading north on the signed Lakes Trail. Treading uphill you meet an unsigned trail on the left (west), leading downhill, which is part of the Long Meadow Trail (Hike 26). Continue around the curve to a junction at 0.1 mile with a spur trail leading left (north-

Lakes Trail

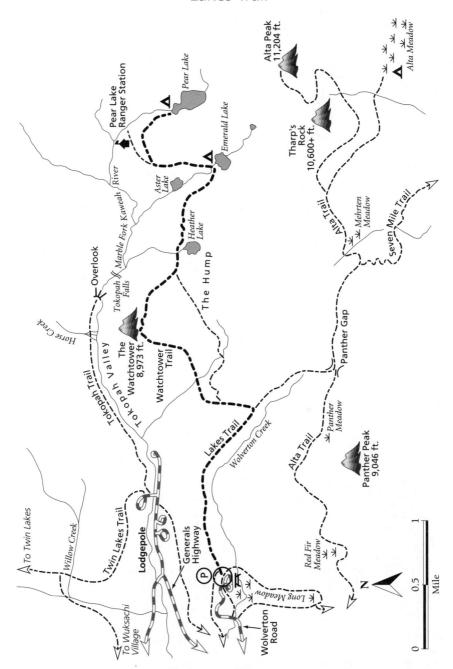

Alta Peak 11,204 ft.

Alta Meadow

Pear Lake

Pear Lake Ranger Station

Tharp's Rock 10,600+ ft.

Emerald Lake

Aster Lake

Alta Trail

Mehrten Meadow

Seven Mile Trail

Heather Lake

Marble Fork Kaweah River

The Hump

Overlook

Tokopah Falls

Horse Creek

Tokopah Trail

Panther Gap

Tokopah Valley

The Watchtower 8,973 ft.

Watchtower Trail

Alta Trail

Panther Meadow

Panther Peak 9,046 ft.

Lakes Trail

Wolverton Creek

Willow Creek

To Twin Lakes

Twin Lakes Trail

Lodgepole

Generals Highway

To Wuksachi Village

Red Fir Meadow

Long Meadow

Wolverton Road

N

0   0.5   1   Mile

west) to Lodgepole. Make a right (east) turn, staying on the Lakes Trail, and almost immediately pass another junction with the Long Meadow Trail.

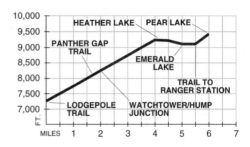

Your path travels up a moraine deposited by the Tokopah Glacier millions of years ago. As you continue, the trail nears the tinkling sounds of Wolverton Creek and a lush meadow appears on the right.

The trail curves to the southeast, travels through a couple of clearings in the dense woodland, and crosses a creeklet. Reach the junction with the Panther Gap Trail at 1.8 miles and make a left (north) turn. The path crosses the small watercourse again, and meets the Hump Trail at 2 miles, which is a steeper and more tiring route to the lakes. For this trip, take the Watchtower Trail, part of which is on the side of a cliff and which has better views.

Ascend to a meadow, easily crossing its creek on stones. The grade steepens, and you may see a marmot or hear one of their loud "chirps." The trail switchbacks and deposits you next to the Watchtower, a colossal granite spire on the south side of Tokopah Valley.

After examining the Watchtower and Tokopah Falls, 1,500 feet below you, continue east on a shelf blasted out of the rock. Views up and down the valley seem endless. The trail is wide and easy to follow as it climbs, then descends to meet the other end of the Hump Trail. Enter a thinly forested area, and at 4.1 miles reach Heather Lake, with its namesake—red heather—lining its banks. A short trail to the north leads to an open air pit toilet, where toilet paper is not supplied. Camping is not allowed at Heather Lake.

The Watchtower stands sentinel over the trail to Tokopah Falls.

You can visit lovely Aster Lake from the Lakes Trail, but no camping is allowed here.

The trail heads up the ridge separating Heather Lake from Aster and Emerald Lakes. It switchbacks and winds first up, then down the rise. Marmots and pikas scramble among the rocks as you approach. The trail drops to pretty Emerald Lake, in its granite amphitheater, at 5 miles. Camping is allowed in numbered sites only. A bear box and solar toilet are available. You can wander down the slabs to lovely Aster Lake, but camping is not allowed here.

The rocky course then climbs the side of the ridge separating Aster and Emerald Lakes from Pear Lake. Flower gardens of penstemon and other rock-loving plants bloom here in summer, attracting a multitude of tiny, flitting hummingbirds. A view down the canyon opens up to the west of the Watchtower, Little Baldy (Hike 29), and Big Baldy Ridge (Hike 44). Reach the trail leading to the Pear Lake Ranger Station at 5.5 miles. Take the fork to the right (east), which rises a bit more and contours around the tip of the promontory. The route crosses granite slabs to arrive at Pear Lake at 6 miles.

Alta Peak stands like a sentinel to the south of this immense bowl and the serrated ridgetop to the west is striking. Camping is allowed only in the numbered campsites, as at Emerald Lake. A bear box and solar toilet are located here as well. You may notice lurking marmots quietly creeping up on your campsite. Be sure to suspend your pack, or you might wake up to find holes gnawed through it in the morning.

When it is time to return to civilization, retrace your steps (12 miles).

Alta Peak • Alta Meadow

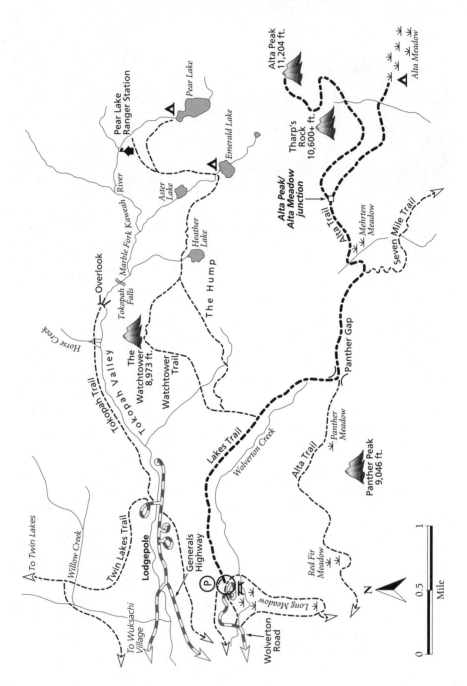

Alta Peak 11,204 ft.

Alta Meadow

Pear Lake Ranger Station

Pear Lake

Emerald Lake

Aster Lake

Tharp's Rock 10,600+ ft.

Alta Peak/ Alta Meadow junction

Alta Trail

Mehrten Meadow

Heather Lake

Marble Fork Kaweah River

Tokopah Falls

Overlook

Horse Creek

Tokopah Trail

Tokopah Valley

The Watchtower 8,973 ft.

Watchtower Trail

The Hump

Seven Mile Trail

Panther Gap

Lakes Trail

Wolverton Creek

Panther Meadow

Alta Trail

Panther Peak 9,046 ft.

To Twin Lakes

Willow Creek

Twin Lakes Trail

Lodgepole

Generals Highway

To Wuksachi Village

Red Fir Meadow

Long Meadow

Wolverton Road

N

1

.5

Mile

0

24 Alta Peak

Highlights:	Although the Alta Trail formally begins in the Giant Forest, this shorter route allows hearty day hikers a 360-degree view from an 11,000-foot-plus peak.
Type of hike:	Out-and-back, day hike or backpack.
Total distance:	13 miles.
Difficulty:	Difficult.
Best months:	July through October.
Maps:	USGS Lodgepole; Sequoia National Park Lodgepole and Wolverton; or TOPO! Sequoia Kings Canyon CD-ROM.
Permits:	Obtain a permit at the Lodgepole Visitor Center if you plan to backpack here.
Special considerations:	A risk of being struck by lightning exists on the summit of Alta Peak. If dark clouds are nearby, or hail, rain, thunder, or static electricity is in the air, descend immediately.
Parking and facilities:	Restrooms and water are available at the south side of the parking area. The trail begins on the north side of the parking lot.

Finding the trailhead: Drive 1.6 miles south from Lodgepole on the Generals Highway, or 0.5 mile north from the General Sherman Tree parking area, to signed Wolverton Road. Follow the road 1.5 miles to the parking area at its end.

Key points:
- 0.0   Trailhead.
- 0.1   Pass the Lodgepole Trail junction.
- 1.8   Reach the Lakes/Panther Gap Trail junction.
- 2.7   Cross Panther Gap.
- 3.7   Pass the Seven Mile Trail junction.
- 4.7   Reach the Alta Meadow Trail junction.
- 6.5   Arrive on the summit.

The hike: Begin by following the Lakes Trail (Hike 23) to the Lakes/Panther Gap Trail junction at 1.8 miles, and continue straight ahead (south), toward the gap. The route alternates through sunny meadows and shady forest, then

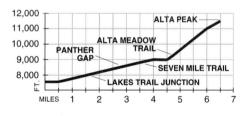

crosses several small, fern-lined forks of the headwaters of Wolverton Creek.

After ascending a few switchbacks, you arrive at Panther Gap at 2.7 miles, where you enjoy views across the Middle Fork Canyon to the Castle Rocks, as well as of the Great Western Divide to the east and Moro Rock to the west. Turn left (east) onto the Alta Trail. The path winds up shaded switchbacks, then climbs along an open cliffside with more views across the canyon and down the canyon to Panther Peak and Moro Rock.

While contouring around a small ridge, you reach the junction of the Seven Mile Trail at 3.7 miles. Take the path uphill, to the left (east). Reenter the forest; then the trail brings you to Mehrten Meadow. An easy rock-hop of its creek allows you to reach a few flat areas where you can camp.

Another climb past a trailside spring and unnamed meadows brings you to the Alta Meadow Trail junction at 4.7 miles. Turn left (northeast) and continue the climb through a rocky landscape, then back into the trees below Tharp's Rock. Views of the Kaweahs and the Great Western Divide open up to the east, and the trail switchbacks, climbing up through granite. A climber's trail appears to the left, leading west to Tharp's Rock, before you wind through the rocks and boulders to a ridgetop. The route proceeds up a long, gravelly hillside and a divot in the summit dome, then climbs precariously perched stones to a register and a 360-degree view at 6.5 miles.

In the north rise Mount Silliman and the majestic Tablelands, with Emerald and Pear Lakes below. In the east the Great Western Divide is visible, from Triple Divide Peak in the north to the peaks surrounding Mineral in the south, with the Kaweah Peaks and Mount Whitney in the background. To the south are Paradise Peak, the Castle Rocks, and Alta Meadow far below. West of you lies the smoggy expanse of the San Joaquin Valley with Little Baldy (Hike 29) and Big Baldy Ridge (Hike 44) easily distinguished.

After taking in the views, retrace your steps to the trailhead (13 miles).

Option: If you wish to take a different route back, continue straight (west) on the Alta Trail from Panther Gap, climbing a bit to Panther Meadow, then descending past Red Fir Meadow. About 2.5 miles from the gap you come to a signed trail junction and make a right (north) turn, switchbacking down to the Long Meadow Trail (Hike 26). Follow the last portion of this trail as described in Hike 26 to the parking area. This optional route will add a little more than a mile onto your hike and a negligible amount of elevation gain.

25 Alta Meadow

Highlights: This expansive meadow attracts numerous types of wildlife, while affording awe-inspiring views of the Great Western Divide and Alta Peak.

See Map on Page 98

Type of hike: Out-and-back, day hike or backpack.
Total distance: 11.2 miles.
Difficulty: Difficult.
Best months: July through October.
Maps: USGS Lodgepole; Sequoia National Park Lodgepole and Wolverton; or TOPO! Sequoia Kings Canyon CD-ROM.
Permits: Obtain a permit at the Lodgepole Visitor Center if you plan to backpack here.
Parking and facilities: Restrooms and water are available at the south side of the parking area. The trail begins on the north side of the parking lot.

Finding the trailhead: Drive 1.6 miles south from Lodgepole on the Generals Highway, or 0.5 mile north from the General Sherman Tree parking area, to Wolverton Road. Follow the road 1.5 miles to the parking area at its end.

Key points:
    0.0   Trailhead.
    0.1   Pass the Lodgepole Trail junction.
    1.8   Reach the Lakes/Panther Gap Trail junction.
    2.7   Cross Panther Gap.
    3.3   Pass Mehrten Meadow.
    3.6   Pass the Seven Mile Trail junction.
    4.7   Reach the Alta Peak Trail junction.
    5.6   Arrive at Alta Meadow.

The hike: Begin by following the Lakes Trail (Hike 23) to the Lakes/Panther Gap Trail junction at 1.8 miles. Then follow the route to Alta Peak (Hike 24) to the junction with the Alta Peak Trail at 4.7 miles. From this point continue straight (southeast) through a sandy zone dotted with phlox, and then reenter the woods.

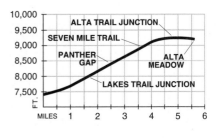

The path is nearly level for some distance, then dips slightly to cross a small creek before arriving at the head of Alta Meadow at 5.6 miles. The trail passes campsites on the southwest side of the upper portion of the meadow among the firs, then crosses to the north side of the meadow and travels downhill past colorful wildflowers in summer. The peaks of the Kaweahs and the Great Western Divide serve as a dramatic backdrop, while Alta Peak and Tharp's Rock stand guard in the northwest. Deer and coyote frequent this area, and you may even spot a bear.

The trail reenters the forest where it continues as an unmaintained route to Moose Lake, becoming increasingly hard to follow after exiting the forest. When you have thoroughly enjoyed this magical setting, return to the trailhead (11.2 miles).

Option: If you wish to take a different route back, continue straight (west) on the Alta Trail from Panther Gap, climbing a bit to Panther Meadow. Descend past Red Fir Meadow. About 2.5 miles from the gap you come to a signed trail junction and make a right (north) turn, switchbacking down to the Long Meadow Trail (Hike 26). Follow the last portion of this trail as described in Hike 26 to the parking area. This optional route will add a little more than a mile onto your hike and a negligible amount of elevation gain.

26 Long Meadow Trail

Highlights:	This surprisingly pretty trek around a large meadow is a good warm-up hike.
Type of hike:	Loop, day hike.
Total distance:	2.5 miles.
Difficulty:	Easy.
Best months:	June through October.
Maps:	USGS Lodgepole; Sequoia National Park Lodgepole and Wolverton; or TOPO! Sequoia Kings Canyon CD-ROM.
Permits:	None.
Special considerations:	This trail is used by horseback riders. Remember proper trail etiquette by stepping off the trail on the downhill side and waiting quietly until the horses have passed. Stay in plain view of the horses; they may think you are a wild animal and bolt if you are hidden behind a rock or tree.
Parking and facilities:	Restrooms and water are available at the south side of the parking area. The trail begins on the north side of the parking lot.

Finding the trailhead: Drive 1.6 miles south from Lodgepole on the Generals Highway, or 0.5 mile north from the General Sherman Tree parking area, to Wolverton Road. Follow the road 1.5 miles to the parking area at its end.

Key points:
- 0.0 Trailhead.
- 0.1 Pass the Lodgepole and Lakes Trail junctions.
- 0.4 Make the Wolverton Creek crossing.
- 1.4 Pass the spur trail to the Alta Trail.
- 2.2 Arrive at Wolverton Road.

The hike: The journey starts by ascending concrete steps, heading north on the signed Lakes Trail. Treading uphill you meet an unsigned trail on the left (west), leading downhill, which is your return route. Continue around the curve to a junction at 0.1 mile with a spur trail leading northwest to Lodgepole. Make a right (east) turn, and then almost immediately make another right onto the signed Long Meadow Trail.

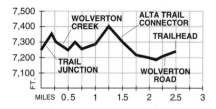

Your path descends through a thick forest, but is still a little too close to the parking area for peace and quiet. The trail passes a large wooden building and crosses a dirt road leading to a spring before reaching the thin log crossing of Wolverton Creek at 0.4 mile.

After a short uphill, the trail dips to step across a small tributary, then enters an open, drier portion of the meadow. You may see deer or even a bear along the trail ahead. As you near the trees, stop to check out the breathtaking view behind you of Silver Peak, a pinnacle on the southwest ridge of Mount Silliman. Passing through meadow goldenrod and lupines, the trail

Long Meadow Trail

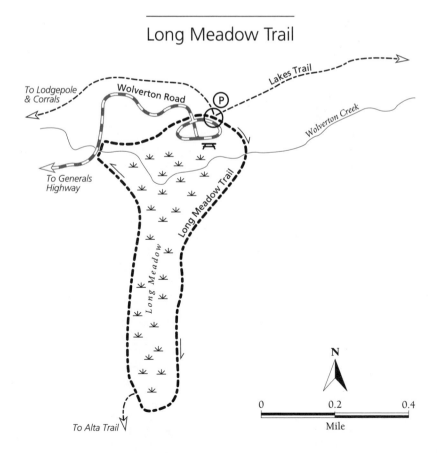

enters the shady forest and skirts the meadow, which is colored in various shades of green. Shooting stars, leopard lilies, and many other flowers bloom here in summer.

The trail leads up a few small switchbacks, then dips, rises, and dips again to cross two small brooks. It then curves to the north. You might hear the toy horn call of the red-breasted nuthatch coming from the surrounding trees.

At 1.4 miles, the path meets a spur trail that leads uphill (left/south) to the Alta Trail. Continue northward, following the western edge of the meadow through an open forest. The trail exits the forest near the site of a former ski lift, and widens to a dirt road. Meadow goldenrods cover the area as the road passes a stockpile of boulders and rocks before it takes you to Wolverton Road and Wolverton Creek at 2.2 miles. Turn right (north) and follow the paved road just across the creek to pick up the trail on the other side.

After following the creek for a short distance, the trail rises above the north end of the meadow and passes the western edge of the parking area. Reenter the woods, cross Wolverton Road, and climb to meet the Lakes Trail. Make a right (south) turn to arrive back at the parking area at 2.5 miles.

27 Tokopah Falls

Highlights:	This hike takes you to the head of the glacially carved Tokopah Valley, which culminates at Tokopah Falls.
Type of hike:	Out-and-back, day hike.
Total distance:	3.8 miles.
Difficulty:	Easy.
Best months:	June through October.
Maps:	USGS Lodgepole; Sequoia National Park Lodgepole and Wolverton; or TOPO! Sequoia Kings Canyon CD-ROM.
Permits:	None.
Parking and facilities:	Restrooms are available next to the nature center and back at the Lodgepole Visitor Center. Water is available at the east end of the parking area and at the visitor center as well. The trail begins just east of the parking area on the north side of Log Bridge (now reconstructed, but with its original name) and on the right (east) side of the road.

Finding the trailhead: Follow the Generals Highway to Lodgepole, which is approximately 27 miles south of the Big Stump entrance in Kings Canyon National Park, or a little more than 20 miles north of the Ash Mountain entrance in Sequoia National Park. Take the road (not identified with a name or number) east into Lodgepole, past the visitor center, to Lodgepole Campground. Let the person at the gate know you are going to the trailhead. Proceed to the parking area on the left (north) side of the road, before Log Bridge and across the road from the Walter Fry Nature Center.

104

Key points:
- 0.0   Trailhead.
- 1.4   Cross Horse Creek.
- 1.9   Reach the Tokopah Falls overlook.

The hike: The trail begins by following the north bank of the Marble Fork of the Kaweah River, and traverses a section of granite that a trailbed has been chiseled into. The smooth rock can sometimes be slippery—be careful.

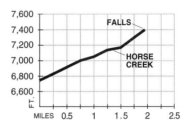

As you enter the forest, you may be aware of the colorful tents and the sounds of civilization in the campground across the river. Within a short distance those reverberations fade away. Spur trails lead down to the river throughout this hike; be sure to keep to the left at these junctions, and keep to the right on the return trip.

Tokopah Valley was shaped by a glacier, much as Yosemite Valley and the Cedar Grove area of Kings Canyon were. A view of the Watchtower, the large, pointed granite monolith on the south wall of the valley, opens up to your right. This crag, which was too solid to be ground down by the ice sheet, seems to constantly change shape as you travel on toward the falls.

Continue through firs and lodgepole pines, passing small meadows where you may see a deer or bear. The trail leads up and over a couple of small ledges before reaching the first branch of Horse Creek at 1.4 miles. Three

Tokopah Falls spills from the head of the glacially carved Tokopah Valley.

Tokopah Falls

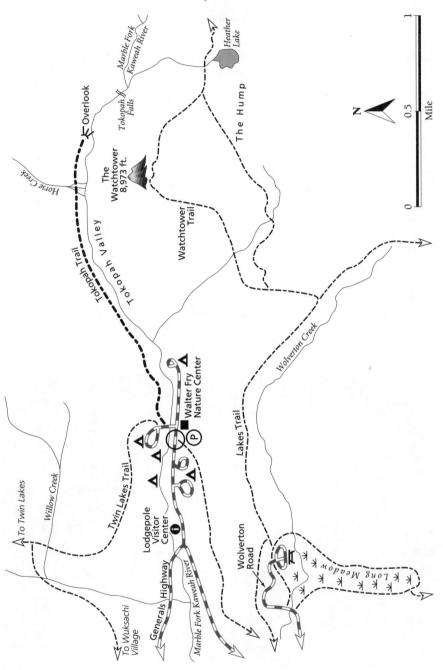

footbridges aid in your crossing of the many-forked creek; then the trail cuts across a usually dry wash. This tributary runs only in early spring and can be crossed on stones if water is present.

Before long you leave the forest and have a view of the falls in its entirety. The trail then winds through willows and boulders, and is edged with brilliant red penstemon in summer. As you near the overlook, you may see marmots and even a pika among the talus blocks and boulders. At the overlook, at 1.9 miles, a sign warns visitors not to continue up the canyon due to injuries and deaths that have occurred in the past.

After enjoying the falls, return the way you came (3.8 miles).

Option: You can explore the many spur trails leading down to the Marble Fork, which offers wading and swimming opportunities. Exercise caution during peak runoff periods and in swift-moving areas of the river.

28 Twin Lakes Trail

Highlights:	This shady trail leads past rushing creeks and gorgeous Cahoon Meadow to alpine lakes nestled below the lofty Twin Peaks.
Type of hike:	Out-and-back, backpack or a long, hard day hike.
Total distance:	13.6 miles.
Difficulty:	Moderate.
Best months:	Mid-June through October.
Maps:	USGS Lodgepole and Mount Silliman, Sequoia National Park Lodgepole and Wolverton, or TOPO! Sequoia Kings Canyon CD-ROM.
Permits:	If you plan to stay overnight, obtain a permit at the Lodgepole Visitor Center.
Parking and facilities:	Restrooms are available next to the nature center and back at the Lodgepole Visitor Center. Water is available at the east end of the parking area and at the visitor center as well. The trail begins just east of the parking area on the north side of Log Bridge (now reconstructed, but retaining its original name). The trailhead is just beyond the trail to Tokopah Falls, on the right (east) side of the road at the large trail sign.

Finding the trailhead: Follow the Generals Highway to Lodgepole, which is approximately 27 miles south of the Big Stump entrance in Kings Canyon National Park, or a little more than 20 miles north of the Ash Mountain entrance in Sequoia National Park. Take the road (not identified with a name or number) east into Lodgepole, past the visitor center, to Lodgepole Campground. Let the person at the gate know you are going to the trailhead. Proceed to the parking area on the left (north) side of the road, before Log Bridge and across the road from the Walter Fry Nature Center.

Key points:
- 0.0   Trailhead.
- 1.5   Pass the trail to Wuksachi Village.
- 2.0   Cross Silliman Creek.
- 2.5   Pass Cahoon Meadow.
- 4.2   Climb over Cahoon Gap.
- 4.8   Pass the JO Pass Trail junction.
- 6.8   Reach Twin Lakes.

The hike: The path to Twin Lakes immediately begins climbing up the glacial moraine on the north side of Tokopah Valley. Ascend past seeps and flowers, then bear clover and ponderosa pines, high above the campgrounds. As the route turns north, the trail becomes almost level and enters a dense and shady forest of firs. After crossing Willow Creek on

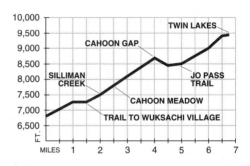

a small log, the trail reaches a junction at 1.5 miles with a footpath leading to the newly constructed Wuksachi Village.

Continue straight ahead (north) and dip across a seasonal creek before rising up switchbacks to the top of a small ridge. A short downhill brings you to Silliman Creek at 2 miles. In early season, caution must be exercised during this crossing; later in the year the creek is easily traversed on stones. This creek is the water supply for Lodgepole—do not contaminate it in any way.

The route then heads up a steep incline and along another long switchback. As you near the creek rushing down from Cahoon Meadow, wildflowers and meadow grasses spill over the adjacent hillside. Just over the next rise, at 2.5 miles, you arrive at the expansive meadow itself. A side trail to the left (northwest) leads down to a meadowside campsite.

The path continues uphill through the woods, crossing several seasonal brooks and passing small meadows filled with Bigelow's sneezeweed in summer. After a few short switchbacks, you reach Cahoon Gap at 4.2 miles. The trail descends to a Clover Creek tributary and crosses on stones. A bear box and a couple of rocky campsites are located on the north side of the creek, to your right (east). The area on the left side of the trail is closed to camping for restoration.

Follow the route over a small rise to another bear box and large, flat campsites at the East Fork of Clover Creek. Again, the area on the left (west) of the trail is closed to camping due to restoration. Some maps show a trail departing to the west at this point, but it is no longer discernible.

Meet the JO Pass Trail on your left (north) at 4.8 miles. Take the trail to the right (northeast) and rock-hop over Clover Creek. The path ascends only slightly at first, through an area of wildflowers in summer. Then you begin to climb in earnest, leaving the cover of the thick forest for only occasional spots of shade. Continuing up the steep switchbacks on the increasingly

Twin Lakes Trail

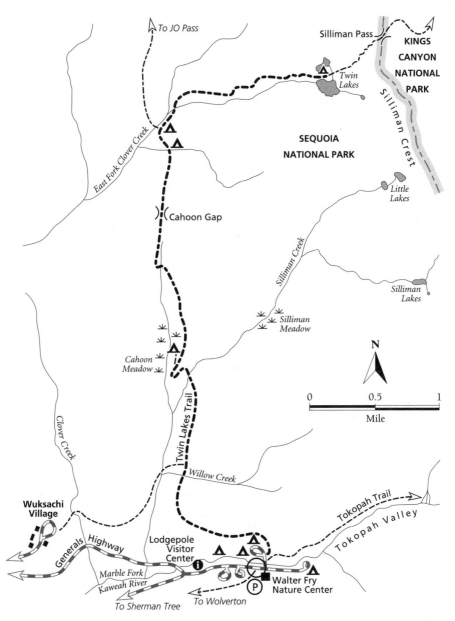

rocky trail, you cross areas of granite slabs and small, seasonal creeklets. At 6.8 miles, you triumphantly arrive at shady, tree-lined Twin Lakes.

Bear boxes, campsites, and a backcountry toilet are located in this picturesque setting. The Twin Peaks tower over the smaller lake, while granite cliffs wall in the larger body of water. Both lakes are rimmed with tall grasses and red heather. After you have enjoyed your stay, return the way you came (13.6 miles).

Options: This trail can also be accessed from the newly constructed Wuksachi Village, which will add about half a mile onto your hike, while taking off about 120 feet of elevation gain.

Silliman Pass can also be accessed from the lakes—an elevation gain of 785 feet in just less than 1 mile.

29 Little Baldy

Highlights:	The summit of Little Baldy gives a spectacular view of the Silliman Crest, the Kaweah Peaks, and the lower portion of the Great Western Divide.
Type of hike:	Out-and-back, day hike.
Total distance:	3.4 miles.
Difficulty:	Easy.
Best months:	June through October.
Maps:	USGS Muir Grove and Giant Forest; USFS John Muir Wilderness and Sequoia–Kings Canyon Wilderness; or TOPO! Sequoia Kings Canyon CD-ROM.
Permits:	None.
Special considerations:	A risk of being struck by lightning exists on the summit of Little Baldy. If dark clouds are nearby, or if hail, rain, thunder, or static electricity are in the air, descend immediately.
Parking and facilities:	No facilities are available at this trailhead. Parking is available on both sides of the road, and the trail, marked by a large sign, begins on the east side.

Finding the trailhead: Drive 6.6 miles north from Lodgepole on the Generals Highway, or 1.5 miles south from Dorst Campground, to the signed Little Baldy Saddle.

Key points:
- 0.0 Trailhead.
- 0.1 Pass the abandoned trailbed.
- 0.4 Enjoy a view of Big Baldy and Chimney Rock.
- 1.0 Arrive in the quiet wooded area.
- 1.3 Reach views of the Great Western Divide.
- 1.7 Attain the summit of Little Baldy.

The hike: The trail begins by climbing a few stone steps, then a short switchback that is not shown on some maps. At 0.1 mile—the end of this switchback—you may be able to discern an old, abandoned trailbed that leads back to the highway.

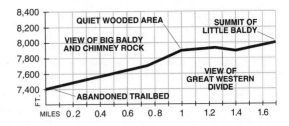

Next, you climb a long traverse through a thick forest of tall pine and fir trees. As you near the next switchback at 0.4 mile, a view opens up to the west of Big Baldy and Chimney Rock. Many wildflowers grow here in summer and you may even see marmots among the large boulders above the path.

Little Baldy

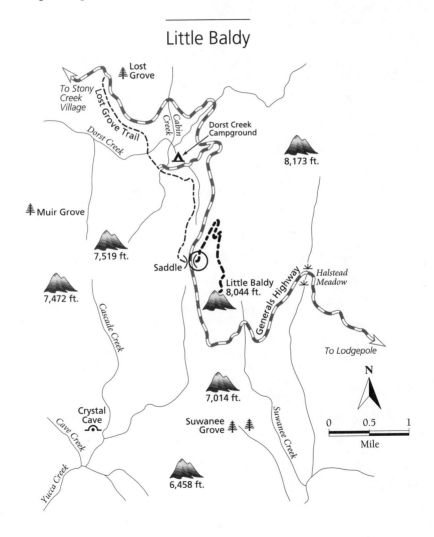

Continuing on this open, sometimes rocky portion of the trail, you meet two more switchbacks and the trail levels off. Enter a very quiet wooded area at 1 mile—a good place to stop and listen to the silence.

After leaving this peaceful place and rounding a hilltop at 1.3 miles, you begin to have views east of the Kaweahs and the Great Western Divide. Traveling through intermittent forest, the trail comes to the base of Little Baldy's granite dome, contours around the south side and on to the summit, which is reached at approximately 1.7 miles. Spanish Mountain and Obelisk are visible to the north, and to the east are Mount Silliman, Alta Peak, the Kaweah Group, and the Great Western Divide all the way south to Farewell Gap. In the foreground to the south-southeast is the tip of Moro Rock and the Castle Rocks. On a clear day (possibly after a rain storm has cleared the air), you may even be able to see the San Joaquin Valley to the west, serving as a backdrop to Big Baldy Ridge and Chimney Rock.

After enjoying the view, retrace your steps to the trailhead at approximately 3.4 miles.

Option: Spending the night on Little Baldy is possible with a wilderness permit. If you do spend the night, bring water—there is none along the trail.

---

30 Muir Grove

Highlights:	This hike takes you to a less frequently visited sequoia grove, with views of Big Baldy and Chimney Rock along the way.
Type of hike:	Out-and-back, day hike.
Total distance:	4 miles.
Difficulty:	Easy.
Best months:	June through October.
Maps:	USGS Muir Grove; USFS John Muir Wilderness and Sequoia–Kings Canyon Wilderness; or TOPO! Sequoia Kings Canyon CD-ROM.
Permits:	None.
Parking and facilities:	Restrooms and water are available just across the road from the trailhead. The signed trail begins on the west side of the road between the group campground entrance and the parking area at the amphitheater.

Finding the trailhead: Drive either 5 miles south from Stony Creek Village on the Generals Highway, or 8.2 miles north of Lodgepole, to the Dorst Campground entrance. Follow signs along the road through the campground to the amphitheater and to a parking area at 0.9 mile, just past the group campground entrance.

Key points:
- 0.0 Trailhead.
- 0.1 Reach the trail fork.
- 0.6 Make the first creek crossing.
- 1.0 Pass the side trail to the dome overlook.
- 1.6 Make the second creek crossing.
- 2.0 Reach Muir Grove.

The hike: The trail begins by dipping to cross a Dorst Creek tributary on a wooden footbridge, then rises to pass above the group campground. Descend a switchback, meeting a north-trending trail leading to Dorst Creek at 0.1 mile. Follow the fork to the left (west), the signed Muir Trail, around a fern-filled

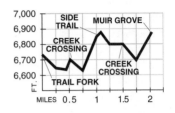

meadow on your right (north). The trail travels through a thick fir forest and you may hear the peaceful song of the hermit thrush.

Pass over granite slabs and step over another tributary at 0.6 mile before coming to a trail fork. At the beginning of a couple of longer switch-

Muir Grove

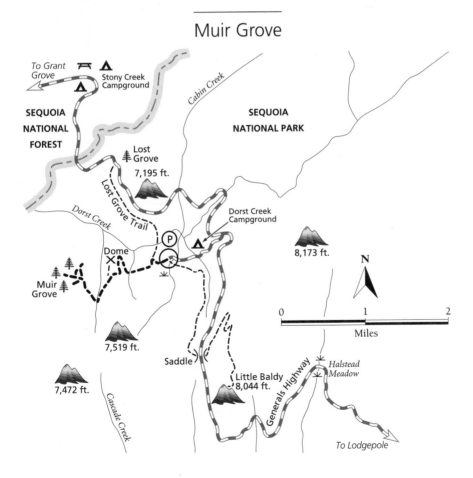

backs, there appears to be a climber's trail continuing straight, toward the base of the granite dome above, which is feebly blocked by some branches. Turn left (south), traveling uphill, and at 1 mile arrive at a path leading to the high point of this dome, with its view of Big Baldy and the east face of Chimney Rock. You can also see the sequoias of Muir Grove on the ridge due west of here.

The trail passes into the trees again, then enters a rocky area, traversing a very steep portion of loose rock, which should be done with caution. After reentering the forest, the trail comes to another tributary at 1.6 miles, which can be crossed by those with good balance on a large fallen tree. If you prefer a lower crossing, use some stones located a few steps past the tree to aid your passage.

The path narrows and becomes slightly overgrown, but is easy to follow. Continuing up along the steep hillside, you reach a gigantic sequoia at the entrance to Muir Grove at 2 miles.

Several paths await exploration in the grove. A short track to the left (south) leads into a group of sequoias and abruptly stops. The pathway to your right (north) travels uphill, splits and rejoins, then leads to a sequoia hollowed out by fire, before ending at a lupine-covered hillside. The footpath that proceeds straight (west) into a group of sequoias fizzles out just beyond them. And finally, the route heading downhill to the southwest is the last remnant of the continuation of this trail. This path used to lead on to Skagway Grove, Hidden Spring, and Crystal Cave, but hasn't been maintained in more than 20 years. The route now ends about 50 feet from an immense sequoia that fell across the trail, sealing its fate of returning to a natural state.

After you have explored the grove, return the way you came (4 miles).

Hikes in the Grant Grove Area

The first two hikes in this chapter start at the Big Stump picnic area, just north of the Big Stump entrance to Kings Canyon National Park on California Highway 180. The South Boundary Trail and Manzanita and Azalea Trails begin near the Grant Grove Visitor Center. Hikes 35, 36, and 37 begin at the General Grant Tree parking area. The last two hikes begin at Panoramic Point.

31 Big Stump Loop

Highlights: This interpretive trail takes you through an area that was heavily logged in the 1880s and now serves as a reminder of how important it is to protect the environment. Although the General Grant National Park was established in 1890, and later incorporated in Kings Canyon National Park in 1940, Big Stump Basin was not included until 1965. An abundance of birds and small animals greet you along this trail, even though it is quite close to California Highway 180.

Type of hike: Loop, day hike.

Total distance: 2 miles.

Difficulty: Easy.

Best months: May through October.

Maps: USGS General Grant Grove; Kings Canyon National Park Grant Grove; or TOPO! Sequoia–Kings Canyon CD-ROM.

Permits: None.

Parking and facilities: Restrooms, picnic tables, and barbecues are available at the parking area. The trail begins on the south side of the parking area, near the restrooms. An interpretive booklet for this trail is sold at the trailhead from a coin-operated machine, and also is for sale at the Grant Grove Visitor Center in Grant Grove Village.

Finding the trailhead: From the Big Stump entrance station on CA 180, drive 0.6 miles to the Big Stump parking area, which is on the left (southwest) side of the road.

Key points:
- 0.0   Trailhead.
- 0.3   Reach the first trail fork.
- 0.6   Reach the second trail fork.
- 1.0   Cross CA 180.
- 1.3   Take the side trail to the Sawed Tree.

The hike: The trail heads downhill and almost immediately comes to the Resurrection Tree. This giant's top was destroyed by lightning and it is now "resurrecting" a new one. In a short distance you reach the Shake Pile, a toppled sequoia that was chiseled apart to make fence posts, roof shingles, and grape stakes. Though

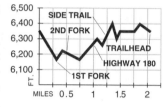

extremely rot- and fire-resistant, sequoia wood is very brittle, and because of the immense size of these trees, they often shattered when they were felled.

At 0.3 mile, you arrive at a fork in the trail; take the route to the left (east). Walk to the Burnt Monarch, known as Old Adam by the loggers. This huge, burned-out sequoia was used to store snow for ice in the summer months, while the logging mill was in operation.

The trail brings you next to two sequoias planted in 1888. At just over one hundred years of age, they have reached great height, but not the girth of the old "giants." An abandoned road grade joins the trail just beyond these trees. Farther down the trail you reach a meadow and the site of the Smith-Comstock mill. All that remains are the wood posts of the foundation sticking up

The Mark Twain Stump is all that remains of a giant sequoia that was cut so that a New York museum could mount a display.

Big Stump Loop

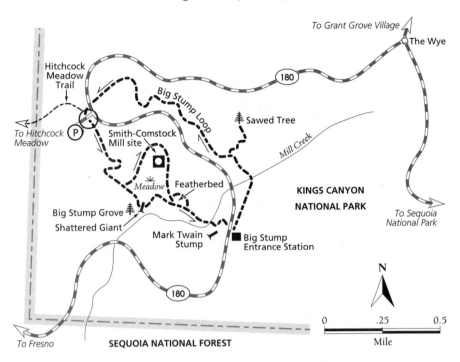

To Grant Grove Village
The Wye
Hitchcock Meadow Trail
180
Big Stump Loop
Sawed Tree
To Hitchcock Meadow
P
Smith-Comstock Mill site
Mill Creek
Meadow
Featherbed
KINGS CANYON NATIONAL PARK
Big Stump Grove
Shattered Giant
Mark Twain Stump
Big Stump Entrance Station
To Sequoia National Park
180
N
0   .25   0.5
Mile
To Fresno   SEQUOIA NATIONAL FOREST

through the grass to your right (west). Notice the piles of reddish-brown sawdust that still prevail more than one hundred years after they were created.

A bit farther down the path is a side trail to the Featherbed. This trench was dug out and lined with branches from felled trees to cushion the fall of one of the "Big Trees." Other featherbeds can be seen in the basin by those who are observant.

At 0.6 mile, you reach the second trail fork and go right (northwest), traveling around the little meadow to the Shattered Giant. This tree was smashed into so many pieces that it was practically unsalvageable. Now it serves as a trail bridge over the tiny tributary flowing through the meadow.

Backtrack to the previous junction and make a right (southeast) turn. Pass another portion of the small Featherbed loop, and cross little Mill Creek on a wooden bridge, arriving at the Mark Twain Stump. This sequoia was felled in 1891 so that the American Museum of Natural History in New York could have a slice to exhibit. There are steps leading to the top of the stump, and standing in the center gives you an even better idea of how large these trees really are. Also visible are the healed-over burn scars from throughout the tree's life.

From the Mark Twain Stump, the trail makes a short climb to CA 180 at 1 mile. Follow the crosswalk and continue uphill on the other side of the road. Traveling through the forest, you reach the side trail to the Sawed Tree at 1.3 miles. Turn right (northeast), and take the path up a few brief switchbacks to this survivor. When loggers realized this tree could not be felled in the direction they wanted, they moved on, and the tree still continues to heal.

Retrace your steps back to the main trail, noticing an abandoned trail section to the left (south) at the last switchback. This route is passable until just before it reaches the main trail, where it is blocked by thorny ceanothus or snowbrush.

Resume on the main trail to your right (northwest), through more forest and manzanita clearings, to a short downhill. The path then follows along a stringer meadow to a large culvert that allows you to pass under CA 180 and join the Hitchcock Meadow Trail. Turn to the left (south) and climb a few feet to the parking area at 2 miles.

32 Hitchcock Meadow Trail

Highlights:	This hike takes you through an area where giant sequoias were logged before the turn of the century, and culminates at a small waterfall.
Type of hike:	Out-and-back, day hike.
Total distance:	2.6 miles.
Difficulty:	Easy.
Best months:	May through October.
Maps:	USGS General Grant Grove; Kings Canyon National Park Grant Grove; or TOPO! Sequoia Kings Canyon CD-ROM.
Permits:	None.
Parking and facilities:	Restrooms, picnic tables, and barbecues are available at the parking area. The trail begins on the north side of the parking area, near its entrance.

Finding the trailhead: From the Big Stump entrance station on California Highway 180, drive 0.6 miles to the Big Stump parking area, which is on the left (southwest) side of the road.

Key points:
- 0.0 Trailhead.
- 0.5 Reach the spur trail in Hitchcock Meadow.
- 0.7 Pass the South Boundary Trail junction.
- 1.1 Make the Sequoia Creek crossing.
- 1.3 Reach Viola Falls.

The hike: The trail heads downhill to the northwest, past the Big Stump Trail. A chorus of various birds serenades you as the path descends and enters the Sequoia National Forest. You may hear or see robins, nuthatches, fox sparrows, warblers, and chickadees. There are also many squirrels and chipmunks in the area.

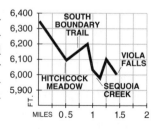

Hitchcock Meadow Trail

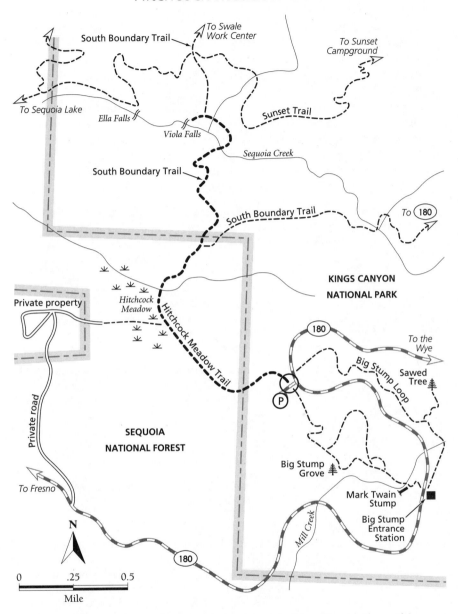

There are numerous giant sequoia stumps along the trail, as this area was heavily logged before General Grant National Park was established in 1890. That small park was later incorporated into Kings Canyon National Park in 1940.

Approach Hitchcock Meadow, and what appears to be a spur trail leading to private property, at 0.5 mile. A peaceful creek flows through the grasses, and dandelions edge the sunny trail.

Follow the route uphill, through the shade and the large sugar pine cones that litter the forest floor. You may come across Douglas squirrels cutting and dropping cones from the treetops high above. A short, welcome downhill along a stringer meadow brings you to the junction with the South Boundary Trail (Hike 33) at 0.7 mile. Proceed straight (north) on the South Boundary Trail; beyond the junction the trail leaves the national forest and reenters the park. After topping the next ridge, descend several switchbacks to Sequoia Creek at 1.1 miles.

Cross the creek on a small plywood bridge, and continue to the short side trail leading to Viola Falls. Hiking high above the creek, you come to a large boulder overlooking the falls at 1.3 miles. This is a good place to relax or have lunch. There is a very steep, eroded path just past the boulder leading down to the small pool that the falls cascade into; you can descend if you wish.

After enjoying the falls, retrace your steps back to the trailhead at 2.6 miles.

Option: If you wish to also see Ella Falls, continue north on the South Boundary Trail to its junction with the Sunset Trail. Make a left (west) turn, and follow that trail downhill to 50-foot Ella Falls, which is reached in another 0.7 mile. This adds an elevation gain of 420 feet to the return trip.

33 South Boundary Trail

Highlights:	This little-traveled trail gives you quiet seclusion and takes you to a small waterfall before giving you a glimpse of the outskirts of the private community of Wilsonia.
Type of hike:	Day hike, loop.
Total distance:	4.6 miles.
Difficulty:	Moderate.
Best months:	May through October.
Maps:	USGS General Grant Grove; Kings Canyon National Park Grant Grove; or TOPO! Sequoia Kings Canyon CD-ROM.
Permits:	None.
Parking and facilities:	Restrooms and water are available just outside the Grant Grove Visitor Center. There are also two lodges, two restaurants, a gift shop, a grocery store, and a post office in Grant Grove Village. To reach the trailhead, walk back from the parking lot to the visitor center and California Highway 180. Cross the highway in the crosswalk leading to the trail.

Finding the trailhead: From the Big Stump entrance station, drive north on CA 180 to Grant Grove Village. Turn right (east) at the visitor center. If parking near the visitor center is full, drive through the parking lot to a smaller parking area next to Bradley Meadow. The trailhead is 3.1 miles from the Big Stump entrance.

Key points:
    0.0   Trailhead.
    0.6   Reach the trail sign in the Azalea Campground.
    1.6   Pass the Sunset Trail junction.
    1.8   Reach Viola Falls.
    2.0   Make the first crossing of Sequoia Creek.
    2.4   Reach the Hitchcock Meadow Trail junction.
    3.0   Make the second crossing of Sequoia Creek.
    3.4   Reach the junction with the dirt road.
    3.5   Make the first CA 180 crossing.
    4.4   Reach the second CA 180 crossing.

The hike: The trail begins by following the paved path leading down to the amphitheater. About 50 feet from the road, you intersect a signed trail

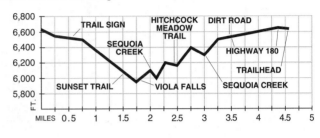

leading to the Grant Tree, and make a right (north) turn.

The trail leads you through Azalea Campground and can be faint in places. The route crosses a small creek on a wooden bridge through a verdant green meadow. Continue through the campground, following the crosswalks across four paved roads, then travel downhill along a stringer meadow just across from the Columbine Picnic Area. Watch to the left (west) for a faint path that heads uphill next to a very large stump. Turn left (west) and follow this spur trail up to the main road through the campground. Upon reaching the road, make a right (north) turn, follow along the right side of the pavement, and stay to the left where the road forks. Continue around the loop to a large, dirt turnout next to campsite 110. The signed South Boundary Trail heads downhill to the right (northwest) at 0.6 mile.

The wide trail, an old fire road, descends quite steeply through a mixed forest. As you begin to see buildings, look to the left (south) for a small trail sign that is easy to miss. Follow the trail above the Swale Work Center, a former campground now used by the Hot Shot fire and rescue crew. Rounding the southern end of the work center, the narrow footpath rejoins the old fire road and travels through a long, peaceful meadow frequented by robins and juncos.

At 1.6 miles you meet the Sunset Trail. A side trip to Ella Falls can be made from this junction (see Option), but to do this loop, continue straight (south). At two large sequoias you meet the side trail to Viola Falls and make a right (southwest) turn. Hiking high above the creek, you come to a large boulder overlooking the falls at 1.8 miles. This is a good place to relax or have lunch. There is a very steep, eroded path just beyond the boulder leading down to the small pool that the falls cascade into, which you can descend if you wish. After enjoying the falls, retrace your steps back to the main trail and resume your trek south.

South Boundary Trail

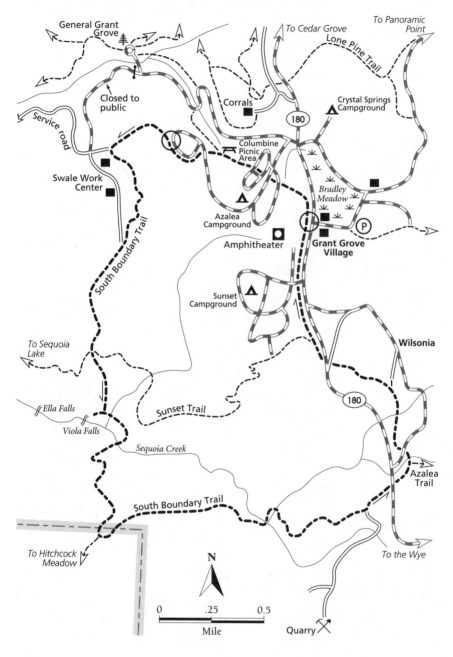

General Grant Grove

To Cedar Grove

To Panoramic Point

Lone Pine Trail

Closed to public

Corrals

Crystal Springs Campground

180

Service road

Columbine Picnic Area

Swale Work Center

Bradley Meadow

South Boundary Trail

Azalea Campground

Amphitheater

Grant Grove Village

P

Sunset Campground

Wilsonia

To Sequoia Lake

180

Ella Falls

Sunset Trail

Viola Falls

Sequoia Creek

Azalea Trail

South Boundary Trail

To Hitchcock Meadow

To the Wye

N

0   .25   0.5

Mile

Quarry

At 2 miles, cross Sequoia Creek on a small plywood bridge and join a portion of the Hitchcock Meadow route (Hike 32). Proceed up several switchbacks to the top of the ridge and the park boundary. After a slight decline through the Sequoia National Forest you reach the next junction at 2.4 miles. Follow the South Boundary Trail to the left (east).

Traveling uphill, the trail follows a stringer meadow through the dense forest and reenters the park. Top a ridge and descend again to Sequoia Creek, crossing on a wooden footbridge at 3 miles. The trail then climbs again, this time through a more openly forested zone.

After a short downhill stretch, you will meet a dirt road at 3.4 miles. The portion of road to the right (south) crosses Sequoia Creek, then leads to an old quarry. Follow the segment of road leading straight (northeast), coming to CA 180 at 3.5 miles. (The trail to the south of this road shown on some maps is now impassable due to fallen trees and branches.)

There is no crosswalk here on the highway, so carefully dash to the other side, then on to a three-way junction. The Azalea Trail is straight ahead. Take the left fork, heading north and crossing Sequoia Creek again, this time on stones. Almost immediately beyond the creek, you cross one of the roads entering the private community of Wilsonia. Winding through the forest, the trail crosses a Sequoia Creek tributary on a plywood bridge and passes some private cabins before turning to the west. Cross yet another tributary on a hewn log and begin to clamber uphill, intersecting a dirt road running down to a small, concrete block structure on your left (southwest). A few more steps and the trail again reaches CA 180, passing between two large rocks at 4.4 miles.

A crosswalk is absent here also; carefully make your way to the other side of the highway. The trail resumes a few yards north on the west side of the roadway. Travel through an open area, joining the Sunset Trail at a group of large, rotting logs. Continue north, descending to a good-sized emerald meadow and the edge of Sunset Campground. Cross the main campground road next to a mileage sign, and follow the trail back up toward the crosswalk at the visitor center, joining the paved path leading up from the amphitheater. Arriving at the trail's end, you will have hiked 4.6 miles.

Option: If you also wish to see Ella Falls, make a right (west) turn at the first Sunset Trail junction. Follow the trail downhill for 0.7 mile to 50-foot Ella Falls. This will add an elevation gain of 280 feet on the return trip.

34 Manzanita and Azalea Trails

Highlights: This hike is best early in the day, as it traverses a dense slope of manzanita to the top of Park Ridge, then returns to Grant Grove Village via the azaleas along Sequoia Creek.

Type of hike: Loop, day hike.

Total distance: 4.3 miles.

Difficulty: Moderate.

Best months: June through October.

Maps: USGS General Grant Grove; Kings Canyon National Park Grant Grove; or TOPO! Sequoia Kings Canyon CD-ROM.

Permits: None.

Parking and facilities: Restrooms and water are available just outside the Grant Grove Visitor Center. There are also two lodges, two restaurants, a gift shop, a grocery store, and a post office in Grant Grove Village. To reach the trail, walk up a small road at the southeast end of the parking area to a sign stating "To Manzanita Trail." Go a few yards up the hill to where a small sign in front of a large cabin directs you onto the trail.

Finding the trailhead: From the Big Stump entrance station on California Highway 180, drive north to Grant Grove Village and turn right (east) at the visitor center. If parking near the visitor center is full, drive through the parking lot to a smaller parking area next to Bradley Meadow. The trailhead is 3.1 miles from the Big Stump entrance.

Key points:
0.0 Trailhead.
0.7 Reach the Cedar Springs Trail junction.
1.0 Pass the Round Meadow Trail junction.
1.8 Reach the three-way junction.
2.4 Make the first crossing of Sequoia Creek.
2.8 Make the second crossing of Sequoia Creek.
3.3 Cross Sequoia Creek a third time.
3.7 Reach the first CA 180 crossing.
4.1 Cross CA 180 a second time.

The hike: The trail begins by climbing under power lines, curving northward. Meet a service road leading to a water tank; follow the "Manzanita Trail" sign. As you enter the forest the sound of singing birds replaces the sounds of civilization.

Continuing through the trees, the trail passes an old dirt road heading downhill to a small structure and a large water tank. Proceed through a grassy, flowered area to a junction with the Cedar Springs Trail at 0.7 mile. This trail leads back through a residential area and becomes the Crystal Springs Trail on the other side of the Panoramic Point Road.

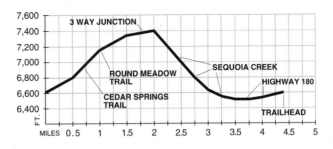

The grade steepens as you travel up a long switchback, and as you round a curve the path intersects the Round Meadow Trail at 1 mile. This trail leads to the Panoramic Point Road and Round Meadow. Continue on the Manzanita Trail, and enter a slope thick with its namesake. An expansive vista of the San Joaquin Valley and the foothills is now to your right (west). As the trail climbs through the dense brush, you will probably come across plump little fox sparrows, or at least hear their sweet song. Nearing the top of Park Ridge, bear clover covers the ground and fills the air with a strong, herbal scent.

Arriving at a three-way junction near the top of Park Ridge at 1.8 miles, just below the service road leading to the fire lookout, go right (southwest) on the Azalea Trail. The trail heads downhill steeply, and before long comes to a short switchback, then traverses a longer one. The route alternates between rocky areas and forest with azaleas lining the path. This trail is one of the best areas in the park to view wild azaleas when they are in bloom.

At 2.4 miles you cross fledgling Sequoia Creek on a footbridge, and follow a steep decline along the watercourse. After another switchback the trail levels a bit more, then crosses Sequoia Creek on another bridge at 2.8 miles. Proceeding on a slighter downhill grade, you arrive at a side trail that rock-hops Sequoia Creek and journeys into Wilsonia, a private community.

Continue straight ahead (west), above the rippling creek, and ascend a small rise. Dropping down the other side on another short switchback, you reach another three-way junction. The South Boundary Trail is straight ahead. Take the right fork, heading north and crossing Sequoia Creek again, this time on stones, at 3.3 miles. Just beyond the creek, you will cross one of the roads entering Wilsonia.

Winding through the forest, the trail crosses a Sequoia Creek tributary on a plywood bridge and passes some private cabins before turning to the west. Pass over yet another tributary on a hewn log and begin to clamber uphill, intersecting a dirt road that runs down to a small, concrete block structure on your left (southwest). A few more steps and the trail reaches CA 180, passing between two large rocks at 3.7 miles.

A crosswalk is absent here, so carefully make your way to the other side. The trail resumes a few yards north on the west side of the highway. Travel through an open area, joining the Sunset Trail at a group of large, rotting logs. Continue north, descending to a good-sized emerald meadow and to the edge of Sunset Campground. Cross the main campground road next to a mileage sign, and follow the trail back toward the crosswalk at the visitor center, joining the paved path from the amphitheater. Arriving at the trail's end, you will have hiked 4.1 miles. If you have parked near the trailhead,

Manzanita and Azalea Trails

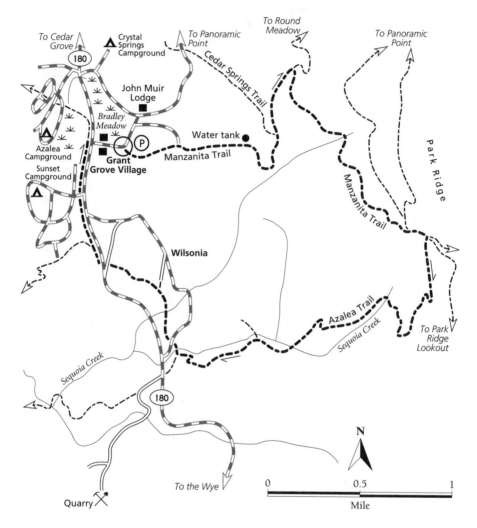

you still have approximately 0.2 mile to go through the visitor center parking lot, for a total of 4.3 miles.

Options: A trip to Panoramic Point or the Park Ridge Lookout can be made from the three-way junction near the top of Park Ridge. A side trip to Panoramic Point will add 3 miles and an elevation gain of 570 feet to your hike. Traveling to Park Ridge Lookout will add about 2 miles and an elevation gain of 250 feet.

35 General Grant Loop

Highlights:	This paved interpretive trail takes you to the General Grant Tree, named for Ulysses S. Grant. The tree has been declared the Nation's Christmas Tree and a living National Shrine to Americans who have died in war. You also pass the historic Gamlin Cabin as you travel through the heart of the General Grant Grove.
Type of hike:	Loop, day hike.
Total distance:	0.8 mile.
Difficulty:	Very easy.
Best months:	May through October.
Maps:	USGS General Grant Grove; Kings Canyon National Park Grant Grove; or TOPO! Sequoia Kings Canyon CD-ROM.
Permits:	None.
Parking and facilities:	Restrooms and water are available at this large parking area. The trail begins on the north side of the parking area at the large sign. A coin-operated machine at the trailhead sells interpretive pamphlets for this hike. Pamphlets are also available at the Grant Grove Visitor Center.

Finding the trailhead: From the Big Stump entrance, drive north on California Highway 180, past Grant Grove Village, to the junction with the General Grant Tree road. Turn left (west), and take the road to the General Grant Tree parking area, which is 4.1 miles from the Big Stump entrance.

Key points:
    0.0   Trailhead.
    0.8   Complete the loop.

The hike: You begin the loop by taking the right fork, and quickly come to the Robert E. Lee Tree, ranked as the 13th largest. Many sequoia groves were explored around the time of the Civil War and some of the trees were given the names of those made famous by that conflict. Not far away and just beyond the east end of the Fallen Monarch is Photo Point, an alcove from which you can take a picture of the entire General Grant Tree from the base to the crown.

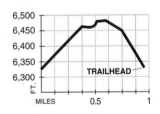

Next, you reach young sequoias that were planted around 1949. The trees contrast in size because of the different amount of water and light each of them receives. A little farther up the trail is a sign describing the other trees that grow in the sequoia grove, such as white fir, incense cedar, sugar pine, and ponderosa pine. Beyond, you reach the Tennessee Tree and Pacific dogwood trees. If you are here in June the dogwoods may be covered with their soft, white blossoms.

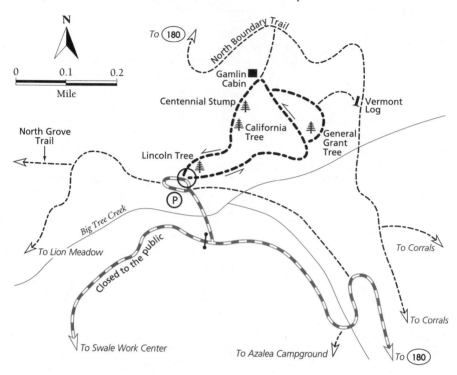

General Grant Loop

N

0   0.1   0.2
Mile

To (180)

North Boundary Trail

Gamlin Cabin

Centennial Stump

Vermont Log

North Grove Trail

California Tree

General Grant Tree

Lincoln Tree

P

Big Tree Creek

To Lion Meadow

Closed to the public

To Corrals

To Corrals

To Swale Work Center

To Azalea Campground

To (180)

You arrive next at this trail's namesake, the General Grant Tree. This tree is the world's third largest living organism and has a greater base diameter than any other sequoia. An unpaved trail circles the General Grant Tree, and meets a side trail to the Vermont Log, which fell in 1985.

Farther up the main trail is the Gamlin Cabin, which was built by the Gamlin brothers in 1872 and served as the first ranger station for General Grant National Park, which was included in Kings Canyon National Park in 1940. Parts of the cabin have been restored, and a concrete foundation has been added to preserve the structure.

If you wish to visit North Grant View, another good photo opportunity, take the trail to the right of Gamlin Cabin a few hundred feet uphill to the North Boundary Trail. Make a left (west) turn at the junction and look to the left (southeast), in the direction of the General Grant Tree. You will be able to see it from top to bottom, as at Photo Point, but from a different perspective.

Beyond the cabin, you arrive at the Fire-Damaged Trees (an interpretive sign here describes the fire-resistant properties of sequoias) and the Centennial Stump. This stump is all that remains of a sequoia that was felled in 1875 so that a 16-foot section could be exhibited at America's Centennial Exhibition in Philadelphia. The tree was cut into segments for transportation and reassembled at the exhibition. Because of this, spectators thought it was many trees put together to resemble a big one and dubbed it the "California Hoax."

Later the stump was known as the "School Stump," as Sunday school classes were held on top of it during the logging era.

Before long you come to the California Tree, which was hit by lightning in 1967. A park forester climbed this tree with a fire hose and put out the blaze to preserve the sequoia grove. The Oregon Tree View is just down the trail and to the right (northwest). Next, you come to the west end of the Fallen Monarch. This tree served as a shelter for the Gamlin brothers and others, it has been used as a hotel and saloon, and the U.S Cavalry, the first to patrol the new park, used it to stable their horses.

As you near the end of the loop you reach the Lincoln Tree and a view of the Twin Sisters, two sequoias that have fused together on the west side of the parking area. Upon reaching the parking area at 0.8 mile, you may notice the group of mature sequoias across the parking lot to your left (east). Known as the Happy Family, these trees are approximately the same age and probably sprouted after a very intense fire cleared the spot where they have grown.

Option: This trail can be combined with the North Boundary and Lone Pine Trails (Hike 38).

36 Sunset Trail

Highlights:	This hike first follows a fire road, closed to private vehicles, through a quiet, less-traveled area of the park, then visits pretty Ella Falls, climbs to Grant Grove Village, and returns to the General Grant Tree parking area.
Type of hike:	Loop, day hike.
Total distance:	5.2 miles.
Difficulty:	Moderate.
Best months:	May through October.
Maps:	USGS Hume and General Grant Grove; Kings Canyon National Park Grant Grove; or TOPO! Sequoia Kings Canyon CD-ROM.
Permits:	None.
Parking and facilities:	Restrooms and water are available at this large parking area. The trail begins at the lower parking area in the far west (reserved for RVs and trailers), at the gate signed "North Grove Loop."

Finding the trailhead: From the Big Stump entrance station, drive north on California Highway 180, past Grant Grove Village, to the junction with the General Grant Tree road, which leads to the General Grant Tree. Turn left (west) and take the road to the General Grant Tree parking area. The trailhead is a total of 4.1 miles from the Big Stump entrance.

Key points:

- 0.0   Trailhead.
- 0.1   Pass the first North Grove Trail junction.
- 0.6   Reach the Dead Giant Trail junction.
- 0.8   Reach the first trail to Sequoia Lake.
- 1.5   The road to Cedar Camp and Sequoia Lake breaks off to the west.
- 2.1   Arrive at the Ella Falls Trail and the second Sequoia Lake Trail junction.
- 2.4   Enjoy the views of Ella Falls.
- 2.9   Pass the South Boundary Trail junction.
- 3.1   Cross the Sequoia Creek tributary.
- 4.1   Join the South Boundary Trail.
- 4.3   Meet the paved trail to the amphitheater.
- 4.9   Use the crosswalk at Big Tree Creek tributary.

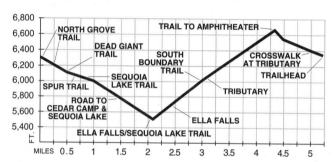

The hike: From the locked gate, follow the closed road downhill through the shady forest. Reach the first junction with the North Grove Trail at 0.1 mile and take the fork to the left (southwest). At 0.3 mile you come to the second junction with the before-mentioned trail; again take the left (southwest) fork and wind around emerald green Lion Meadow.

At 0.6 mile you arrive at the junction with the parallel paths of the Dead Giant Trail. Stay left (south) and continue to descend. At about 0.7 mile you approach a spur path to the right, which dead-ends in a clearing. At 0.8 mile, you reach a trail complete with a mileage sign, which leads to Cedar Camp and Sequoia Lake. The YMCA operates a summer camp along the shore of Sequoia Lake and you are welcome to hike down to it, but you must stay on the trail—this is private property.

The Sunset road/trail winds down three long switchbacks, and at 1.5 miles meets a road that also leads to Cedar Camp and eventually to Sequoia Lake. Continue straight (south) as the road winds and switchbacks to the next junction at 2.1 miles. Here, a small sign pointing east toward Ella Falls directs you onto a trail and closer to the sounds of Sequoia Creek. The road you have just left leads down to Sequoia Lake, as does the trail to the right (west) just a few hundred feet ahead. This is an easier trail to Sequoia Lake and again, if you decide to hike down you must stay on the trail—this is private property.

Take the trail to the left (east) toward Ella Falls. Begin to climb, and reach the cascading, 50-foot Ella Falls on Sequoia Creek at 2.4 miles. This is a great area to stop and rest or have lunch.

Sunset Trail

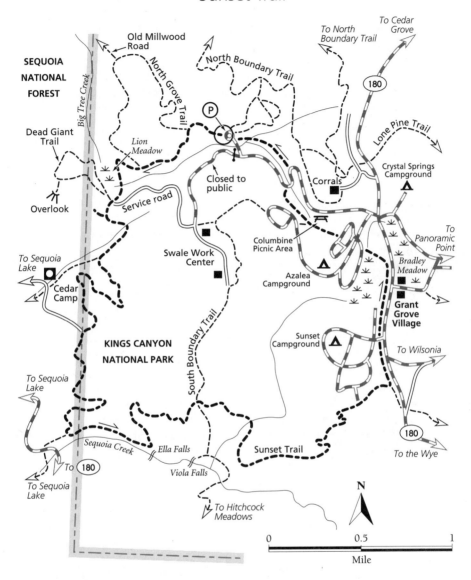

Beyond the falls, several steep switchbacks lead you up through the dense forest. Cross the junction with the South Boundary Trail at 2.9 miles. A side trip to Viola Falls can be made from this point (see the options outlined at the end of the hike description). Follow the Sunset Trail uphill, through the trees and a rocky area, crossing a tributary to Sequoia Creek on a small wooden bridge at 3.1 miles. There is a pretty cascade to your left (northeast) in early season here. The trail continues its steep climb through the forest, then through another rocky, granite zone. You may see pileated woodpeckers nesting in dead snags in the area.

Several more switchbacks through forest bring you to the outer edge of Sunset Campground. The path travels around the south side of the campground and joins a portion of the South Boundary and Azalea Trails at a group of large rotting logs at 4.1 miles. Turn left (north), descending to a good-sized meadow and the east edge of the campground. Cross the main road into the campground. Follow the trail uphill, joining the paved path leading up from the amphitheater toward the crosswalk across CA 180 at 4.3 miles. Turn right (west) and intersect the signed trail leading to the General Grant Tree about 50 yards from the road. Make another right (north) turn on this trail.

The trail leads you through Azalea Campground and can be faint in places. The route crosses a small creek on a wooden bridge and passes through a verdant green meadow. Continue through the campground, following the crosswalks across four paved roads, and head downhill along another stringer meadow just across from the Columbine Picnic Area. The trail becomes more defined as it travels above a tributary of Big Tree Creek that begins in the meadow you have been following.

Cross the road leading to the General Grant Tree parking area in yet another crosswalk at 4.9 miles, and descend along the creek. The trail passes the Michigan Tree before ending at the parking area at 5.2 miles.

Options: If you wish to visit Sequoia Lake, keep in mind that the first trail encountered while on the Sunset Trail is steep, with many switchbacks. This trail first leads 0.3 mile to Cedar Camp, which consists of a campfire pit with logs serving as benches, and a couple of broken-down outhouses. The lake is another 0.4 mile downhill. The return trip is completely uphill, with an elevation gain of 640 feet.

The second trail is shorter and more gradual, only 0.3 mile and with less than 100 feet of elevation gain on the way back. This trail crosses Sequoia Creek a couple of times on small wooden bridges before reaching the lake. Because the YMCA privately owns the property each of these trails travels on, you must stay on the trail and return the way you came. Do not enter the summer camp.

A side trip to Viola Falls will add 0.4 mile and a little more than 100 feet onto your hike.

And last but not least, this loop can be done in a clockwise direction, if you prefer a longer downhill walk.

37 North Grove and Dead Giant Loops

Highlights:	This hike takes you through the northern portion of the General Grant Grove, past an old road leading to a former logging camp, and to an overlook of a beautiful lake.
Type of hike:	Loop, day hike.
Total distance:	2.5 miles.
Difficulty:	Easy.
Best months:	May through October.
Maps:	USGS Hume and General Grant Grove; Kings Canyon National Park Grant Grove; or TOPO! Sequoia Kings Canyon CD-ROM.
Permits:	None.
Parking and facilities:	Restrooms and water are available at this large parking area. The trail begins at the lower parking area in the far west (reserved for RVs and trailers), at the gate signed "North Grove Loop."

Finding the trailhead: From the Big Stump entrance station, drive north on California Highway 180, past Grant Grove Village, to the junction with the road leading to the General Grant Tree. Turn left (west and north) and take the road to the General Grant Tree parking area. The trailhead is 4.1 miles from the Big Stump entrance.

Key points:
- 0.0   Trailhead.
- 0.1   Reach the North Grove Trail junction.
- 0.6   Pass the Old Millwood Road junction.
- 1.1   Arrive at the Sunset Trail junction.
- 1.3   Reach the Dead Giant Trail junction.
- 1.7   Visit the Sequoia Lake overlook.
- 1.9   Return to the Sunset Trail junction.

The hike: From the gate, follow the closed road, which is also part of the Sunset Trail, downhill through the dappled light of the shady forest. At 0.1 mile, you reach the first junction and take the right (northwest) fork onto the North Grove Trail.

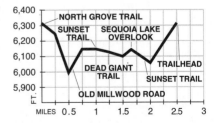

The wide path winds through numerous sequoias while continuing to descend. At 0.6 mile you arrive at the unsigned junction with the Old Millwood Road on the right (northwest), which looks more like a small gully leading into the brush. If you step through the overgrowth, the gully widens to a one-lane dirt road. The Old Millwood Road

133

North Grove and Dead Giant Loops

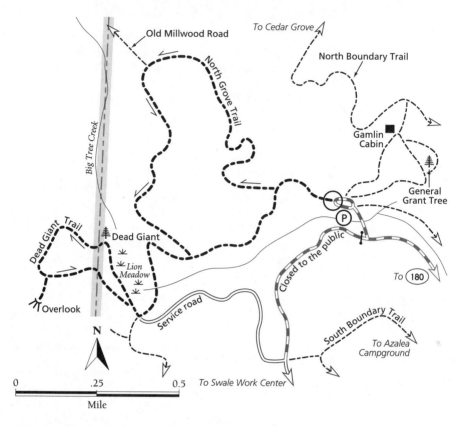

leads 2.3 miles (with an elevation loss of 920 feet) to the site of Millwood, an old logging camp.

The trail begins to climb beyond the junction, which is just before an immense burned sequoia, then continues through more "Giants" back to the closed road. Turn right (west) at the junction with the Sunset Trail at 1.1 miles. Follow the road around pretty Lion Meadow and come to the next junction with the Dead Giant Trail at 1.3 miles. Turn right (northwest) on the first and lower of two parallel paths; the other trail is the return route. The path travels above the edge of the deep green meadow and brings you to the Dead Giant, a large, girdled sequoia that is still standing.

The trail turns to the southwest and climbs uphill past a trail sign to the top of the ridge, through clearings in the manzanita. As the wide track levels and comes to another trail sign indicating a left turn, continue straight (south) to the Sequoia Lake overlook at 1.7 miles. This sapphire blue lake, framed by cedars and pines, is manmade. The Sanger Lumber Company dammed Sequoia Creek in 1889 to supply water for their flume while logging operations were going on in the area. The flume stretched 54 miles to Sanger, and cost $300,000 to construct.

After viewing the lake, return to the trail sign and go right (east). Follow the trail downhill, back into the forest and to the closed road at 1.9 miles. Make a left (north) turn onto the road and follow it past the two junctions with the North Grove Trail, retracing your steps to the trailhead at 2.5 miles.

Option: If you wish to visit the site of Millwood, follow the Old Millwood Road, which quickly narrows to a trail, enters the Sequoia National Forest at an old drift fence, then joins Forest Road 13S63. Proceed on the dirt road southwest to the bridge spanning Mill Flat Creek, a grand total of 2.3 miles. Nothing remains of Millwood, but there are many campsites in the area. Keep in mind that your return trip will be all uphill, with an elevation gain of 920 feet.

Sequoia Lake, created by a nineteenth-century lumber company, is visible from an overlook on the Dead Giant Loop.

38 North Boundary and Lone Pine Trails

Highlights:	Despite being the primary horse trail in the Grant Grove area, this hike is a little-traveled jewel in the early summer and the fall.
Type of hike:	Semi-loop, day hike.
Total distance:	6 miles.
Difficulty:	Moderate.
Best months:	June through October.
Maps:	USGS Hume and General Grant Grove; Kings Canyon National Park Grant Grove; or TOPO! Sequoia Kings Canyon CD-ROM.
Permits:	None.
Special considerations:	Because the North Boundary and Lone Pine Trails are used by horseback riders, please remember proper trail etiquette by stepping off the trail on the downhill side and waiting quietly until the horses have passed. Stay in plain view of the horses—they may think you are a wild animal and bolt if you are hidden behind a rock or tree.
Parking and facilities:	An outhouse and picnic tables are available at the parking area, but no water. The signed trail begins at the northwest end of the parking area, on the south side of the service road heading west.

Finding the trailhead: From the Big Stump entrance station on California Highway 180, drive north to Grant Grove Village. Turn right (east) at the visitor center and drive through the parking lot, past Bradley Meadow, to the junction with Panoramic Point Road, next to the new John Muir Lodge. Make a right (northeast) turn and follow narrow Panoramic Point Road to the Panoramic Point trailhead at the road's end. The trailhead is 5.5 miles from the Big Stump entrance.

Key points:
- 0.0 Trailhead.
- 0.5 Pass an unnamed trail junction.
- 0.9 Reach the Lone Pine Trail junction.
- 1.2 Cross CA 180.
- 1.5 Reach the Abbott Creek crossing.
- 1.9 Meet the junction with the trail to the corrals.
- 3.3 Pass the spur trail to the General Grant Loop.
- 3.8 Arrive at the corrals and a four-way junction.
- 3.9 Cross CA 180 again.
- 4.3 Pass the Crystal Springs Trail junction.
- 4.5 Reach Panoramic Point Road.
- 4.6 Cross an Abbott Creek tributary.
- 5.1 Reach the North Boundary Trail junction.

The hike: The North Boundary Trail starts by winding through the trees, then quickly begins to descend. As the grade steepens, loose rock litters the trail—watch your footing! Small yellow violets and light pink pussypaws bloom along the trail in clearings. Many of the trees in Grant Grove and Sequoia National Park sustained damage or were killed by the caterpillars

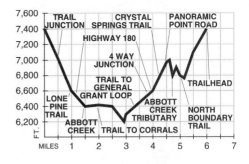

of the tussock moth in 1998. You may notice bare or brown conifers along this portion of the trail due to that outbreak.

After the long downhill, several switchbacks bring you to grassy Round Meadow. At 0.5 mile you reach a wide, grassy trail leading south across the lower end of the meadow to a turnout on Panoramic Point Road. From this turnout an abandoned trail leads to a hilltop once known as Bird's Eye View, which overlooks the San Joaquin Valley. Sadly, this trail is now impassable, though still shown on the General Grant Grove topo. Fortunately, there are other hills and mountaintops from which the valley may be observed.

From Round Meadow, the trail follows Abbott Creek, which eventually flows into Mill Flat Creek near the former site of Millwood, an old logging camp. At 0.9 mile you reach the Lone Pine Trail, on which you will be returning. Continue straight (northwest) as the trail levels and widens. This portion of the trail was a fire road in the early days of General Grant National Park, before this area was included in Kings Canyon National Park in 1940.

The trail descends to a large turnout on CA 180 at 1.2 miles. Take the crosswalk across the highway and pick up the trail on the other side. Continue to descend, crossing Abbott Creek at 1.5 miles on a small wooden bridge.

The path follows the dogwood-lined creek. Round the next ridge, and cross a tributary passing through a small culvert. Pretty green meadows lie downhill to your right (north), and are visible here and there through the trees.

After rounding another ridge, cross another tributary on stones at 1.9 miles and intersect the trail leading to the corrals, which is uphill on the left (south). On the right (west), an abandoned portion of the trail leads downhill. Descend the middle fork, meeting the other end of the abandoned segment, and passing through some controlled burn areas, before you begin to climb.

In forest clearings you may come across blue-eyed Marys and mustang clover blooming in early season. Giant sequoias loom ahead; just before you reach the spur trail to the General Grant Loop at 3.3 miles, you come to General Grant North View (unsigned, near a small boulder), where you can see the entire General Grant Tree from top to bottom.

Upon reaching the junction with the spur trail to the General Grant Loop, take the left (east) fork to the corrals. The trail gently climbs through open forest along the outskirts of the General Grant Grove. Looking to your right (west), you can see many of the "giants" without dealing with the crowds on the General Grant Loop. On your right, after you've passed through the

137

North Boundary and Lone Pine Trails

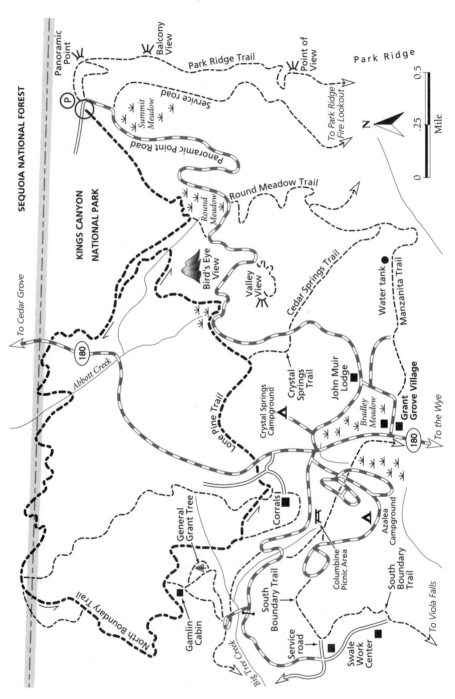

fallen Vermont Log, you can climb stairs to the top of a large boulder, which is an overlook of the General Grant Tree.

Back on the North Boundary Trail, climb through a mixed forest to a longer side trail on the right (south), which eventually leads to the corrals. Take the shorter fork on the left, and arrive at the corrals and a four-way junction at 3.8 miles. Continue east on the signed Lone Pine Trail, cross a service road, and cross CA 180 using the painted crosswalk at 3.9 miles.

The path then traces the northern edge of Crystal Springs Campground, where you may see foraging nuthatches and hear their toy horn-like call. At 4.3 miles, you come to a junction with the Crystal Springs Trail, which leads to the Manzanita Trail. The trail heads to the left (northeast), leading uphill to the Panoramic Point Road at 4.5 miles.

The trail then follows the north side of the road, reaches a trail sign, and leaves the road at 4.6 miles. Cross an Abbott Creek tributary passing through a culvert. From here, the route stays fairly level as it passes the unnamed meadow fed by this tributary and enters the forest. You may hear the tinkling song of the hermit thrush in this lightly traveled area.

The trail crosses Abbott Creek again, and arrives at the junction with the North Boundary Trail at 5.1 miles. Begin the long uphill, retracing your steps past Round Meadow, up the switchbacks, and back to the trailhead at 6 miles.

Option: The General Grant Loop (Hike 35) can be incorporated into this loop, adding an extra 0.8 mile.

39 Park Ridge Trail

Highlights:	This hike first gives you a breathtaking view of the Monarch and Great Western Divides at Panoramic Point, then brings you to another spectacular view at one of the few lookout towers still occasionally staffed in the park.
Type of hike:	Loop, day hike.
Total distance:	5.5 miles.
Difficulty:	Moderate.
Best months:	June through October.
Maps:	USGS Hume and General Grant Grove; Kings Canyon National Park Grant Grove; or TOPO! Sequoia Kings Canyon CD-ROM.
Permits:	None.
Parking and facilities:	An outhouse and picnic tables are available at the parking area, but no water. The paved trail begins at the southeast end of the parking area.

Finding the trailhead: From the Big Stump entrance station, drive north to Grant Grove Village. Turn right (east) at the visitor center and drive through the parking lot, past Bradley Meadow to the junction with Panoramic Point Road, which is next to the new John Muir Lodge. Make a right (northeast) turn and follow Panoramic Point Road to the Panoramic Point trailhead at the road's end. The trailhead is 5.5 miles from the Big Stump entrance.

Key points:
- 0.0   Trailhead.
- 0.2   Reach Panoramic Point.
- 1.7   Arrive at the three-way junction.
- 2.6   Reach the fire lookout.
- 3.9   Return to the three-way junction.
- 5.3   Reach Panoramic Point Road.

The hike: The wide asphalt path begins with a slight uphill, then meets a long switchback leading you to Panoramic Point in just 0.2 mile. You'll find a wonderful 180-degree view here, complete with interpretive signs identifying the distant peaks and Hume Lake to the east. As with the Sanger Lumber Company, which created Se-

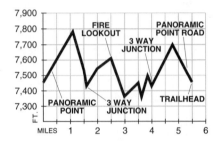

quoia Lake west of here, the Hume-Bennett Lumber Company created Hume Lake in 1909 to provide water for a 17-mile flume extension, added to the existing flume that came from the former logging camp of Millwood. This extension cost $100,000 to construct, and the total length of the flume reached 59 miles to the town of Sanger.

You may notice a "horse trail" sign immediately downhill to your left (north). This connects to the North Boundary Trail. After enjoying the view, take the trail to the right (south), losing the pavement. Just past the huge boulder next to the overlook, the trail inclines slightly as you pass a couple of side trails heading down to a flat area known as Balcony View, a nice place to picnic in cooler weather. You may hear the "whoomp, whoomp, whoomp" call of the male blue grouse as you enter the forest.

As you near the first hilltop along Park Ridge, a vista of the San Joaquin Valley is to the west. Douglas phlox blooms in the sunny, rocky areas in summer. A short downhill brings you back into the woods, before the next climb uphill, with another panorama of the Monarch and Great Western Divides. Another decline on this roller-coaster trail, through more mixed forest, brings you to a switchback and a climb up to a hilltop known as Point of View. Both divides are still visible to the left (east), and you can now see part of the Kaweah Peaks peeking out to the right (south) of Mount Silliman.

The trail now embarks on a long downhill run, passing through alternating burned areas and manzanita, before reaching the dirt service road to the lookout tower. Follow the road a short distance to directional signs,

Park Ridge Trail

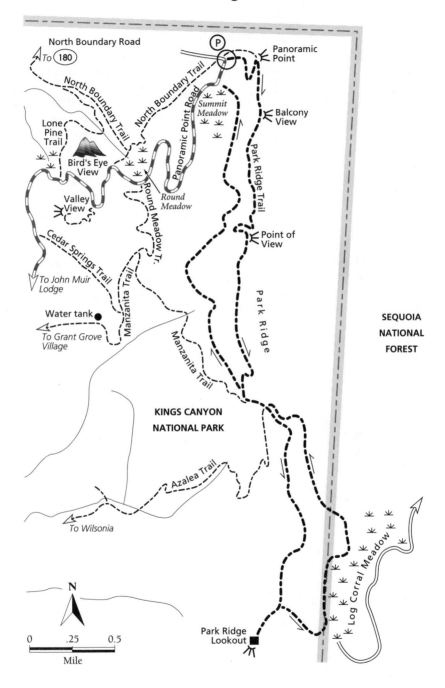

which are both to your left (east) on the road and to your right (west) at a three-way trail junction at 1.7 miles. Head toward the junction with the Manzanita and Azalea Trails to your right (west), and take the Park Ridge Trail south and uphill.

Pass through a densely forested area full of woodland creatures, climbing steadily before dipping through a rocky, exposed stretch. The trail ascends again and soon meets the service road, which you follow to the lookout at 2.6 miles.

If the lookout is staffed, it is polite to ask permission before going up, this being the fire lookout's home during the fire season. From this point, you can enjoy 270-degree view. To the east and southeast, you can see part of the northern portion of the Great Western Divide, Shell Mountain and the Silliman Crest, Mount Stewart and part of the Kaweahs, Alta Peak, and the southern portion of the Great Western Divide. To the south, Big Baldy and Redwood Mountain flank Ash Peaks ridge. To the west are the foothills and the hazy San Joaquin Valley. To the northwest are the Patterson Bluffs near Balch Camp, and Nelson Mountain, and Eagle Peak are visible to the north, near Courtright Reservoir.

After taking in the views, follow the service road downhill, this time continuing on it rather than the trail. In a short distance you enter the Sequoia National Forest and are looking down on beautiful Log Corral Meadow.

The road winds through a logged area, passing fingers of the meadow. Western tanagers and Anna's hummingbirds may be seen flitting through the small trees now growing in the most heavily logged section. Also, a vista of Mounts McGee, Goddard, and Reinstein, as well as the northern Kings Canyon backcountry, appears before you.

The road reenters the dense trees at the park boundary, and at 3.9 miles, passes the three-way junction. Continue on the road as it climbs through a fire-scarred zone and manzanita. There are western views of the smog-ridden valley, and before entering the forest again, you can discern the little-used trail contouring around Valley View, a wooded hilltop, below you to the northwest. The road begins a long, gradual descent, passing pretty Summit Meadow, filled with shooting stars in early summer.

You arrive at the Panoramic Point Road at 5.3 miles; turn right (northeast) and follow it uphill to the parking area at 5.5 miles.

Hikes in the Redwood Canyon Area

The first three hikes in this section begin at Redwood Saddle. The next two begin along the Generals Highway, with the Buena Vista Peak trail located across from the Kings Canyon Overlook, and the Big Baldy Ridge trail beginning near Big Meadows Road.

40 Hart Tree Trail

Highlights:	This interesting jaunt takes you to an old logging camp, a sequoia "log" cabin, a pretty meadow, and a waterfall, all while traveling through the largest sequoia grove left standing on the planet.
Type of hike:	Loop, day hike.
Total distance:	7.2 miles.
Difficulty:	Moderate.
Best months:	May through June and October through November.
Maps:	USGS General Grant Grove, or TOPO! Sequoia Kings Canyon CD-ROM.
Permits:	None.
Parking and facilities:	There is a new outhouse at this trailhead, but no water. The trail begins at the southwest end of the parking area, to the left of the bulletin board, and is signed "Hart Tree" and "Redwood Canyon."

Hart Meadow is a wonderful destination.

Finding the trailhead: Drive 5.3 miles south from the Big Stump entrance on the Generals Highway to Quail Flat. Turn right (south) onto the dirt Redwood Saddle Road, which is across the Generals Highway from the paved Forest Road 13S09 to Hume Lake. Follow Redwood Saddle Road for approximately 1.7 miles to a junction at a large, modern cabin. Take the left (southeast) fork, which leads through a fallen sequoia, and continue for another 0.2 mile to the parking area.

Key points:

0.0	Trailhead.
0.3	Reach the Redwood Canyon Trail junction.
0.5	Pass Barton's Post Camp.
0.8	Reach the Pierce Cabin.
0.9	Enjoy a viewpoint.
1.7	Arrive at a second viewpoint.
1.9	Cross Buena Vista Creek.
3.0	Cross the East Fork of Redwood Creek.
3.5	Reach a creek crossing and waterfall.
4.7	Reach the Fallen Goliath.
5.2	Make the Redwood Creek crossing.
5.3	Arrive at the Sugarbowl Trail junction.
6.9	Return to the Hart Tree Trail junction.

The hike: The wide trail (once a dirt road) heads downhill (south), past a fire hydrant, through mixed firs, pines, and giant sequoias. A view of Buena Vista Peak (Hike 43) can be had as the path rounds a turn and switchbacks. Reach the junction with the Redwood

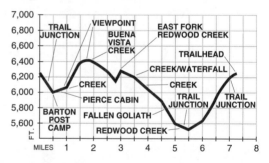

Canyon Trail at 0.3 mile and turn left (north) onto the Hart Tree Trail. The other path will be your return route.

Wild strawberries carpet the forest floor, and after stepping across fledgling Redwood Creek, you arrive at Barton's Post Camp at 0.5 mile. Large sequoia stumps and a few felled trees are the only evidence of the small-scale logging operation that manufactured fence posts here in the late 1800s.

The path rises to cross a small ridge and dips to step across an unnamed brook before reaching the deteriorating Pierce Cabin at 0.8 mile. This fire-hollowed sequoia had shingles, fireplaces, and a door added to make it habitable at one time, but now is sadly collapsing. The path then climbs to a granite and manzanita-covered knob at 0.9 mile, where a few steps off the trail give you an excellent view of the crowns of the sequoias growing on Redwood Mountain to the west.

After the viewpoint, you descend to cross another unnamed creeklet at 1 mile, and then ascend a switchback and travel through oaks. Come to an-

Hart Tree Trail

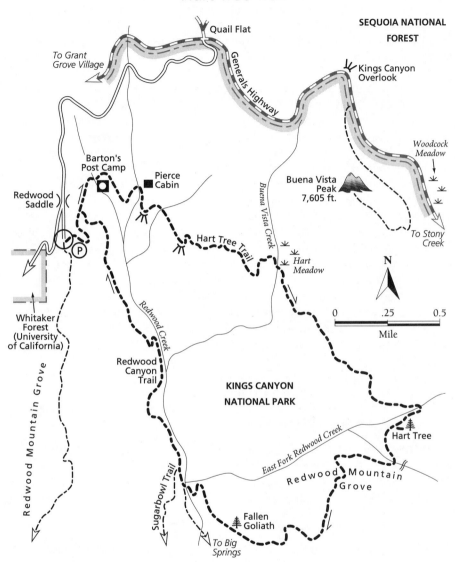

other easily spanned rivulet and climb to a rocky knoll at 1.7 miles, with views of Redwood Mountain to the west and Big Baldy Ridge (Hike 44) and the Redwood Canyon to the south.

The trail then drops down through wild roses to lovely Hart Meadow, with Buena Vista Peak as the backdrop. At 1.9 miles you gingerly advance through a muddy area at the lower end of the meadow, crossing a couple of branches of Buena Vista Creek, which are lined with white mountain violets and sword ferns. The route mounts the next ridge, passes through the entire length of a fire-hollowed sequoia (a bypass is available for those who are claustro-phobic) and winds its way down through fallen "giants" to the East Fork of Redwood Creek at 3 miles. This crossing can be a little tricky in early sea-son if you are not wearing waterproof boots.

After another climb, at 3.2 miles the trail reaches a steep spur path flanked by two signs and leading to the Hart Tree. This behemoth once was ranked as the fourth largest sequoia, before being surpassed by other trees.

The route then descends to a pretty, unnamed creek with a peaceful wa-terfall at 3.5 miles, and an easy crossing on stones. A muddy seep intersects the path on the other side of this creek; beyond, you begin the long decline to the bottom of the canyon, passing over one more tiny brook at 3.9 miles in the process. Along the way you may spot tiny winter wrens darting around the many sequoia trunks near grassy areas.

After passing through large zones of wild rose and bear clover, you reach the immense Fallen Goliath at 4.7 miles. The path continues to descend and arrives at Redwood Creek at 5.2 miles. A campsite is located to the right (north). This crossing can be tricky without waterproof boots in early season, but is easily crossed on stones in the fall. Alders and dogwoods line the creek, the latter decorated with their delicate white blooms in June. In autumn there is an exhilarating color show, with the deciduous trees turning beautiful hues of light green, gold, and red.

On the other side of the creek you come to a junction with the Redwood Canyon Trail and turn right (northwest). At 5.3 miles you pass the junction with the Sugarbowl Trail as the path climbs gradually along meandering Red-wood Creek. The route switchbacks and moves upslope from the watercourse, continuing past many "big trees" and working its way around three sequoias that have fallen across the old roadbed. Reach the junction with the Hart Tree Trail at 6.9 miles. From here, turn left (south) and retrace your steps to the parking area at 7.2 miles.

Options: This hike can be combined with the Sugarbowl Trail (Hike 41), or the Redwood Canyon Trail (Hike 42), for a more challenging day hike or an overnighter.

41 Sugarbowl Trail

Highlights: This hike takes you through the main portion of the largest sequoia grove on earth, and returns along serene Redwood Creek.
Type of hike: Loop, day hike.
Total distance: 6.4 miles.
Difficulty: Moderate.
Best months: May through June and October through November.
Maps: USGS General Grant Grove, or TOPO! Sequoia Kings Canyon CD-ROM.
Permits: None.
Parking and facilities: There is a new outhouse at this trailhead, but no water. The trail begins at the southwest end of the parking area, to the right of the bulletin board, and is signed "Sugarbowl Trail."

Finding the trailhead: Drive 5.3 miles south from the Big Stump entrance on the Generals Highway to Quail Flat. Turn right (south) onto the dirt Redwood Saddle Road, which is across the Generals Highway from the paved Forest Road 13S09 to Hume Lake. Follow Redwood Saddle Road for approximately 1.7 miles to a junction at a large, modern cabin. Take the left (southeast) fork, which leads through a fallen sequoia and continues for another 0.2 mile to the parking area.

Key points:
0.0 Trailhead.
1.1 Pass the first switchback.
2.2 Reach The Sugarbowl.
4.0 Cross an unnamed creek.
4.5 Reach the Redwood Canyon Trail junction.
6.1 Reach the Hart Tree Trail junction.

The hike: This trek begins by climbing south on a ridge on the north side of Redwood Mountain. Pass numerous sequoias and a "Research Area—Do Not Disturb" sign. The path (once a dirt road) crosses from one side of the ridge to the other, winding through a controlled burn zone and passing a few sequoia stumps, evidence of small-

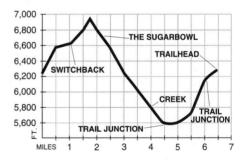

scale logging that took place in the late 1800s. At 1.1 miles, you ascend a small switchback and come to clearings above slopes covered in mustang clover. Before long you have a view of Buena Vista Peak (Hike 43), to the northeast, Big Baldy Ridge (Hike 44) to the east, and Sawtooth Peak to the southeast, high above the Mineral King Valley.

Sugarbowl Trail

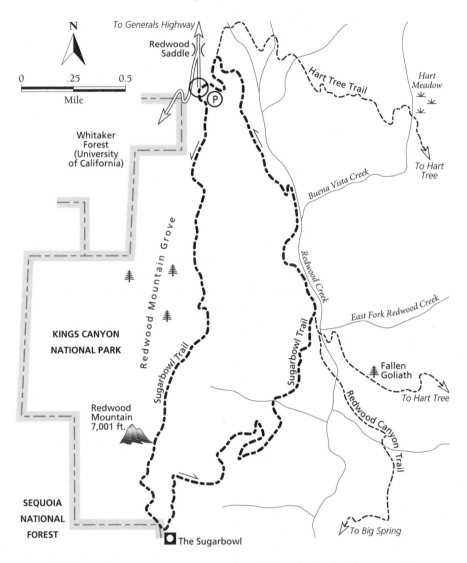

At 2.2 miles, you arrive at a flat area completely dominated by "giants," which is a nice place for a rest stop or snack. You have entered what was known to old-time loggers as "The Sugarbowl," due to the large concentration of sequoias here.

The trail descends to an old mileage sign nailed to a fir tree before turning north and dropping past areas of metamorphic rock and manzanita. Enter a cedar thicket, and you may be greeted by a flock of curious mountain chickadees with their wheezy call. Bear clover becomes the main ground cover as the path works its way down a couple of long switchbacks. At 4 miles, you easily cross a small creek lined with very young sequoias, and soon the parental trees come into view.

The route passes through an area thick with infant sequoias and arrives at the bottom of the canyon, intersecting the Redwood Canyon Trail at 4.5 miles. Make a left (north) turn and follow the wide track that climbs gradually beside meandering Redwood Creek. Alders and dogwoods line the creek, the latter decorated with delicate white blooms in June. In autumn there is an exhilarating color show, with the deciduous trees turning beautiful hues of light green, gold, and red.

The route switchbacks and moves upslope from the watercourse, continuing past many "big trees," and working its way around three sequoias that have fallen across the old roadbed. You will reach the junction with the Hart Tree Trail at 6.1 miles. From here, turn left (south), ascend a switchback, pass an out-of-place fire hydrant, and arrive at the parking area at 6.4 miles.

Options: This hike can be combined with the Hart Tree Trail (Hike 40), or the Redwood Canyon Trail (Hike 42), for a more challenging day hike or an overnighter.

42 Redwood Canyon

Highlights:	This hike takes you down Redwood Canyon, past Lilburn Cave, to Redwood Cabin, with an option to trek farther on a seldom traveled or maintained portion of trail.
Type of hike:	Out-and-back, day hike.
Total distance:	8.8 miles.
Difficulty:	Moderate.
Best months:	May through June and October through November.
Maps:	USGS General Grant Grove, or TOPO! Sequoia Kings Canyon CD-ROM.
Permits:	None.
Parking and facilities:	There is a new outhouse at this trailhead, but no water. The trail begins at the southwest end of the parking area, to the left of the bulletin board, and is signed "Hart Tree" and "Redwood Canyon."

Finding the trailhead: Drive 5.3 miles south from the Big Stump entrance on the Generals Highway to Quail Flat. Turn right (south) onto the dirt Redwood Saddle Road, which is across the Generals Highway from the paved Forest Road 13S09 to Hume Lake. Follow Redwood Saddle Road for approximately 1.7 miles to a junction at a large, modern cabin. Take the left (southeast) fork, which leads through a fallen sequoia and continues for another 0.2 mile to the parking area.

Key points:
- 0.0   Trailhead.
- 0.3   Pass the first Hart Tree Trail junction.
- 1.9   Pass the Sugarbowl Trail junction.
- 2.0   Pass the second Hart Tree Trail junction.
- 2.2   Cross Redwood Creek.
- 2.6   Cross an unnamed creek.
- 3.5   Reach a seasonal creek.
- 3.6   Arrive at the Lilburn Cave entrance.
- 4.4   Reach Redwood Cabin.

The hike: The wide trail (once a dirt road) heads downhill, past a fire hydrant, through mixed firs, pines, and giant sequoias. Enjoy a view of Buena Vista Peak (Hike 43) as the path rounds a

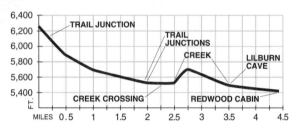

turn and switchbacks. Reach the first junction with the Hart Tree Trail at 0.3 mile and make a right (southeast) turn onto the Redwood Canyon Trail. Alders and dogwoods line the creek, the latter decorated with delicate white blooms in June. In autumn, hikers are treated to an exhilarating color show, with the deciduous trees turning beautiful hues of light green, gold, and red.

The route descends past many "big trees" and works its way around three sequoia logs that have fallen across the old roadbed. Move down a switchback and travel along meandering Redwood Creek before passing the junction with the Sugarbowl Trail at 1.9 miles. At 2 miles, you will come to the second junction with the Hart Tree Trail. Continue straight (southeast) on the mostly flat track, and cross Redwood Creek next to a large campsite at 2.2 miles. This portion of the creek can be completely dry in late season. The trail then ascends to a muddy intersection with a small brook at 2.6 miles; a drier crossing lies a few steps upstream.

The path rises, traverses a ridge, and then descends back toward Redwood Creek. At 3.5 miles, the trail crosses the bed of a seasonal creek. Around the next curve you can spot the entrance to Lilburn Cave, with a tall cedar growing above it, to the left (east) at 3.6 miles. This cave is the longest in California and periodically is flushed with water. It is also thought to feed Big Springs, farther down the canyon. Unless you are an experienced spelunker and have permission from the National Park Service, do not enter the cave.

Dip to cross another seasonal creekbed, then ascend gently to Redwood Cabin at 4.4 miles. This reconstructed cabin was originally built by a tungsten miner by the name of Lilburn, and is now used by research groups. Several picnic tables are located here, and it is a picturesque spot to rest or have lunch. The trail is not regularly maintained past the cabin, but if you are feeling adventurous and wish to continue, a description follows.

After enjoying the peaceful atmosphere of this small dwelling, return the way you came (8.8 miles).

Redwood Canyon

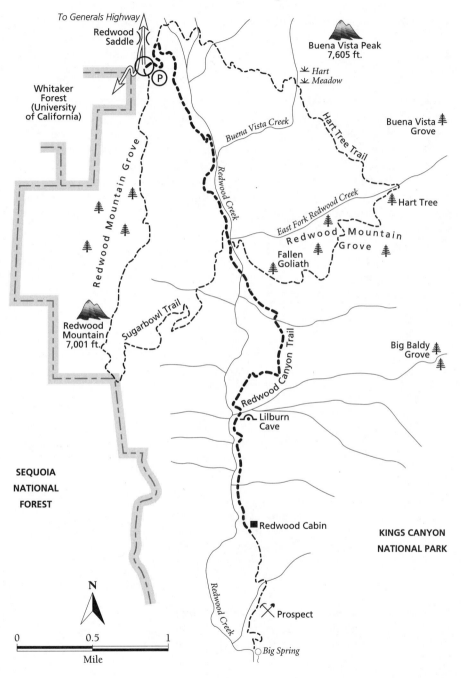

To Generals Highway

Redwood
Saddle

Whitaker
Forest
(University
of California)

P

Buena Vista Peak
7,605 ft.

Hart
Meadow

Buena Vista Creek

Hart Tree Trail

Buena Vista
Grove

Redwood Creek

Redwood Mountain Grove

East Fork Redwood Creek

Hart Tree

Redwood   Mountain   Grove

Fallen
Goliath

Sugarbowl Trail

Redwood
Mountain
7,001 ft.

Big Baldy
Grove

Redwood Canyon Trail

Lilburn
Cave

SEQUOIA

NATIONAL

FOREST

Redwood Cabin

KINGS CANYON

NATIONAL PARK

N

Redwood Creek

Prospect

Big Spring

0   0.5   1
Mile

Option: From Redwood Cabin, the dim path heads uphill through a small gap, widens to a one-lane road, and passes an overgrown side road to the old tungsten prospect. Beyond this, the route becomes covered with blow-downs that you must carefully pick your way through. Contour into the canyon of a seasonal stream and advance through its wide rock-strewn bed. The route comes upon a very old sign stating that the Cherry Flat Trail is 3 miles away. That portion of trail has not been maintained for many years and is now impassable.

Oaks, firs, and cedars shade the continuation of the wide path as the roadbed begins to descend sharply. Young firs and cedars encroach on the trail and soon begin to impede your progress. About 0.1 mile above Big Springs, a log blocks the path and the small trees become impenetrable. The flow of the spring is audible, but the foliage is so thick you cannot view it. Hopefully, this portion of the trail will be cleared sometime in the future.

When you are ready to turn around, return the way you came. This side trip will add 400 feet of elevation loss and 0.9 mile onto your hike, meaning more uphill on the way back.

43 Buena Vista Peak

Highlights:	This short trek takes you to the top of a small peak with quite a nice view of Kings Canyon and Sequoia National Parks.
Type of hike:	Out-and-back, day hike.
Total distance:	2 miles.
Difficulty:	Easy.
Best months:	Late May through October.
Maps:	USGS General Grant Grove, or TOPO! Sequoia Kings Canyon CD-ROM. (This trail does not appear on maps.)
Permits:	None.
Special considerations:	A risk of being struck by lightning exists on the summit of Buena Vista Peak. If dark clouds are nearby, or hail, rain, thunder, or static electricity is in the air, descend immediately.
Parking and facilities:	No restrooms or water are available at this trailhead. The nearest facilities are located in Grant Grove Village, 6.7 miles to the north.

Finding the trailhead: Follow the Generals Highway south for approximately 6.5 miles from the Big Stump entrance. The signed, dirt parking area is on the west side of the road, just south of the Kings Canyon Overlook turnout.

Key points:
0.0   Trailhead.
1.0   Reach the summit of Buena Vista Peak.

The hike: The trail begins on the west side of the parking area next to a group of tall pines. First head west, then quickly curve south on the flower-bordered path. The route climbs and dips, winding through many oddly shaped and balanced boulders. You rise again and gain a view to the northeast, observing Spanish Mountain, Obelisk, Mount Goddard,

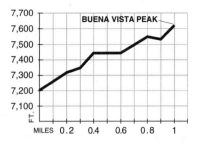

and the Monarch Divide. To the east you can see the fire lookout perched atop Buck Rock.

After passing through a sunny area of granite slabs, the trail sags again and enters a forested zone before the last incline. The path makes a barely noticeable switchback and passes through a large patch of lupine mixed with a few other blossoms in summer. Travel up a wide ledge to a large flat, from which you can reach three viewpoints. The finest vista is from the northernmost point, the summit of Buena Vista Peak, which is on your right (north) at 1 mile.

Buena Vista Peak

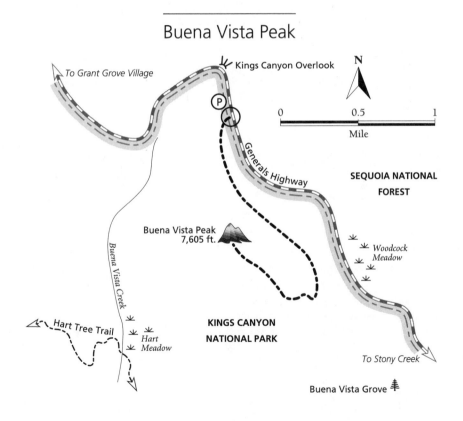

From the top, peaks to the north in the Sierra National Forest are visible, as well as crests in northern Kings Canyon National Park to the northeast. East is Buck Rock with its lookout tower, Shell Mountain, and Mount Silliman, with the Great Western Divide as a backdrop. To the south is Big Baldy, and west are Redwood Canyon, Redwood Mountain, and the haze-enveloped San Joaquin Valley.

After you have enjoyed your journey's goal, backtrack to your car (2 miles).

Option: This hike can be combined with Big Baldy Ridge (Hike 44), which is just down the Generals Highway.

44 Big Baldy Ridge

Highlights:	This trip takes you to a striking 360-degree view of Kings Canyon and Sequoia National Parks from the summit of Big Baldy, then on to a less-visited view of the west face of Chimney Rock.
Type of hike:	Out-and-back, day hike.
Total distance:	5.6 miles.
Difficulty:	Moderate.
Best months:	June through October.
Maps:	USGS General Grant Grove, or TOPO! Sequoia Kings Canyon CD-ROM.
Permits:	None.
Special considerations:	A risk of being struck by lightning exists on the summit of Big Baldy. If dark clouds are nearby, or hail, rain, thunder, or static electricity are in the air, descend immediately. There are also steep drop-offs around the summit—exercise caution.
Parking and facilities:	There are no facilities at this trailhead. The closest facilities are at Stony Creek Village, 4.8 miles south on the Generals Highway. The trailhead begins on the southwest side of the parking area.

Finding the trailhead: Drive either 8.4 miles south from the Big Stump entrance on the Generals Highway, or 4.8 miles north from Stony Creek Village, to the signed parking turnout on the southwest side of a large, blind curve just west of Big Meadows Road. If the parking area is full, more parking is available in a large turnout on the south side of the road to the east.

Key points:
0.0 Trailhead.
2.1 Reach the Big Baldy summit.
2.8 Enjoy the view of Chimney Rock.

The hike: The trail enters the forest and almost immediately meets a trail coming up from the Montecito Sequoia Lodge. (This is private property. Unless you are a lodge guest, do not enter this area.) Wind through some large boulders, chinquapin, and snowbrush beneath tall firs and pines. The ascent proceeds through an open, rocky area, edged with

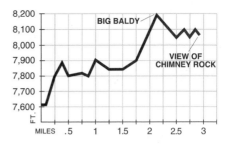

manzanita, then goes back into the woods. The route dips slightly and climbs again, passing many colorful wildflowers, most notably skyrockets and penstemons in summer.

Entering another granitic area, round a small dome and proceed up the ridge. As the trail levels a bit, a view of the summit opens to the south. Reenter the trees and rise again, reaching a penstemon-lined switchback, then contour around the east side of the high point, just below the ridgecrest. The path swings up toward the summit, passing a notch in the ridge that gives you a glimpse of the extreme drop-off.

At 2.1 miles you reach the top—8,209 feet—and spectacular views. To the north are Nelson Mountain and Eagle Peak near Courtright Reservoir, along with Spanish Mountain, Obelisk, Castle Peak, Mount Goddard, and the jagged peaks in northern Kings Canyon National Park. Buena Vista Peak (Hike 43) is nearest to you in the north. To the east, the Great Western Divide and the Kaweah Peaks serve as a backdrop for Mount Silliman and Alta Peak (Hike 24). To the southeast are the peaks surrounding Mineral King, including Sawtooth Peak, and to the west are Redwood Canyon, Redwood Mountain, and the smog-shrouded San Joaquin Valley.

The trail continues south along the west side of the short, stout summit pinnacles, and down around the east side of the next dome through rocky terrain. Descend to a saddle with a view of a pond and a meadow in the Pierce Valley to the west, and of the Sunrise Bowl just below to the east. A metal-roofed structure and radio tower are found here. The path rounds another dome and travels through open forest to a portion of trail completely covered by crushed rock. A tree has fallen across the trail here, and you may have to make your way over the obstacle if it has not been cleared away by your visit.

The path then enters a forested area populated by many birds, including nuthatches, western bluebirds, and western tanagers. The trail continues to climb as it exits the forest, with a nice view of Chimney Rock and Little Baldy (Hike 29) through the trees. Wind up through talus blocks on the west side to the top of this lower outcrop of Big Baldy Ridge, which is at 8,169 feet and 2.8 miles. Views to the east of Chimney Rock and Little Baldy are exceptional, with the Great Western Divide in the background. To the west are lower Redwood Canyon, the Eshom Valley, and the San Joaquin Valley.

Enjoy the views, and then backtrack to the parking area at 5.6 miles.

Big Baldy Ridge

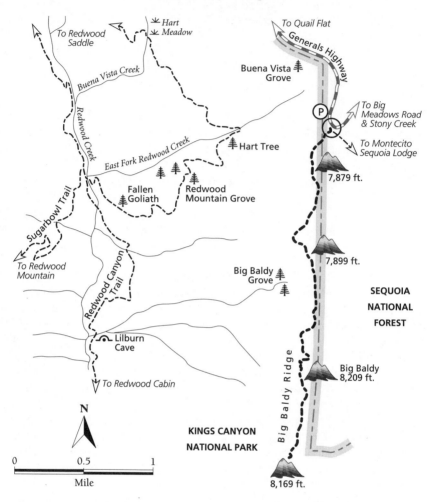

Option: This hike can be combined with Buena Vista Peak (Hike 43), which is north on the Generals Highway.

Hikes in the Cedar Grove and Monarch Divide Areas

Hikes in this chapter begin along California Highway 180, and are listed from west to east, starting just outside the park boundary and continuing to the trailheads at Road's End.

45 Deer Cove Trail to Grizzly Lakes

Highlights:	This steep trek is definitely a challenge, but it leads to a beautiful destination.
Type of hike:	Out-and-back, backpack.
Total distance:	17.8 miles.
Difficulty:	Difficult.
Best months:	Mid-June through October.
Maps:	USGS Cedar Grove; USFS John Muir Wilderness and Sequoia-Kings Canyon Wilderness; or TOPO! Sequoia Kings Canyon CD-ROM.
Permits:	None.
Special considerations:	Be alert for rattlesnakes on the lower portion of this trail. Also, mountain lions frequent this area; you are advised not to hike solo.
Parking and facilities:	There are no facilities at this trailhead. The trail begins at the north end of the parking area at the trail register.

Finding the trailhead: Follow California Highway 180 for approximately 29 miles north and east from Grant Grove, past Boyden Cave and the Grizzly Falls Picnic Area, to the Deer Cove Trailhead on the north side of the road, just outside the Kings Canyon park boundary.

Key points:
- 0.0   Trailhead.
- 1.7   Reach Deer Cove.
- 3.3   Arrive at Deer Cove Saddle and Forest Trail 30E03.
- 5.0   Reach Wildman Meadow.
- 5.7   Meet the Happy Gap Trail (Forest Trail 30E02).
- 6.4   Intersect the second trail to Frypan Meadow.
- 8.9   Reach Upper Grizzly Lake.

The hike: Forest Trail
30E01 begins ascend-
ing immediately,
switchbacking up a
steep hillside through
oaks, manzanita, and
bear clover. Pass a
seep spring, which be-

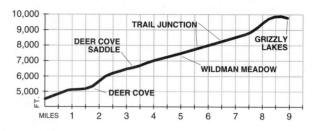

comes a small creek below the trail. Dry-slope wildflowers bloom along
the path in sunny areas, and cedars and pines soon join the already present vegetation.

As you gain elevation, views across the canyon include the Cedar Grove
area and the South Fork of the Kings River. To the southeast is Palmer
Mountain, and a small portion of the Great Western Divide is visible between
it and Sentinel Dome. Due south is Lookout Peak (Hike 76), with the Lightning Creek drainage to its west. East of you, on the north side of the canyon,
is Stag Dome.

The route parallels Deer Cove Creek as it continues to climb, then drops
down to an easy crossing at Deer Cove at 1.7 miles. A slight trace of an abandoned section of trail can be seen heading north, covered by blowdowns.
Resume the task of traveling switchbacks through a shadier slope of bear
clover, brush, and trees to a trail junction at the Deer Cove Saddle at 3.3
miles. The trail to the left (west), Forest Trail 30E03, leads steeply down to
Choke Creek, while you continue northeast up the ridge and gain a view of
the Grizzly Creek drainage to the north. The crest of terra cotta-colored crags
to your left (west) is the Grand Dike. Straight up the drainage you can spot
the pointed cap of Mount Harrington.

The trail narrows and you may spot more traces of the abandoned trail
to your right (south) before switchbacking up another steep slope support-
ing bear clover and few trees. After an arduous climb, cross over to the north
side of the ridge and reach the southern tip of Wildman Meadow, amidst
the shade of firs. About midway through the meadow, at 5 miles, is a sign
identifying it, and a dim trail that leads northeast to Frypan Meadow. (Some
maps show Wildman Meadow in the wrong location; other trails in this area
may be slightly off on some maps as well.) Across the meadow is a packers'
campsite with a hitching post.

Continue on the trail, skirting the meadow, and at 5.7 miles reach a junction with the trail to Burns Meadow and Happy Gap (Forest Trail 30E02).

After an easy climb, you reach a more defined trail leading to Frypan
Meadow near the park boundary at 6.4 miles. Take the path to the left (northwest), toward Grizzly Lakes. The route steps across two seasonal brooks, then
dips to a shallow ford of the East Fork of Grizzly Creek. The trail follows the
willow-lined creek uphill, then swings to the west, climbing steeply and occasionally switchbacking past meadows filled with shooting stars, pink and
blue forget-me-nots, corn lilies, and drier slopes of buck brush and scarlet gilia.

The sometimes faint trail leads northeast, nearing the East Fork of Grizzly Creek. The steep path then winds its way up the ridge that separates

Deer Cove Trail to Grizzly Lakes

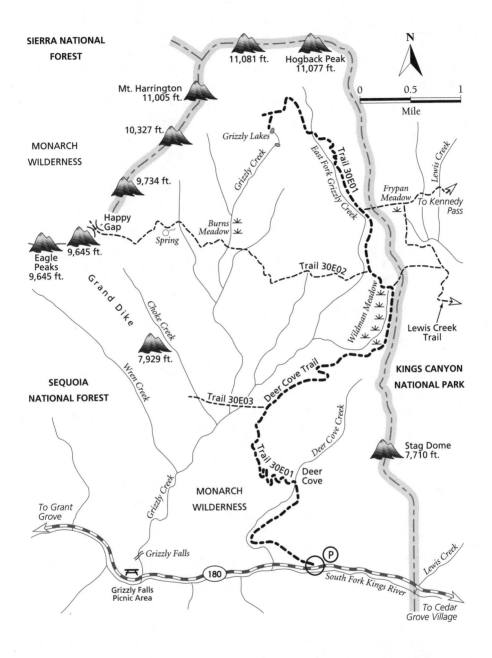

SIERRA NATIONAL FOREST

11,081 ft.

Hogback Peak
11,077 ft.

N

0   0.5   1
Mile

Mt. Harrington
11,005 ft.

10,327 ft.

Grizzly Lakes

MONARCH
WILDERNESS

9,734 ft.

Grizzly Creek

East Fork Grizzly Creek

Trail 30E01

Lewis Creek

Frypan
Meadow

To Kennedy
Pass

Happy
Gap

Burns
Meadow

Spring

Eagle
Peaks
9,645 ft.

9,645 ft.

Trail 30E02

Grand Dike

Choke Creek

7,929 ft.

Wildman Meadow

Lewis Creek
Trail

SEQUOIA
NATIONAL FOREST

Wren Creek

Trail 30E03

Deer Cove Trail

KINGS CANYON
NATIONAL PARK

Deer Cove Creek

Stag Dome
7,710 ft.

Trail 30E01

Deer
Cove

Grizzly Creek

MONARCH
WILDERNESS

To Grant
Grove

Grizzly Falls

P

Grizzly Falls
Picnic Area

180

South Fork Kings River

Lewis Creek

To Cedar
Grove Village

Grizzly Creek from its east fork, giving you views across the canyon of the Great Western Divide to the southeast, the Kaweahs, Tablelands, and Silliman Crest farther to the south, and Shell Mountain in the Jennie Lakes Wilderness. The higher of the two Grizzly Lakes comes into view below. At 8.9 miles, the trail drops down to the blue-green body of water, lined on the east by huge boulders and on the northwest by an expansive meadow. Mount Harrington towers above. Campsites can be found on the southwest and forested side of the lake.

After your stay, retrace your steps to the trailhead at 17.8 miles.

Option: A side trip to Frypan Meadow can be easily incorporated into this trip if you wish.

46 Lewis Creek Trail

Highlights:	This challenging route leads to a picturesque meadow and views of northern Kings Canyon National Park from a high pass on the Monarch Divide.
Type of hike:	Out-and-back, backpack.
Total distance:	19.6 miles.
Difficulty:	Difficult.
Best months:	June through October.
Maps:	USGS Cedar Grove; Kings Canyon National Park Cedar Grove; or TOPO! Sequoia Kings Canyon CD-ROM.
Permits:	Obtain a permit at Cedar Grove Road's End.
Special considerations:	This trail can be very hot—be sure to get an early start. Also, this trail is used by horseback riders; please remember proper trail etiquette by stepping off the trail on the downhill side and waiting quietly until the horses have passed. Stay in plain view of the horses; they may think you are a wild animal and bolt if you are hidden behind a rock or tree. Be alert for rattlesnakes on the lower portion of this trail. And, finally, mountain lions frequent this area; you are advised not to hike solo.
Parking and facilities:	The nearest restrooms and water are located 1.3 miles east of the trailhead at Cedar Grove Village. The trail begins on the north side of California Highway 180 near a bulletin board.

Finding the trailhead: Follow CA 180 north and east from Grant Grove for approximately 30.7 miles. The trailhead is just beyond the park boundary opposite the Lewis Creek parking area, which is on the south side of the road.

Key points:

0.0 Trailhead.
1.9 Pass the Hotel Creek Trail.
3.4 Cross Comb Creek.
4.5 Cross Lewis Creek.
6.0 Pass the trail junction.
6.2 Reach Frypan Meadow.
9.8 Arrive at Kennedy Pass.

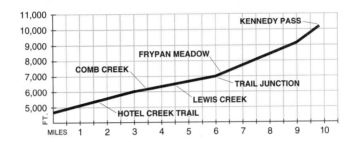

The hike: The trip begins by ascending short switchbacks through a canopy of oaks, pines, and cedars, with an understory of bear clover. After a long curve through willow, then manzanita, the path climbs longer switchbacks, dips through a fire-scarred area, and gains a view of the Monarch Divide.

At 1.9 miles you reach the junction with the Hotel Creek Trail (Hike 48), under ponderosa pines and cedars. Take the left (north) fork, dipping to cross an unnamed creek; a large log aids in your crossing during high water. The trail switchbacks again, and bends into the side canyons of seasonal brooks before dropping down to shady Comb Creek at 3.4 miles. A difficult wade in early season, this creek is more easily crossed on thin logs later in the year.

More switchbacks and a hot, sunny climb through bear clover and sparse pines lie ahead. Another descent brings you to pretty Lewis Creek and a campsite at 4.5 miles. An easy rock-hop in late season, the Lewis Creek crossing is a torrential wade earlier in the year.

The route winds steeply uphill once more, meeting the obscure path to Wildman Meadow at 6 miles. After a bit more of a climb you dip slightly to Frypan Meadow and a few fir-shaded campsites at 6.2 miles. Beyond, a path leads west to Grizzly Lakes, while you head east, toward Kennedy Pass.

The trail ascends through the forest and across branches of Lewis Creek, then traverses high above its east fork. Traveling up switchbacks, then climbing an exposed slope of manzanita, you have a vast panorama to the south of the Great Western Divide, the Kings-Kaweah Divide, and Shell Mountain in the Jennie Lakes Wilderness.

Your route passes through a grove of aspen, intersecting seasonal creeks, before the last push to the pass. The final abrupt climb leads through scattered whitebark pines, then arrives at Kennedy Pass at 9.8 miles. The vista to the north, across the Middle Fork of the Kings River, of the northern Kings

Lewis Creek Trail

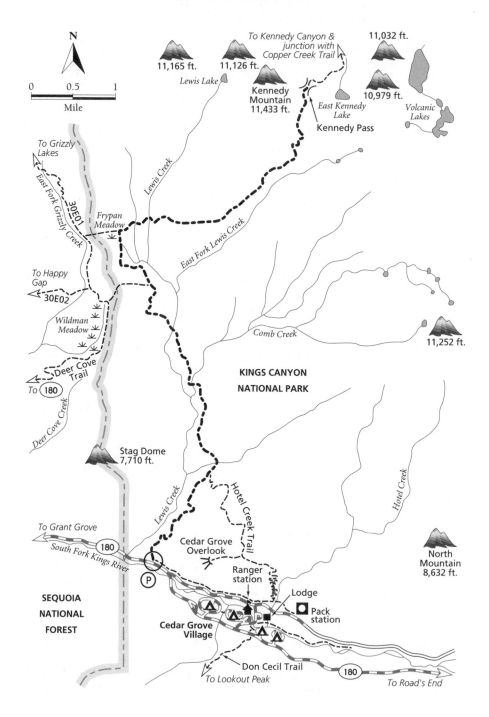

N

0   0.5   1
Mile

11,165 ft.

11,126 ft.

Lewis Lake

To Kennedy Canyon &
junction with
Copper Creek Trail

11,032 ft.

Kennedy
Mountain
11,433 ft.

*East Kennedy
Lake*

10,979 ft.

*Volcanic
Lakes*

Kennedy Pass

Lewis Creek

To Grizzly
Lakes

East Fork Grizzly Creek

30E01

*Frypan
Meadow*

East Fork Lewis Creek

To Happy
Gap

30E02

*Wildman
Meadow*

Comb Creek

11,252 ft.

**KINGS CANYON
NATIONAL PARK**

Deer Cove
Trail

To 180

Deer Cove Creek

Stag Dome
7,710 ft.

Lewis Creek

Hotel Creek Trail

Hotel Creek

To Grant Grove

180

South Fork Kings River

P

Cedar Grove
Overlook

Ranger
station

Lodge

Pack
station

North
Mountain
8,632 ft.

**SEQUOIA
NATIONAL
FOREST**

**Cedar Grove
Village**

Don Cecil Trail

To Lookout Peak

180

To Road's End

Canyon backcountry, is breathtaking. Below you to the right (east) lies rock-bound East Kennedy Lake.

After taking in the views, retrace your steps to the trailhead at 19.6 miles.

Option: For an extended backpacking trip, continue down switchbacks past East Kennedy Lake, then travel down the canyon, along Kennedy Creek. Cross the creek to loop back around to the south and climb Dead Pine Ridge. The route dips down to cross the West Fork of Dougherty Creek, passes a cross-country route to the Volcanic Lakes, then drops to join the Copper Creek Trail (Hike 54), north of Granite Pass. Make a right (south) turn, and follow this trail back to Road's End, where you should have a car waiting for you. This would add 23 miles onto your trip, and a considerable amount of elevation gain. A good topographic map of the area is recommended for this trek.

47 Don Cecil Trail

Highlights:	This old path, named after a shepherd, was the route sheepherders and cattlemen took to Cedar Grove long ago. Though it is steep and narrow in some areas, it affords splendid views of the Monarch Divide and the Cedar Grove area.
Type of hike:	Out-and-back, day hike.
Total distance:	8.8 miles.
Difficulty:	Difficult.
Best months:	Late May through June, October through mid-November.
Maps:	USGS Cedar Grove; Kings Canyon National Park Cedar Grove; USFS John Muir Wilderness and Sequoia–Kings Canyon Wilderness; or TOPO! Sequoia Kings Canyon CD-ROM.
Permits:	None.
Special considerations:	Mountain lions frequent this area. You are advised not to hike solo.
Parking and facilities:	The nearest restrooms and water are located downhill near Cedar Grove Village, which can be reached by a spur trail on the north side of the road. A large turnout for parking is located on the north side of the road, just west of the trailhead.

Finding the trailhead: From Grant Grove, follow California Highway 180 north, then east, for approximately 32 miles to Cedar Grove Village. The trailhead and parking turnout are located just beyond the access road to Cedar Grove Village.

Key points:
- 0.0 Trailhead.
- 0.3 Cross the dirt road.
- 0.8 Reach the Sheep Creek bridge.
- 2.9 Cross the West Fork of Sheep Creek.
- 4.4 Reach the Summit Meadow trailhead.

The hike: The wide trail begins climbing immediately, through oaks, cedars, and ponderosa pines. Large gray squirrels and small chickarees (Douglas squirrels) scamper about the area gathering acorns in the fall.

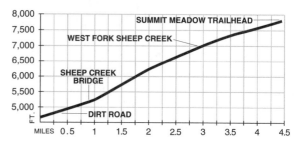

Come to a service road at 0.3 mile, which leads to a heliport and water tanks. Listen first for approaching cars before crossing the road. The path continues to ascend, crosses a seasonal creekbed, and gains views of the Monarch Divide to the north.

The trail descends into the shady canyon of Sheep Creek, arriving at the footbridge across the creek at 0.8 mile.

You first notice the small waterfall streaming down below the bridge, then the stair-step cascades above it. This is a nice place to linger, but it is the water supply for Cedar Grove—please do not contaminate it in any way.

Beyond the creek, the trail narrows and steeply switchbacks up slopes covered in bear clover, with increasing vistas to the north. Upon reaching a ridgecrest, a view of Mounts Clarence King, Gardiner, and Rixford opens up to the northeast. Leave the switchbacks and oaks behind as the trail narrows further and traverses a precipitous slope among rocks and outcroppings.

The footpath nears the tinkling sounds of the West Fork of Sheep Creek, widens a bit, and levels in a peaceful glen along the watercourse before crossing it on a hewn log at 2.9 miles. Deer frequent this area and you may see a large herd if you visit in the fall. The narrow route then travels up a couple of long switchbacks to the boulder-strewn ridge emanating from Lookout Peak. As you near the peak, you can see the notch just below the summit. Looking back to the northeast, Mounts Clarence King, Gardiner, and Rixford are joined by Palmer Mountain, Mount Farquhar, North Guard, and Mount Brewer on the Great Western Divide. Cedar Grove is also visible far below.

As you trudge on, the slopes below you gradually become less steep, and the path widens before it reaches the park boundary signs. One last climb up a small hill brings you to the Summit Meadow Trailhead at 4.4 miles. The Lookout Peak Trail is to your right (west), next to a fire ring and a metal trail stake. On the other side of a large fallen log to your left (southeast), an unmaintained extension of this trail proceeds toward private property.

Don Cecil Trail

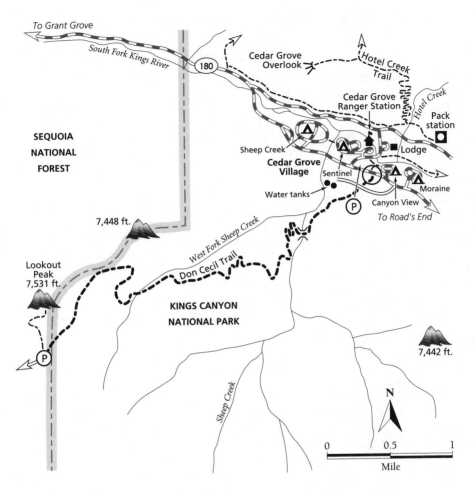

Return the way you came, this time a welcome downhill, to the trailhead at 8.8 miles.

Option: This hike can be done in conjunction with Lookout Peak (Hike 76).

48 Hotel Creek Trail

Highlights:	This trip takes you to the Cedar Grove Overlook, giving you views across the Kings Canyon to the south, and of the lofty Monarch Divide to the north.
Type of hike:	Loop, day hike.
Total distance:	6.9 miles.
Difficulty:	Moderate.
Best months:	Late May through June, and October through mid-November.
Maps:	USGS Cedar Grove; Kings Canyon National Park Cedar Grove; or TOPO! Sequoia Kings Canyon CD-ROM.
Permits:	None.
Special considerations:	This trail can get hot—be sure to get an early start. The route also is used by horseback riders. Please remember proper trail etiquette by stepping off the trail on the downhill side and waiting quietly until the horses have passed. Stay in plain view of the horses; they may think you are a wild animal and bolt if you are hidden behind a rock or tree. Be alert for rattlesnakes on the lower portion of this trail. Also, mountain lions frequent this area; you are advised not to hike solo.
Parking and facilities:	The nearest restrooms and water are located at Cedar Grove Village. The trail begins to the right of the wooden bulletin board.

Finding the trailhead: From Grant Grove, follow California Highway 180 north, then east, for approximately 32 miles to the Cedar Grove Village turnoff and turn left (north). Proceed on the Cedar Grove Village road, past the village, to a T junction with the unnamed road to the pack station at 0.5 mile. The parking area is just to the right (east) of this intersection, on the north side of the road.

Key points:
- 0.0   Trailhead.
- 1.6   Reach the trail to the overlook.
- 2.0   Arrive at the Cedar Grove Overlook.
- 3.8   Reach the Lewis Creek Trail junction.
- 5.5   Reach the junction with the horse trail.

The hike: The trail begins by heading to the east through oaks and ponderosa pines; the west-trending horse trail will be your return route. As you make your way to the first of many switchbacks, you may come across a few deer

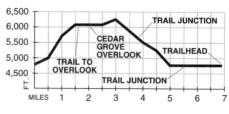

Hotel Creek Trail

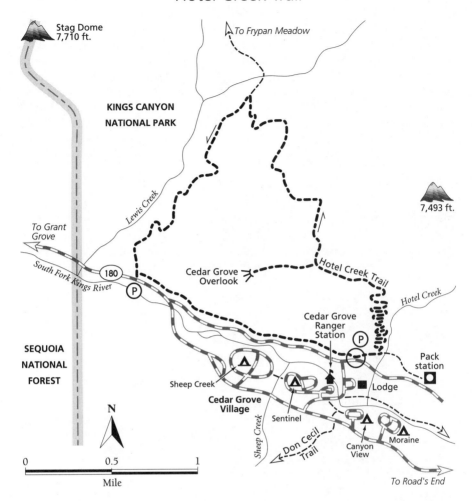

browsing. At the junction with the first switchback and the continuation of the horse trail, follow the short track down to Hotel Creek for a look at its pretty cascade, then climb back up and begin switchbacking up the canyon wall. Partial shade is provided by oaks and manzanita on the hot and dusty trail; the views across the canyon improve as you hike. Heavily wooded Cedar Grove is far below, and the South Fork of the Kings River appears as a silver ribbon twisting through the trees.

After the trail levels a bit and passes through a grassy clearing, pines come into view once again. Contour into the gorge of a seasonal creek, cross a ridge, and reach the junction with the overlook trail at 1.6 miles. Turn left (west) and dip down through hillsides of verdant bear clover, then make the short ascent to the overlook at 2 miles. Avalanche Peak, Palmer Mountain, and Sentinel Dome flank Thunder and Table Mountains on the Great Western

Divide to the southeast, while Lookout Peak peers over a ridge to the southwest. To the north is the impressive Monarch Divide, with the Eagle Peaks, Mount Harrington, Hogback Peak, Kennedy Mountain, and Comb Spur all visible from this rocky knob.

After enjoying the view, retrace your steps to the main trail and make a left (north) turn. The route descends through ponderosa pines, with vistas of the striking peaks to the north. The path crosses two seasonal drainages, then passes through a fire-scarred area before mounting a small ridge. Several switchbacks lead down to the junction with the Lewis Creek Trail at 3.8 miles on the other side of the ridge. Turn left (south) on the Lewis Creek Trail, dropping through pines, cedars, and oaks high above Lewis Creek. The dusty path descends many switchbacks, giving you a view to the west of Stag Dome.

At 5.5 miles you reach the horse trail just above the Lewis Creek Trailhead, and make a left (east) turn. The trail climbs and drops repeatedly all the way back to the parking area, and is within sight of pavement at all times. If you have had enough uphill, follow CA 180 to the signed road leading to the pack station and turn left (east). Follow the road or trail past an outhouse and back to the parking area, with nice views of the river along the way.

49 Roaring River Falls to Zumwalt Meadow

Highlights:	First visiting billowing Roaring River falls, then peaceful Zumwalt Meadow, this hike offers ideal opportunities for a picnic lunch or just relaxing.
Type of hike:	Semi-loop, day hike.
Total distance:	3.9 miles.
Difficulty:	Easy.
Best months:	Late May through October.
Maps:	USGS The Sphinx; Kings Canyon National Park Cedar Grove; or TOPO! Sequoia Kings Canyon CD-ROM.
Permits:	None.
Parking and facilities:	There are no facilities at this trailhead. Parking is available on the south side of California Highway 180, on either side of the bridge spanning the Roaring River. The trail begins on the south side of the parking area, east of the bridge.

Finding the trailhead: From Grant Grove, follow CA 180 north, then east, for approximately 32 miles to Cedar Grove Village. Continue for 3.1 miles past the Cedar Grove Village turnoff to the Roaring River Falls parking area on the right (south).

Key points:

- 0.0 Trailhead and River Trail junction.
- 0.1 Reach Roaring River Falls.
- 0.2 Return to the River Trail junction.
- 1.6 Pass the suspension bridge.
- 1.7 Reach the Zumwalt Meadow Trail junction.
- 2.3 Pass the River Trail junction.
- 2.5 Return to the Zumwalt Meadow Trail junction.
- 3.8 Reach the Roaring River Falls trail junction.

The hike: This partially paved trail begins by following the Roaring River. In a few hundred feet you reach the River Trail which you will take to Zumwalt Meadow. For now, continue straight (south) to the falls, which are at 0.1 mile.

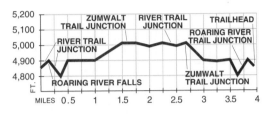

The roar of rushing water plunging into a blue-green pool fills this granite bowl as you approach the overlook. Shrubs and small trees cling to cliffs that seem to reach straight up to the sky. When the falls are at their peak,

Roaring River Falls is the first stop on the way to Zumwalt Meadow.

mist douses those standing at the overlook. Only the lower portion of Roaring River Falls is visible; the upper cascades are inaccessible. (Do not venture up the canyon on side trails—others have been injured or killed trying to do so.)

After enjoying the falls, backtrack to the River Trail junction at approximately 0.2 mile, and make a right (east) turn. The rocky, open trail travels close to the road at first, but soon enters a shady forest along the Kings River. Continuing through both forest and clearings laced with the scent of incense cedar, you climb a couple of rocky

Roaring River Falls to Zumwalt Meadow

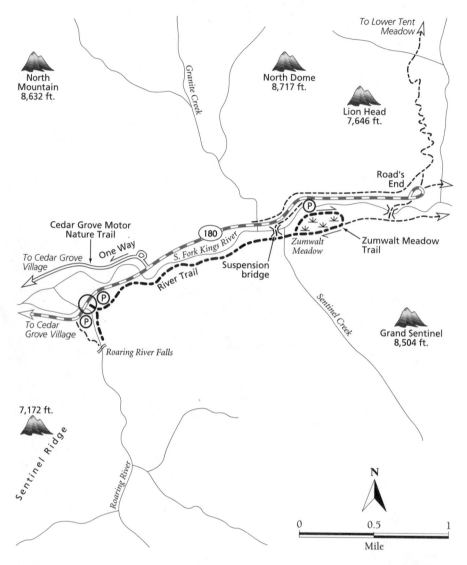

knolls and come to the suspension bridge that leads to the Zumwalt Meadow Trail parking area at 1.6 miles. An interpretive pamphlet describing numbered stops along the loop can be purchased at the parking area and at park visitor centers.

Continue straight (east), cross the usually dry Sentinel Creek (though you should be prepared to rock-hop if the creek is flowing), and meet the Zumwalt Meadow Trail junction at 1.7 miles. Turn left (northeast) and cross a seasonal creek on a small footbridge. North Dome and Lion Head can be seen above the trees to the north, while the Grand Sentinel towers above the meadow to the south. The trail travels along a boardwalk through the fragile meadow area, then enters a shady forest while following the Kings River. Many are the tree-framed views of the meadow, accompanied by the peaceful splashing and rippling of the river. You may see a hummingbird, a dipper, or even a deer if the trail isn't crowded.

Pass two spur trails on your left (east), which connect with the River Trail as the path begins to leave the forest. After passing between two large boulders, the route reaches the junction with the River Trail itself at 2.3 miles. Turn right (west) and begin a short climb. You will enjoy views of Zumwalt Meadow as you wind through a moonscape of talus at the base of the Grand Sentinel. The trail dips and rises once more, and again crosses the seasonal creek.

At 2.5 miles, return to the Zumwalt Loop junction and complete the loop portion of the trip. Retrace the remaining portion of the trail, back to the Roaring River parking area, for a grand total of 3.9 miles.

Options: If you wish to make this a shuttle trip, have a car waiting at the Zumwalt Meadow parking area. After completing the loop, cross the river on the suspension bridge to your right (north) to reach the parking area. This will cut a little more than 1.5 miles off your hike.

For a different view of Roaring River Falls, follow the footpath south from the parking area on the west side of the river. The dim and rocky path travels uphill through the oaks, then veers left (east) along large boulders. Granite steps then lower you onto an overlook. The falls are visible to the right (south), and you also can see the river boiling past you and downstream to the left (north).

Both the Roaring River Falls trail and the Zumwalt Meadow Trail can be done as separate, shorter hikes.

50 Road's End to the Bailey Bridge

Highlights:	This easy walk takes you through peaceful forest and sunny manzanita flats while winding along the crystalline South Fork of the Kings River.
Type of hike:	Loop, day hike.
Total distance:	4.5 miles.
Difficulty:	Easy.
Best months:	Late May through mid-November.
Maps:	USGS The Sphinx; Kings Canyon National Park Cedar Grove; or TOPO! Sequoia Kings Canyon CD-ROM.
Permits:	None.
Parking and facilities:	Restrooms and an information center are located at the east end of the parking area. Water is available from a spigot next to the information center. The trail begins next to a mileage sign at the entrance to the parking area.

Finding the trailhead: From Grant Grove, follow California Highway 180 north, then east, for approximately 32 miles to Cedar Grove Village. Continue for 5.6 miles past the Cedar Grove Village turnoff to the Road's End parking area.

Key points:
- 0.0   Trailhead.
- 0.1   Cross the bridge over the Kings River.
- 2.1   Reach the Avalanche Creek crossing.
- 2.5   Arrive at the Bubbs Creek Trail junction.
- 2.6   Reach the Bailey bridge.
- 4.3   Reach the Copper Creek bridge.

The hike: The trail begins by winding through the shady forest, then descends in the sun to cross the South Fork of the Kings River on a long, narrow footbridge at 0.1 mile. Upon reaching the

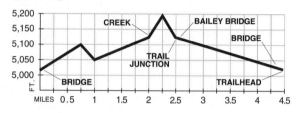

other side you come to a junction; the trail to your right (west) leads to Zumwalt Meadow. The route is to the left (east), passing through huge boulders before nearing the river.

Traveling a few feet down the trail, you can see the large flat rock known as Muir's Pulpit along the north side of the stream. The track undulates through more boulders and dense forest near the water, then exits the woodland to pass through grassy, manzanita-filled clearings and fire-scarred areas.

The Grand Sentinel looms above you to the right (south), while North Dome, Lion Head, Buck Peak, and Glacier Monument are visible to your left (north). Pass an enormous boulder on your right with the initials W.B. 1912 painted on the side. Before reentering the forest, you may catch a glimpse of The Sphinx, high on the south wall of the canyon ahead.

The route crosses the many branches of Avalanche Creek easily on large stones at 2.1 miles, and proceeds through ferns before meeting the Bubbs Creek Trail at 2.5 miles. The wooden bridge spanning the creek is visible to the right (east), but you turn left (north), passing side trails leading to the river. Arrive at the Bailey bridge at 2.6 miles. (Bailey is the name of this type of prefabricated steel bridge—it is not the surname of a pioneer.)

The middle of the bridge is a great place to view the river upstream and downstream, and to look into the beautiful aquamarine pools directly below. On the other side, you continue left (west), join the trail leading from the Mist Falls and Paradise Valley, and enter an area thick with green horsetails. The path crosses a rocky knoll, then advances through manzanita clearings in the pockets of forest. Large gray squirrels scamper about, especially in the fall, when they are gathering acorns and pine cones for the winter. Side trails lead left (south) to the river here and there, while the Grand Sentinel towers above on the south side of the canyon.

Road's End to the Bailey Bridge

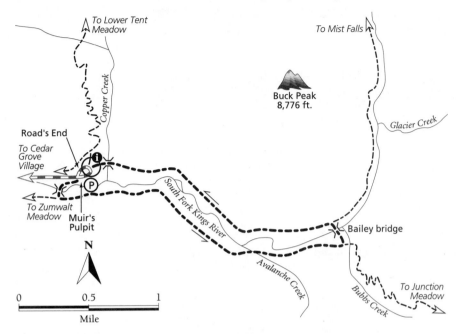

Reach the Copper Creek bridge at 4.3 miles, north of the site of Kanawyer's Store, which served cattlemen and sheepherders heading into the backcountry in the early days. The old supply point was visited by John Muir, but was torn down in the late 1920s. A picture of the store during its heyday is on display in the Cedar Grove Ranger Station.

At 4.5 miles, you reach the parking area and the end of your journey.

51 Junction Meadow

Highlights:	This journey takes you up the Bubbs Creek Canyon, past The Sphinx, and on to verdant and expansive Junction Meadow.
Type of hike:	Out-and-back, backpack.
Total distance:	20.6 miles.
Difficulty:	Difficult.
Best months:	July through October.
Maps:	USGS The Sphinx and Mount Clarence King; USFS John Muir Wilderness and Sequoia–Kings Canyon Wilderness; or TOPO! Sequoia Kings Canyon CD-ROM.
Permits:	Obtain a permit at Cedar Grove Road's End. Bear-proof food storage containers are required.
Special considerations:	Be alert for rattlesnakes on the lower portion of this trail.
Parking and facilities:	Restrooms and an information center are located at the east end of the parking area. Water is available from a spigot next to the information center. The trail begins next to a mileage sign at the entrance to the parking area.

Finding the trailhead: From Grant Grove, follow California Highway 180 north, then east, for approximately 32 miles to Cedar Grove Village. Continue for 5.6 miles past the Cedar Grove Village turnoff to the Road's End parking area.

Key points:
- 0.0 Trailhead.
- 0.1 Cross the bridge over the Kings River.
- 2.1 Reach the Avalanche Creek crossing.
- 2.5 Arrive at the Bubbs Creek Trail junction.
- 4.5 Reach the Avalanche Pass Trail junction.
- 7.5 Arrive at the Charlotte Creek campsites.
- 10.3 Reach Junction Meadow.

The hike: Begin by following the trail from Road's End to the Bailey bridge (Hike 50), reaching the Bubbs Creek Trail junction at 2.5 miles. Turn right (southeast). The route crosses the Bubbs Creek delta on four wooden bridges and traces the tum-

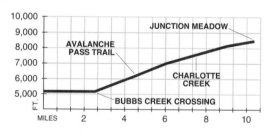

bling creek up the canyon before ascending many switchbacks, where you gain views back down to Cedar Grove and up the canyon of the South Fork

Junction Meadow can serve as a jumping-off point for exploration of rugged East Creek Canyon.

of the Kings River. To the south rises The Sphinx, an oddly carved granite obelisk towering above the oaks and pinyon pines.

After the laborious switchbacks, the path dips, rises, then dips again to meet the Avalanche Pass Trail at 4.5 miles, at a wooden bridge spanning Bubbs Creek. Campsites and a bear box are located on the north side of the trail at this junction.

Beyond the first campsites the trail undulates through willows, sage, and wildflowers with very little shade. Pyramid-shaped University Peak can be spotted at the head of the canyon, and after climbing steeply you enter a shady, forested area and cross Charlotte Creek on a double-log bridge. Side trails lead to your right (south) to spacious campsites and a bear box at 7.5 miles. The path then resumes its undulating course, this time with more shade, and passes through large areas of bracken fern and boulders. One last steep climb brings you to several campsites along sword fern-lined Bubbs Creek just before Junction Meadow at 10.3 miles.

To view the meadow, continue through the drift fence gate and enter the huge spread of grasses and flowers. Willows line the creek and deer can sometimes be seen feeding in the area. A side trail leads to a packers' campsite, and about 0.3 mile from the campsites you meet the trail to East Lake and Lake Reflection.

After enjoying your stay, return the way you came (20.6 miles).

Option: This hike can be used as a base camp for excursions up the steep East Creek Canyon, where bears have become a big problem for campers. The Bubbs Creek crossing can be difficult, so use extreme caution.

Junction Meadow • Vidette Meadow

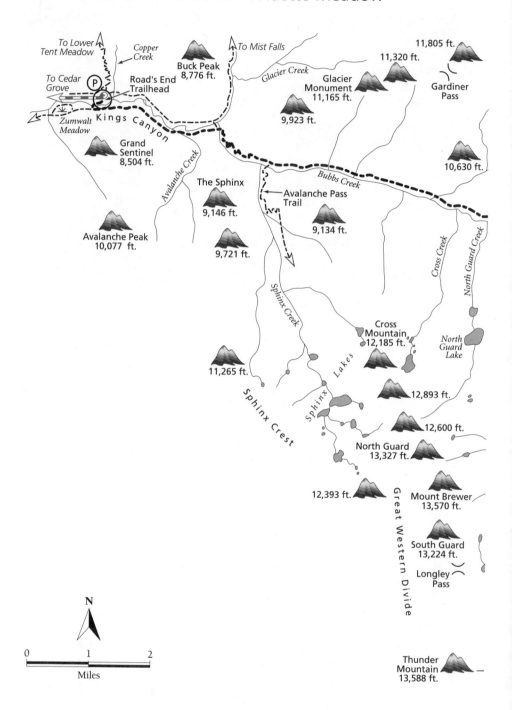

To Lower Tent Meadow

Copper Creek

Buck Peak 8,776 ft.

To Mist Falls

Glacier Creek

11,805 ft.

11,320 ft.

Glacier Monument 11,165 ft.

Gardiner Pass

To Cedar Grove

Road's End Trailhead

P

9,923 ft.

10,630 ft.

Zumwalt Meadow

Kings Canyon

Grand Sentinel 8,504 ft.

Avalanche Creek

Bubbs Creek

The Sphinx 9,146 ft.

Avalanche Pass Trail

Cross Creek

North Guard Creek

Avalanche Peak 10,077 ft.

9,721 ft.

9,134 ft.

Sphinx Creek

Cross Mountain 12,185 ft.

North Guard Lake

11,265 ft.

Sphinx Lakes

12,893 ft.

12,600 ft.

Sphinx Crest

North Guard 13,327 ft.

12,393 ft.

Great Western Divide

Mount Brewer 13,570 ft.

South Guard 13,224 ft.

Longley Pass

N

0   1   2

Miles

Thunder Mountain 13,588 ft.

Upper Bubbs Creek

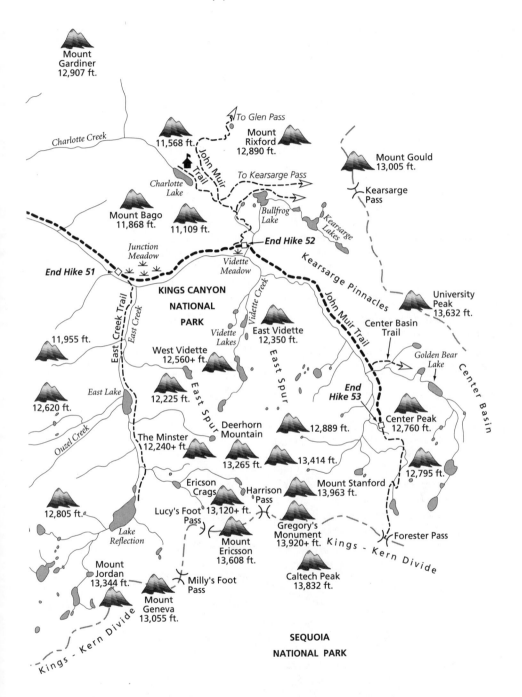

Mount Gardiner 12,907 ft.

Charlotte Creek

11,568 ft.

To Glen Pass

Mount Rixford 12,890 ft.

Mount Gould 13,005 ft.

John Muir Trail

To Kearsarge Pass

Kearsarge Pass

Charlotte Lake

Mount Bago 11,868 ft.

11,109 ft.

Bullfrog Lake

Kearsarge Lakes

Junction Meadow

End Hike 52

End Hike 51

Vidette Meadow

Kearsarge Pinnacles

University Peak 13,632 ft.

KINGS CANYON

NATIONAL

PARK

Vidette Creek

East Creek Trail

East Creek

Center Basin Trail

11,955 ft.

Vidette Lakes

East Vidette 12,350 ft.

John Muir Trail

Golden Bear Lake

Center Basin

West Vidette 12,560+ ft.

East Spur

12,225 ft.

East Lake

12,620 ft.

Ouzel Creek

The Minster 12,240+ ft.

Deerhorn Mountain

East Spur

12,889 ft.

End Hike 53

Center Peak 12,760 ft.

13,265 ft.

13,414 ft.

12,795 ft.

12,805 ft.

Ericson Crags

Harrison Pass

Mount Stanford 13,963 ft.

Lucy's Foot Pass

13,120+ ft.

Gregory's Monument 13,920+ ft.

Kings - Kern Divide

Forester Pass

Lake Reflection

Mount Ericsson 13,608 ft.

Mount Jordan 13,344 ft.

Milly's Foot Pass

Caltech Peak 13,832 ft.

Mount Geneva 13,055 ft.

Kings - Kern Divide

SEQUOIA

NATIONAL PARK

52 Vidette Meadow

Highlights:	This trip takes you to a meadow nestled beneath the Kearsarge Pinnacles, University Peak, and East Vidette.
Type of hike:	Out-and-back, backpack.
Total distance:	26 miles.
Difficulty:	Difficult.
Best months:	July through September.
Maps:	USGS The Sphinx, Mount Clarence King, and Mount Brewer; USFS John Muir Wilderness and Sequoia–Kings Canyon Wilderness; or TOPO! Sequoia Kings Canyon CD-ROM.
Permits:	Obtain a permit at Cedar Grove Road's End. Bear-proof food storage canisters are required.
Parking and facilities:	Restrooms and an information center are located at the east end of the parking area. Water is available from a spigot next to the information center. The trail begins next to a mileage sign at the entrance to the parking area.

See Map on Page 176

Finding the trailhead: From Grant Grove, follow California Highway 180 north, then east, for approximately 32 miles to Cedar Grove Village. Continue for 5.6 miles past the Cedar Grove Village turnoff to the Road's End parking area.

Key points:
- 0.0 Trailhead.
- 0.1 Take the bridge across the Kings River.
- 2.1 Make the Avalanche Creek crossing.
- 2.5 Reach the Bubbs Creek Trail junction.
- 4.5 Pass the Avalanche Pass Trail junction.
- 7.5 Reach the Charlotte Creek campsites.
- 10.3 Pass Junction Meadow.
- 13.0 Arrive at Vidette Meadow and the John Muir Trail.

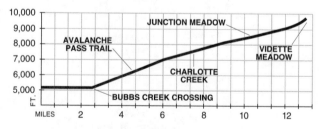

The hike: Begin by following the trail from Road's End to the Bailey bridge (Hike 50), reaching the Bubbs Creek Trail junction at 2.5 miles. Then follow the route to Junction Meadow (Hike 51), to the junction with the East Creek Trail, which is just beyond Junction Meadow at 10.3 miles. Continue past the junction on the trail heading east, gaining views north of the rugged spires on the south face of Mount Bago.

As the trail rises up switchbacks out of the meadow, you'll have views up the East Creek Canyon, with South Guard, Mount Brewer, and North Guard visible as you climb. East Vidette also comes into view ahead of you to the southeast as the route loses much of its shade, still switchbacking, and passes thundering cascades on Bubbs Creek.

The path winds its way over a few more rises, covered with a multitude of flowers, where you may hear the mysterious single-noted song or bubbly warble of the Townsend's solitaire. As you near the end of this hike, you reach the first campsites (equipped with a bear box) along the north end of Vidette Meadow. The Kearsarge Pinnacles rise to the east, and University Peak stands guard over the far end of the meadow. East Vidette towers above to the southeast, while the tip of West Vidette stands to the southwest.

The path continues ascending to the John Muir Trail at 13 miles. More campsites and bear boxes lie ahead, along with an easy crossing of the creek flowing down from Kearsarge and Bullfrog Lakes.

After a pleasant stay, retrace your steps to the trailhead at 26 miles.

53 Upper Bubbs Creek

Highlights:	Visit timberline along Bubbs Creek, with views of Forester Pass and the Kings-Kern Divide to the south, and of Mount Gardiner and the King Spur to the north.
Type of hike:	Out-and-back, backpack.
Total distance:	31 miles.
Difficulty:	Difficult.
Best months:	July through September.
Maps:	USGS The Sphinx, Mount Clarence King, Mount Brewer, and Mount Williamson; USFS John Muir Wilderness and Sequoia–Kings Canyon Wilderness; or TOPO! Sequoia Kings Canyon CD-ROM.
Permits:	Obtain a permit at Cedar Grove Road's End. Bear-proof food storage canisters are required.
Parking and facilities:	Restrooms and an information center are located at the east end of the parking area. Water is available from a spigot next to the information center. The trail begins next to a mileage sign at the entrance to the parking area.

See Map on Page 176

Finding the trailhead: From Grant Grove, follow California Highway 180 north, then east, for approximately 32 miles to Cedar Grove Village. Continue for 5.6 miles past the Cedar Grove Village turnoff to the Road's End parking area.

Key points:

- 0.0   Trailhead.
- 0.1   Cross the bridge spanning the Kings River.
- 2.1   Make the Avalanche Creek crossing.
- 2.5   Reach the Bubbs Creek Trail junction.
- 4.5   Pass the Avalanche Pass Trail junction.
- 7.5   Pass the Charlotte Creek campsites.
- 10.3   Reach Junction Meadow.
- 13.0   Arrive at Vidette Meadow and the John Muir Trail.
- 15.5   Reach the viewpoint beyond the last campsite.

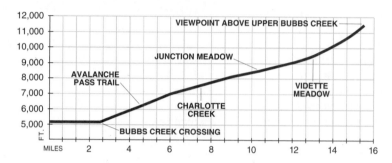

The hike: Begin by following the trail from Road's End to the Bailey bridge (Hike 50), reaching the Bubbs Creek Trail junction at 2.5 miles. Then, follow the route to Junction Meadow (Hike 51), passing the East Creek Trail junction at 10.3 miles. Continue to Vidette Meadow (Hike 52) and the campsites near the John Muir Trail junction at 13 miles.

From the campsites at Vidette Meadow, follow the John Muir Trail south, switchbacking up the slope through the lodgepole pine forest. The path leads through a gate in a drift fence, climbs through a more exposed area of sage and Indian paintbrush, then reenters the trees and passes through another gate.

The trail enters an area of granite, meadows, and willows lining meandering Bubbs Creek, with views up the canyon of Forester Pass and across the canyon of the East Spur and East Vidette. The forest cover comes into play again, and at about 15 miles you reach the point where the dim Center Basin Trail branches off of your route to the east. This former track of the John Muir Trail, which continues over Junction Pass to meet the Shepherd Pass Trail, is now more of a cross-country route than a discernible passage. Just beyond the junction, the John Muir Trail approaches campsites, which are downhill from the trail (west).

After crossing the creek emanating from the Center Basin, you come to the last small campsite. Continue climbing, past a pretty meadow, then up short switchbacks to a rocky knoll with great views just west of Center Peak at 15.5 miles. To the southwest is Mount Keith, to the south are Junction Peak and Forester Pass, a portion of the Kings-Kern Divide, and to the right (west) of that, Mount Stanford. As you turn to the west you can see East Spur and East Vidette, and in the northeast, Mount Gardiner and Mount Cotter, the latter being the southern tip of the King Spur. Due north are the Kearsarge

Pinnacles and University Peak. And, of course, the high mountain just east of you is Center Peak.

After you have thoroughly enjoyed this impressive view, retrace your steps to the Road's End parking area at 31 miles.

Option: If you wish to hike all the way to Forester Pass, you will add approximately 700 feet of elevation gain and 5 miles to your hike.

The view of Upper Bubbs Creek and Forester Pass is spectacular.

54 Copper Creek Trail

Highlights:	This rigorous excursion leads to a high lake basin near the lofty crest of the Monarch Divide.
Type of hike:	Out-and-back, backpack.
Total distance:	20 miles.
Difficulty:	Difficult.
Best months:	July through October.
Maps:	USGS The Sphinx; Kings Canyon National Park Cedar Grove; or TOPO! Sequoia Kings Canyon CD-ROM.
Permits:	Obtain a permit at Cedar Grove Road's End.
Special considerations:	This trail can be very hot—be sure to get an early start. This trail is also used by horseback riders; please remember proper trail etiquette by stepping off the trail on the downhill side and waiting quietly until the horses have passed. Stay in plain view of the horses; they may think you are a wild animal and bolt if you are hidden behind a rock or tree. Be alert for rattlesnakes along the lower portion of this trail. And, finally, mountain lions frequent this area, so you are advised not to hike solo.
Parking and facilities:	Restrooms and an information center are located at the east end of the day use parking area. Water is available from a spigot next to the information center. The trail begins on the north side of the overnight parking area, next to several bear boxes.

Finding the trailhead: From Grant Grove, follow California Highway 180 north, then east, for approximately 32 miles to Cedar Grove Village. Continue for 5.6 miles past the Cedar Grove Village turnoff, past the Road's End parking area and ranger station, to the overnight parking area on the north side of the loop.

Key points:
- 0.0   Trailhead.
- 4.0   Reach Lower Tent Meadow.
- 5.5   Reach Upper Tent Meadow.
- 9.5   Take the Granite Lake Trail.
- 10.0   Arrive at Granite Lake.

The hike: The trail begins by switchbacking in the shade of conifers and oaks, then travels up a more exposed slope of manzanita below North Dome. You may hear the bubbly song of the Townsend's solitaire as you ascend. You will enjoy views up and down the canyon

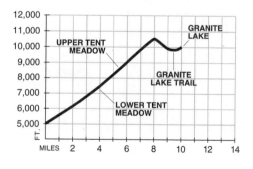

Copper Creek Trail

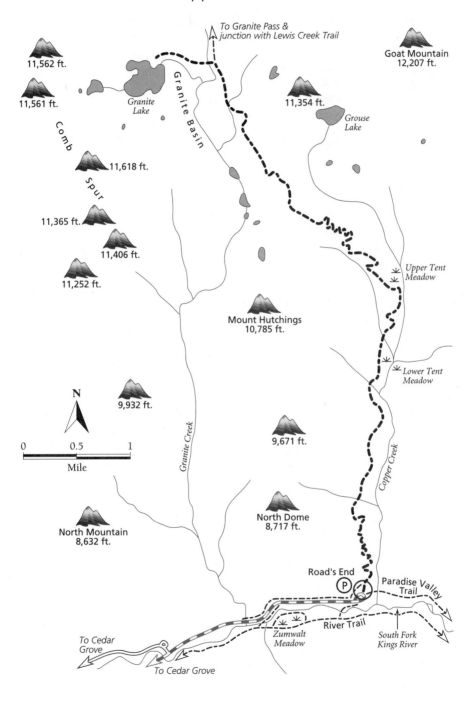

To Granite Pass &
junction with Lewis Creek Trail

Goat Mountain
12,207 ft.

11,562 ft.

11,561 ft.

*Granite
Lake*

Granite Basin

11,354 ft.

*Grouse
Lake*

**C
o
m
b**

11,618 ft.

**S
p
u
r**

11,365 ft.

11,406 ft.

Upper Tent
Meadow

11,252 ft.

Mount Hutchings
10,785 ft.

Lower Tent
Meadow

N

9,932 ft.

9,671 ft.

Granite Creek

Copper Creek

0   0.5   1
Mile

North Dome
8,717 ft.

North Mountain
8,632 ft.

Road's End

Paradise Valley
Trail

P

River Trail

*Zumwalt
Meadow*

*South Fork
Kings River*

To Cedar
Grove

To Cedar Grove

as you climb, with The Grand Sentinel and The Sphinx standing out across the deep valley.

The path reenters the trees as you rise out of the Kings Canyon and winds uphill, high above Copper Creek, crossing seasonal brooks in the process. The forest cover becomes quite thick, then you are greeted by a grove of quaking aspen before reaching the thin stringer of Lower Tent Meadow at 4 miles. A few campsites with a bear box are located near a year-round creek here.

Another steep uphill with switchbacks brings you to willow- and aspen-filled Upper Tent Meadow at 5.5 miles, where campsites and a bear box are also located. More switchbacks lead to the crossing of a saddle between Mount Hutchings and Goat Mountain, with a magnificent view east of Mounts Clarence King, Cotter, and Gardiner, and south of the Great Western Divide.

The trail then drops down into the lower portion of the Granite Basin. Travel through woods, past small ponds, and through meadows to the side trail leading to Granite Lake at 9.5 miles. Turn left (west) and follow the path to the large body of water, where you will also find campsites and wonderful views of Mount Hutchings to the south, Goat Mountain to the east, and Comb Spur to the west.

After you have enjoyed your visit, backtrack to the parking area at 20 miles.

Option: For an extended backpacking trip, return to the main trail and continue north from the lake, over Granite Pass, to a junction with a west-trending path to Volcanic Lakes and Kennedy Creek. Make a left turn on this path, pass a cross-country route to the Volcanic Lakes, and then dip across the West Fork of Dougherty Creek. A stiff climb leads up to Dead Pine Ridge, then the route drops down into the canyon of Kennedy Creek, where a lengthy ascent up the gorge brings you past East Kennedy Lake. Switchbacks deposit you at Kennedy Pass and the Lewis Creek Trail (Hike 46). Follow the trail down to the Lewis Creek trailhead, where you should have a car waiting for you. This would add just less than 23 miles to your trip, and a considerable amount of elevation gain. You will need a good topographic map of the area for this journey.

55 Paradise Valley

Highlights:	This outing takes you past the delightful Mist Falls and into tranquil Paradise Valley, which is nestled along the South Fork of the Kings River.
Type of hike:	Out-and-back, day hike or backpack.
Total distance:	13 miles.
Difficulty:	Difficult.
Best months:	Mid-June through October.
Maps:	USGS The Sphinx; Kings Canyon National Park Cedar Grove; or TOPO! Sequoia Kings Canyon CD-ROM.
Permits:	Obtain a permit to spend the night from the information center at Cedar Grove Road's End. Bear-proof food storage canisters are required.
Special considerations:	This trail can be very hot—be sure to get an early start. The trail also is used by horseback riders; remember proper trail etiquette by stepping off the trail on the downhill side and waiting quietly until the horses have passed. Stay in plain view of the horses; they may think you are a wild animal and bolt if you are hidden behind a rock or tree. And, finally, mountain lions frequent this area; you are advised not to hike solo.
Parking and facilities:	Restrooms and an information center are located at the east end of the day use parking area. Water is available from a spigot next to the information center. The trail begins next to the information center.

Finding the trailhead: From Grant Grove, follow California Highway 180 north, then east, for approximately 32 miles to Cedar Grove Village. Continue for 5.6 miles past the Cedar Grove Village turnoff to the Road's End parking area on the south side of the loop, or past the ranger station to the overnight parking area, on the north side of the loop.

Key points:
- 0.0 Trailhead.
- 1.9 Arrive at the trail fork.
- 4.1 Reach Mist Falls.
- 6.5 Arrive in Paradise Valley.

The hike: Follow the return portion of the trail from Road's End to the Bailey bridge (Hike 50), in reverse. This takes you to the trail fork at 1.9 miles, just before the bridge. Take the left (north) fork uphill, soon gaining

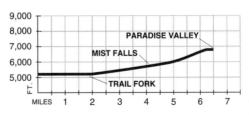

a view of the confluence of Bubbs Creek and the South Fork of the Kings River. The path dips and rises through the shade of cedars, oaks, and firs through an understory of ferns and horsetails, as it passes below Buck Peak.

Paradise Valley

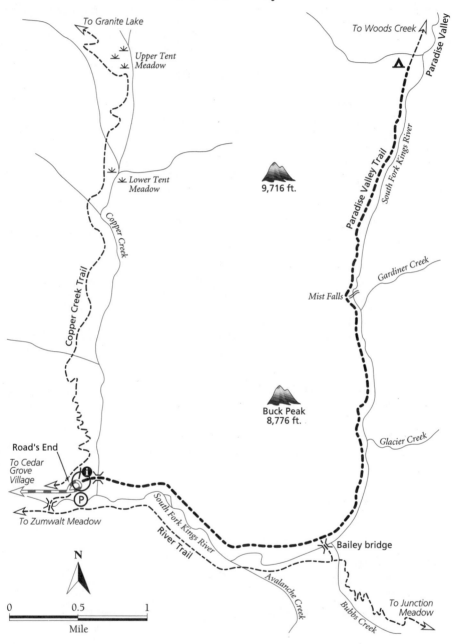

To Granite Lake

Upper Tent Meadow

To Woods Creek

Paradise Valley

Lower Tent Meadow

Copper Creek

9,716 ft.

Paradise Valley Trail

South Fork Kings River

Copper Creek Trail

Gardiner Creek

Mist Falls

Buck Peak
8,776 ft.

Glacier Creek

Road's End

To Cedar Grove Village

To Zumwalt Meadow

South Fork Kings River

River Trail

Bailey bridge

N

Avalanche Creek

Bubbs Creek

To Junction Meadow

0   0.5   1
Mile

After climbing and switchbacking through a mixed forest, a view of The Sphinx opens to the south, down the canyon behind you. The path ascends a bit more, with views of lacy cascades on the river below, before reaching the deluge of the Mist Falls at 4.1 miles. In early season, a refreshing mist unfurls through the air, making this a wonderfully cool rest stop.

The trail continues to climb through granite, ascending several switchbacks. Climbing through oaks, the route soon levels off, passing through willows and alders, then conifers, as it enters Paradise Valley at 6.5 miles. The South Fork of the Kings River is quite peaceful here, as it meanders through aspens, cottonwoods, and grassy flower-filled meadows. The first set of campsites in this long valley are located here at its southern terminus, equipped with bear boxes and a pit toilet. This makes a good place to rest for backpackers as well as for day hikers.

If you are spending the night, you can explore farther up the valley after setting up camp. When you are ready to return, follow the trail back to the parking area at 13 miles.

Option: The Mist Falls are a nice destination for a shorter hike and a picnic lunch on the large slabs of granite below the falls. Exercise caution—do not climb on any slippery rocks near the water.

56 Rae Lakes Loop

Highlights:	This hike is one of the most popular in Kings Canyon National Park, taking you up the Kings Canyon and Woods Creek to alpine lakes, over a nearly 12,000-foot pass, and back down the scenic Bubbs Creek Canyon.
Type of hike:	Loop, backpack.
Total distance:	43.6 miles.
Difficulty:	Difficult.
Best months:	Mid-July through mid-October.
Maps:	USGS The Sphinx and Mount Clarence King; USFS John Muir Wilderness and Sequoia–Kings Canyon Wilderness; or TOPO! Sequoia Kings Canyon CD-ROM.
Permits:	Obtain a permit at Cedar Grove Road's End. Bear-proof food storage canisters are required.
Special considerations:	This trail can be very hot—be sure to get an early start. The trail is also used by horseback riders; please remember proper trail etiquette by stepping off the trail on the downhill side and waiting quietly until the horses have passed. Stay in plain view of the horses; they may think you are a wild animal and bolt if you are behind a rock or tree. And, finally, mountain lions frequent this area—you are advised not to hike solo.
Parking and facilities:	Restrooms and an information center are located at the east end of the day use parking area. Water is available from a spigot next to the information center. The trail begins next to the information center.

Finding the trailhead: From Grant Grove, follow California Highway 180 north, then east, for approximately 32 miles to Cedar Grove Village. Continue for 5.6 miles past the Cedar Grove Village turnoff, then past the Road's End parking area on the south side of the loop, to the overnight parking area on the north side of the loop.

Key points:

0.0	Trailhead.
1.9	Reach the Bailey bridge trail fork.
4.1	Pass Mist Falls.
6.5	Reach Paradise Valley.
8.9	Make the river crossing.
14.5	Enter Castle Domes Meadow.
16.0	Reach the John Muir Trail/Pacific Crest Trail junction.
21.0	Arrive at Dollar Lake.
22.5	Reach the middle Rae Lake.
27.5	Cross Glen Pass.
30.1	Pass the Kearsarge Pass/Charlotte Lake trail junction.
30.4	Pass the Bullfrog Lake trail junction.
31.2	Reach Vidette Meadow.
33.9	Pass Junction Meadow.
36.5	Cross Charlotte Creek.
39.5	Pass the Avalanche Pass Trail.
41.5	Reach the trail junction.
43.5	Pass the trail junction.

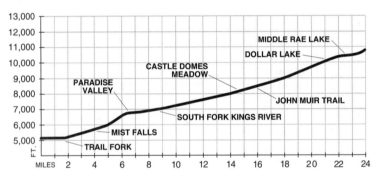

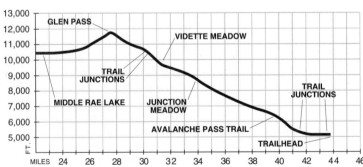

The Painted Lady and Mount Rixford tower over the middle Rae Lake.

The hike: Begin by following the second portion of the trail from Road's End to the Bailey bridge (Hike 50), in reverse. This brings you to the trail fork at 1.9 miles, just before the Bailey bridge. From here, follow the trail to Paradise Valley (Hike 55) to the campsites at 6.5 miles. Beyond the camps, the trail dips and rises through the shade, continuing up the river valley.

At about 7.5 miles, you reach a second and smaller campground, also with a bear box and pit toilet. The trail advances through a fire-scarred area and a sunny meadow; switchbacks and a few ups-and-downs bring you to the last campsites in the valley, just beyond the signed stock crossing. A pit toilet and large bear boxes are located among the ample campsites.

Just east of the campground, at 8.9 miles, you will cross the South Fork of the Kings River. Large logs aid your crossing in early season, but later in the year, an easy rock hop is to the left. On the other side of the river, the path travels through a shady woodland, crossing a brook on a small log footbridge.

The pleasant, shady trail soon turns rocky and begins to climb above Woods Creek. The forest cover thins and the trail ascends short switchbacks to avoid rocky outcroppings. At times the route descends close to the creek, then soars high above, just to dip down again.

After a long uphill through manzanita and chinquapin, the path drops down to aspen-lined Castle Domes Meadow at 14.5 miles, with Window Peak and the Castle Domes towering above. The trail reenters the forest shade and continues dipping and rising, passing a couple of aspen-shrouded campsites.

The John Muir Trail/Pacific Crest Trail intersection is just beyond the signed stock crossing at 16 miles. Turn right (south) on the John Muir Trail. Cross Woods Creek on a bouncy suspension bridge; on the other side are large campsites with bear boxes. The ruins of one of fur trapper Shorty Lovelace's cabins are also located near this crossing.

From the campsites, the trail climbs moderately as the forest cover thins, then continues its undulating and switchbacking course through aspens

Rae Lakes Loop

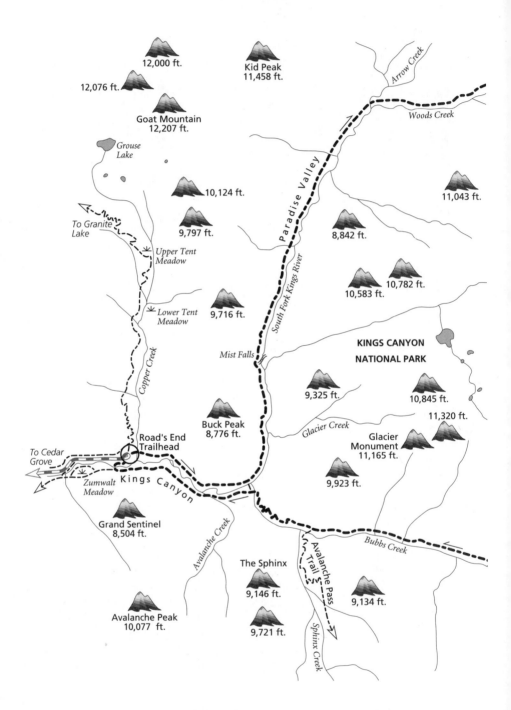

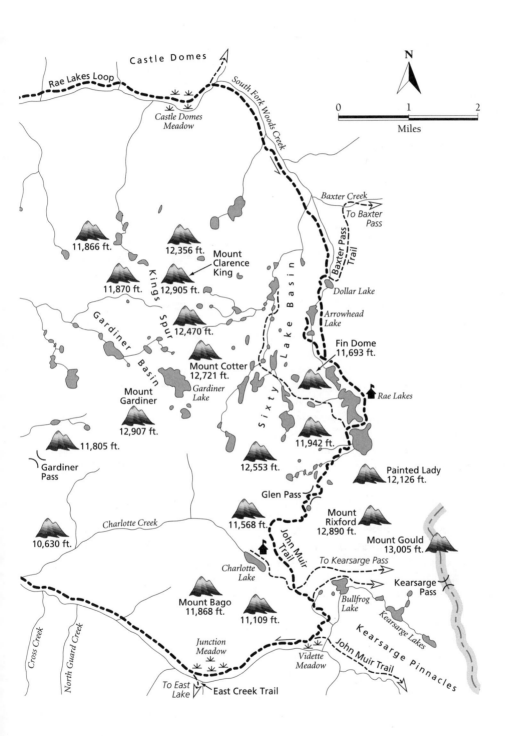

Castle Domes

Rae Lakes Loop

Castle Domes
Meadow

South Fork Woods Creek

N

0   1   2
Miles

Baxter Creek
To Baxter
Pass

Baxter Pass Trail

11,866 ft.

12,356 ft.

Mount
Clarence
King

11,870 ft.   12,905 ft.

Kings Spur

Dollar Lake

Arrowhead
Lake

Sixty Lake Basin

Gardiner Basin

12,470 ft.

Fin Dome
11,693 ft.

Mount Cotter
12,721 ft.

Gardiner
Lake

Rae Lakes

Mount
Gardiner

12,907 ft.

11,942 ft.

11,805 ft.

Gardiner
Pass

12,553 ft.

Painted Lady
12,126 ft.

Glen Pass

Charlotte Creek

11,568 ft.

Mount
Rixford
12,890 ft.

Mount Gould
13,005 ft.

10,630 ft.

John Muir Trail

To Kearsarge Pass

Kearsarge
Pass

Charlotte
Lake

Bullfrog
Lake

Kearsarge Lakes

Mount Bago
11,868 ft.

11,109 ft.

Kearsarge Pinnacles

Cross Creek

North Guard Creek

Junction
Meadow

Vidette
Meadow

John Muir Trail

To East
Lake   East Creek Trail

and junipers. In the summer, colorful wildflowers bloom along the hillsides, while in the fall the aspens put on a show of their own.

Soon you come to the ford of a small creek, with a log crossing for times of high water on your right (west). The climbs become a little steeper before the path descends to a stock gate at a bridged crossing of the outlet flowing down from Sixty Lake Basin, which is in a verdant meadow. Still climbing steeply, the trail gradually rounds a ridge, passing the dim Baxter Pass Trail and reaching Dollar Lake at 21 miles.

Rounding the west side of Dollar Lake, the trail crosses the South Fork of Woods Creek below Diamond Peak, then passes Arrowhead Lake and a side trail leading to campsites and bear boxes along its east shore. Fin Dome stands like a beacon as you near the Rae Lakes, passing a side trail leading to the west shore of Arrowhead Lake. The path ascends past the northern tip of the lowest lake, then passes a side trail that leads to campsites and bear boxes near the shore of the middle Rae Lake at 22.5 miles. The small backcountry ranger station is to the left (east) of the trail. Travel high above the lake before dropping down to meet another side trail that leads to campsites and bear boxes near the lake's south end. Fin Dome towers above the lake in the west, while Mount Gould, Painted Lady, and Mount Rixford are visible to the south.

The trail continues through a meadowy section, advancing past an obscure path to Dragon Lake before crossing the land bridge between the middle and the highest of the Rae Lakes. A rock hop leads across the tiny stream connecting the two lakes. The trail passes the steep trail to Sixty Lake Basin and turns to the south, traveling above the highest Rae Lake. The route ascends switchbacks, passes a pond, and becomes increasingly rocky and steep as it winds through the granite past high and desolate lakes. Numerous switchbacks, some steep and slippery, rise to Glen Pass at 27.5 miles.

After traversing the narrow ridge of the pass, the trail descends first rocky, then sandy switchbacks high above a large, deep-blue lake. Winding down past an aqua-blue tarn, the path enters the trees and undulates on a slope high above Charlotte Lake, with a view of Charlotte Dome to the west. To the north of this dome you can spot the pointed summit of Mount Gardiner.

After passing a trail that connects with the Kearsarge Pass Trail, you intersect the Kearsarge Pass and Charlotte Lake Trails at a four-way junction at 30.1 miles (not shown on some maps). Continue on the John Muir Trail/Pacific Crest Trail, crossing a small rise, then switchback steeply down. At 30.4 miles, meet the Bullfrog Lake and Kearsarge Lakes Trail. Continue southeast, descending more switchbacks on the John Muir Trail, and crossing the outlet of two small lakes located near Bullfrog Lake.

As you continue, you gain views of the Kearsarge Pinnacles, the Kings-Kern Divide, and East and West Vidette. At 31.2 miles you arrive at picturesque Vidette Meadow, with campsites, bear boxes and possibly a few deer.

From this point, follow the routes described for Vidette Meadow (Hike 52), Junction Meadow (Hike 51), and the first portion of the trail from Road's End to the Bailey bridge (Hike 50)—all in reverse—to the parking area at 43.6 miles.

Hikes in the Mineral King and South Fork Areas

All of the hikes in this chapter, with the exception of the last two, begin along the Mineral King Road, and are presented from west to east, and then from north to south. The last two, Ladybug and Whisky Log Camps, and Garfield Grove, begin at the South Fork Campground.

57 Paradise Peak

Highlights:	This trip takes you past the sequoias of Atwell Grove and on to views of the peaks surrounding the Mineral King Valley and the Middle Fork of the Kaweah, as well as the mighty Kaweah Peaks.
Type of hike:	Out-and-back, day hike.
Total distance:	9.8 miles.
Difficulty:	Difficult.
Best months:	Mid-June through October.
Maps:	USGS Silver City; USFS John Muir Wilderness and Sequoia–Kings Canyon Wilderness; or TOPO! Sequoia Kings Canyon CD-ROM.
Permits:	None.
Special considerations:	A risk of being struck by lightning exists on the summit of Paradise Peak. If there are dark clouds nearby, or if hail, rain, thunder, or static electricity are in the air, descend immediately.
Parking and facilities:	From the large parking area, follow the dirt road west, passing a water spigot and restrooms along the way. Turn right (north) on the first side road leading up to Mineral King Road. Follow the paved road to the signed trailhead, which is around a curve and on the north side of the road.

Finding the trailhead: From central Three Rivers, drive north on California Highway 198 approximately 3.9 miles to Mineral King Road and turn right (east). Follow the narrow road for 10.1 miles to the Lookout Point entrance station. Continue east, losing and regaining the pavement before reaching Atwell Mill Campground at approximately 20.2 miles. The signed parking area is just east of the campground, on the south side of the road.

Key points:
- 0.0 Trailhead.
- 2.0 Make the creek crossing.
- 3.3 Reach the Redwood Meadow Trail junction.
- 4.9 Arrive on the Paradise Peak summit.

The hike: Start your journey by climbing several steep and short switchbacks through shady patches of fir, pine, and cedar, and sunny areas of manzanita, bear clover, and ceanothus. Longer switchbacks then take you through a portion of the Atwell Grove of giant sequoias. At approximately 2 miles, jump across a tiny creek lined with sword and bracken fern.

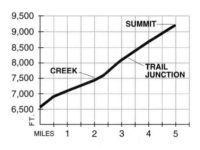

The path continues rising steeply through sun and shade, attaining the top of the ridge at a trail junction at 3.3 miles. The path straight ahead (north) leads steeply downhill to the secluded Redwood Meadow grove. Turn left (west) onto an unsigned trail.

Follow the winding trail uphill through shady woods; it rises gently at first, then reassumes its previous steep and switchbacking manner. Pass an abandoned trail segment branching to the left (southwest), meeting its other end after contouring around a hilltop.

Paradise Peak

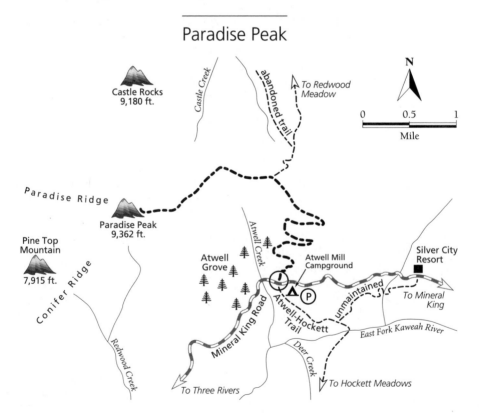

As you near the Paradise Peak summit, the trail becomes a little vague. Follow the "ducks" (cairns that serve as trail markers) through a rocky area and across slabs of granite that are shrouded by flowers in summer. A fallen and shattered tree can make a switchback leading uphill to the north easy to miss. The trail picks up again on the other side of the debris.

At 4.9 miles, you arrive at stone steps leading up to a crevice between tall boulders, topped with a short radio tower. Rock climbing skills are required to reach the very top of Paradise Peak, which once sported a fire lookout. If climbing isn't your thing, views to the north of the Big Baldy Ridge, Little Baldy, Castle Rocks, Moro Rock, and Alta Peak can be seen from the base of the boulders. On your return trip, views through the trees to the northeast include Valhalla, Lion Rock, Mount Stewart, Eagle Scout Peak, and the Kaweahs. To the southeast, you can see Needham Mountain, Sawtooth Peak, Mineral Peak, Rainbow Mountain, Florence Peak, Tulare Peak, Eagle Crest, Vandever Mountain, and Hengst Peak. Retrace your steps to the trailhead, a total of 9.8 miles.

58 Atwell-Hockett Trail to Hockett Meadows

Highlights:	This hike leads you past billowing falls at the East Fork bridge and through the East Fork Grove of giant sequoias to beautiful Hockett Meadows at the northern end of the Hockett Plateau.
Type of hike:	Out-and-back, backpack.
Total distance:	19.8 miles.
Difficulty:	Difficult.
Best months:	June through October.
Maps:	USGS Silver City; USFS John Muir Wilderness and Sequoia–Kings Canyon Wilderness; or TOPO! Sequoia Kings Canyon CD-ROM.
Permits:	Obtain a permit at the Mineral King Ranger Station if camping overnight.
Special considerations:	Four creeks, three of which will definitely require wading in early season, are crossed by this trail.
Parking and facilities:	From the large parking area, follow the dirt road west, past a water spigot and restrooms. The trail begins at a sign prohibiting trailhead parking in the campground.

Finding the trailhead: From central Three Rivers, drive north on California Highway 198 for approximately 3.9 miles to Mineral King Road and turn right (east). Follow the narrow road for 10.1 miles to the Lookout Point entrance station. Continue east, losing and regaining the pavement before reaching Atwell Mill Campground at approximately 20.2 miles. The signed parking area is just east of the campground, on the south side of the road.

Key points:

- 0.0 Trailhead.
- 0.7 Cross Deadwood Creek.
- 1.2 Cross the East Fork of the Kaweah River.
- 2.2 Reach Deer Creek.
- 7.0 Ford Clover Creek.
- 7.5 Cross Corner Creek.
- 8.3 Reach Horse Creek.
- 9.9 Arrive at Hockett Meadows.

The hike: The wide path leads downhill, through the lower portion of the Atwell Grove, and passes the site of the mill at a flywheel in a small meadow.

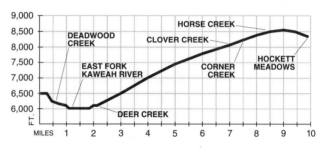

Pass through areas of controlled burns and bear clover, stepping over a small, seasonal creek. At 0.7 mile, cross shallow Deadwood Creek and continue descending. Pass an unmaintained trail to Cabin Cove before arriving at the East Fork of the Kaweah River. A sturdy wooden bridge leads you across the river at 1.2 miles, passing right next to a small, thundering waterfall.

On the other side of the watercourse you begin to climb through ferns and thimbleberry. After an easy crossing of a small brook, you reach the ford of Deer Creek (2.2 miles), which requires a wade above its pretty cascades. Beyond, your route passes through the western portion of the East Fork Grove. The path switchbacks up the slope, then climbs toward the southwest. In sunny areas, blue-eyed Mary, mustang clover, and wallflowers bloom in season. As you pass though an area of rocky granite and mountain pride penstemon, Mineral King Road can be seen snaking up the canyon to the northwest.

After stepping over a few seasonal creeks, the trail enters the Horse Creek Canyon. To the west Cahoon Rock and Homer's Nose come into view. Pass over a couple more seasonal creeks before coming to multi-forked Clover Creek at 7 miles; the middle branch requires a wade in early season. The path crosses another hillside meadow and at 7.5 miles you reach Corner Creek in a large meadow of mountain bluebells. This creek too requires a wade if you are hiking early in the season.

Atwell-Hockett Trail to Hockett Meadows

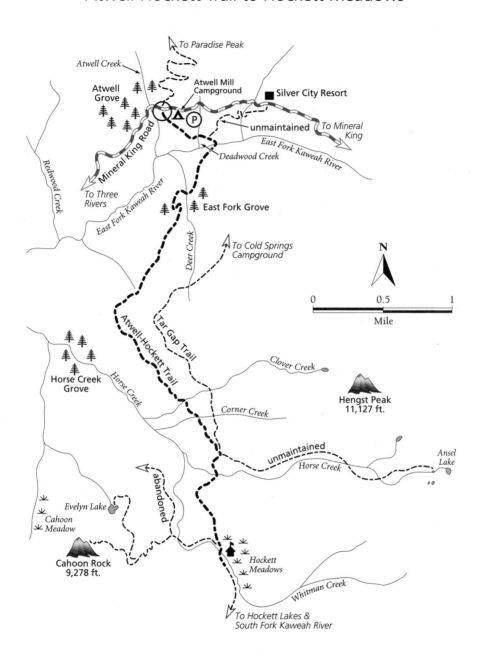

At 8.2 miles you arrive at the junction with the Tar Gap Trail, and pass the unmaintained and virtually imperceptible path heading east along Horse Creek to Ansel Lake. At 8.3 miles, you reach campsites on the north side of Horse Creek, complete with a cable to suspend food bags. A large log aids in crossing the creek, which is a raging torrent in early season.

Beyond the creek, a small bridge leads over a tiny tributary stream. The trail then rises over a ridge, and makes a slight descent through the woods to Hockett Meadows at 9.9 miles.

Two cabins at the backcountry ranger station stand at the north end of the expansive meadow, next to a trail junction and a small tributary of Whitman Creek. A campsite and open-air pit toilet are a short way down the path to the right (west), signed for Evelyn Lake. More campsites and a bear box can be found south of the ranger station, after stepping over the tributary and crossing Whitman Creek on a small bridge.

After your stay, return the way you came (19.8 miles).

59 Evelyn Lake and Cahoon Rock

Highlights:	This excursion takes you from Hockett Meadows to views from the summit of Cahoon Rock, then on to cirque-bound Evelyn Lake.
Type of hike:	Out-and-back, backpack.
Total distance:	29 miles.
Difficulty:	Difficult.
Best months:	June through October.
Maps:	USGS Silver City; USFS John Muir Wilderness and Sequoia–Kings Canyon Wilderness; or TOPO! Sequoia Kings Canyon CD-ROM.
Permits:	Obtain a permit at the Mineral King Ranger Station if camping overnight.
Special considerations:	Four creeks must be crossed on the way to Hockett Meadows; three of them will require wading in early season.
Parking and facilities:	From the large parking area, follow the dirt road west, passing a water spigot and restrooms along the way. The trail begins at a large sign prohibiting trailhead parking in the campground.

Finding the trailhead: From central Three Rivers, drive north on California Highway 198 approximately 3.9 miles to Mineral King Road and turn right (east). Follow the narrow road for 10.1 miles to the Lookout Point entrance station. Continue east, losing and regaining pavement, before reaching Atwell Mill Campground at approximately 20.2 miles. The signed parking area is just east of the campground, on the south side of the road.

Key points:

- 0.0   Trailhead.
- 0.7   Cross Deadwood Creek.
- 1.2   Cross the East Fork of the Kaweah River.
- 2.2   Ford Deer Creek.
- 7.0   Reach Clover Creek.
- 7.5   Cross Corner Creek.
- 8.3   Reach Horse Creek.
- 9.9   Arrive at Hockett Meadows.
- 10.6   Cross Whitman Creek.
- 10.9   Ford a tributary creek.
- 11.5   Reach the trail junction.
- 12.5   Arrive on the Cahoon Rock summit.
- 13.5   Return to the trail junction.
- 14.6   Reach Evelyn Lake.

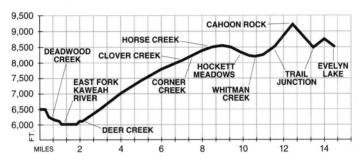

The hike: Begin by following the trail to Hockett Meadows (Hike 58). From the junction just north of the backcountry ranger station, make a right (west) turn, and follow the signed Evelyn Lake Trail along bubbling Whitman Creek. Pass a small campsite and a sign pointing the way to an open-air pit toilet. The path descends slightly to log bridges, aiding in the crossing of a boggy meadow, then on to the main branch of Whitman Creek at 10.6 miles. Cross the creek by hopping boulders just north of the trail, or by using a fallen log.

The trail leads up, past the abandoned Eden Creek Grove Trail, which has become overgrown but still appears on some maps. Pass through a forested area, reaching a meadow and the crossing of a branch of Whitman Creek at 10.9 miles. After traveling up a few winding switchbacks, the trail brings you to the Evelyn Lake Trail junction at 11.5 miles.

For now, continue straight (west) toward Cahoon Rock, following the edge of a picturesque meadow and crossing the soggy tip at its western end. The route switchbacks again and skirts a seasonal creek in a stringer meadow before leading up a final switchback to the summit of Cahoon Rock (12.5 miles).

Views from the top include Mineral King Road and Conifer Ridge to the north; Hengst Peak, White Chief Peak, and Vandever Mountain to the east; Quinn Peak and Sheep Mountain to the southeast; Dennison Ridge to the south; and, of course, Homer's Nose to the west. After enjoying the vista,

Evelyn Lake and Cahoon Rock

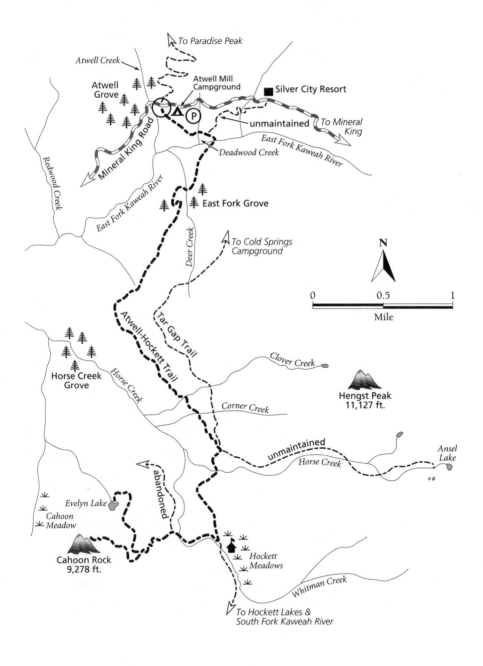

retrace your steps to the trail junction at 13.5 miles, and make a left (northwest) turn. The route travels up a sparsely forested ridge dotted with phlox, giving you a view to the east much like you had at Cahoon Rock.

After crossing over a sunny hilltop, the path winds through the forest until you can spot deep blue Evelyn Lake through the trees, below you on the left (west). The trail steeply switchbacks down to a bench above the lake with a hitching post and campsites, then drops farther, through boulders and chinquapin, to a large campsite near the rocky lakeshore at 14.6 miles.

When you are ready to return, retrace your steps to the trail junction and make a left (east) turn to Hockett Meadows, reaching it at 19.1 miles. Then retrace your steps to the trailhead, for a round-trip total of 29 miles.

60 Cold Springs Nature Trail

Highlights: This easy ramble takes you through meadows and aspen groves along the East Fork of the Kaweah River, gives you nice views of the surrounding peaks, and leads to the site of the former mining settlement of Beulah.

Type of hike: Semi-loop, day hike.
Total distance: 2 miles.
Difficulty: Easy.
Best months: June through October.
Maps: Sequoia National Park Mineral King (not shown on other maps).
Permits: None.
Parking and facilities: Restrooms are located at the picnic area, and water is available in the campground. To reach the trailhead from the picnic area, follow the road west to the Cold Springs Campground entrance and a small parking turnout, and make a left (south) turn. Continue across the bridge and turn left again, now heading east. The signed nature trail begins next to campsite 6.

Finding the trailhead: From central Three Rivers, drive north on California Highway 198 approximately 3.9 miles to Mineral King Road and turn right (east). Follow the narrow road for 10.1 miles to the Lookout Point entrance station. Continue east, and lose and regain pavement before passing Atwell Mill Campground. You will lose and regain the pavement again before you reach Cabin Cove and the Silver City Store and Resort at approximately 20.5 miles. The road loses pavement once more, then becomes paved again, and reaches the Mineral King Ranger Station at 23.2 miles. Park in the small pullout on the north side of the road just before the ranger station and across from the campground, or at the picnic area located across from the ranger station on the south side of the road.

Key points:
- 0.0   Trailhead.
- 0.2   Leave the nature loop.
- 0.8   Arrive at the smelter site.
- 1.0   Reach the site of Beulah.
- 1.8   Return to the nature loop.

The hike: The trail begins by passing through an open, grassy stretch filled with meadow goldenrod, Bigelow's sneezeweed, and many other wildflowers in the summer. Pass the first interpretive sign and enter cottonwoods and aspens. The interpretive signs along the way identify the native plants and trees that grow in the Mineral King Valley.

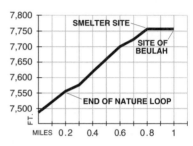

You reach a trail fork and take the path to the left (east); the other will be taken on the return trip. After a few more information posts, at 0.2 mile, you come to the junction with the other portion of the interpretive trail. Continue straight ahead, passing a couple of nice places to rest or eat lunch along the river.

The trail climbs over a small rise before dipping to cross two small brooks on wooden plank bridges in a grassy hillside meadow. A nice view opens down to the sparkling water as the path rises up a couple of switchbacks and enters a grove of firs. You then dip to cross the boggy hillside meadow

Cold Springs Nature Trail

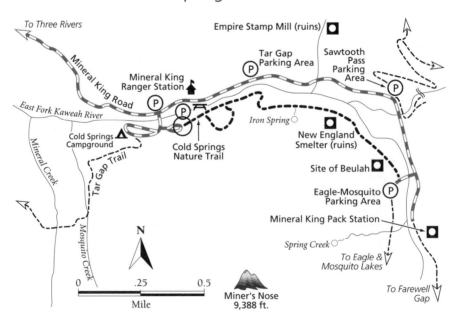

watered by Iron Spring, where Sierra gentians bloom profusely in late summer. Ahead of you and across the valley is Black Wolf Falls, with Empire Mountain and Sawtooth Peak towering above.

The trail then enters a flat area of sagebrush, with views of Florence and Tulare Peaks to the south, and reaches the site of the New England Smelter at 0.8 mile, just before a grove of aspen. A couple of foundation supports are all that is left of the smelter, which operated in the late 1800s.

Mineral Peak becomes visible to the right (south) of Sawtooth Peak before you enter the aspen grove. The route then winds through more sagebrush and flowers as Rainbow Mountain joins Florence and Tulare Peaks, along with Farewell Gap in your view to the south.

Enter a private residential area near tall fir trees, and at 1 mile arrive at the small sign marking the site of Beulah, the community that thrived here during Mineral King's mining days. Most of Beulah was leveled by an avalanche set off by the San Francisco earthquake in 1906. Now only private cabins occupy this former townsite.

The road ahead leads down to the Eagle-Mosquito parking area, passing through private cabins, each signed with family names and the year established. If you venture down to the parking area, stay on the road and respect the private property.

When you are ready to return, retrace your steps to the trail fork at 1.8 miles and stay left (southwest) to travel the other portion of the interpretive trail. Arrive at the trailhead at 2 miles.

Option: If you are staying at Cold Springs Campground, you can use this trail as a route to other trails leaving from the Eagle-Mosquito parking area.

61 Timber Gap

Highlights:	This trek gives you a nice panorama with a little less work than other trails above the Mineral King Valley, and even gives you a peek across the Middle Fork Canyon.
Type of hike:	Out-and-back, day hike.
Total distance:	4.2 miles.
Difficulty:	Moderate.
Best months:	June through October.
Maps:	USGS Mineral King; Sequoia National Park Mineral King; or TOPO! Sequoia Kings Canyon CD-ROM.
Permits:	None.
Parking and facilities:	Parking is available on both sides of the road. Restrooms are in the southern parking area, and there is a "Charge A Call" phone (which only accepts calling cards or collect calls) in the northern parking area. No water is available. The trail begins at the north end of the parking area.

Finding the trailhead: From central Three Rivers, drive north on California Highway 198 for approximately 3.9 miles to Mineral King Road and turn right (east). Follow the narrow road for 10.1 miles to the Lookout Point entrance station. Continue east, losing and regaining the pavement before passing Atwell Mill Campground. You will lose and regain the pavement again before Cabin Cove and the Silver City Store and Resort at approximately 20.5 miles. The road loses pavement once more, then becomes paved again, and reaches the Mineral King Ranger Station at 23.2 miles. The Sawtooth Pass parking area is 0.8 mile farther up the road.

Key points:
0.0 Trailhead.
0.6 Reach the Sawtooth Pass Trail junction.
2.1 Arrive at Timber Gap.

The hike: Begin by climbing through sagebrush and grasses on a bed of crushed rock. A vista of Timber Gap—your destination— is to the north. As you rise up the lower slopes of Empire Mountain, views over the Mineral King Valley become more and more 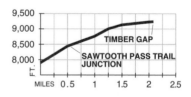 expansive. A cheerful cascade on Monarch Creek appears below hillside meadows to the right (southeast), just before the trail switchbacks and heads north.

The path continues rising and reaches a fork with the Sawtooth Pass Trail at 0.6 mile. Take the route to the left (north), which travels steeply uphill, passes through a few trees, and contours around the precipitous slopes of a

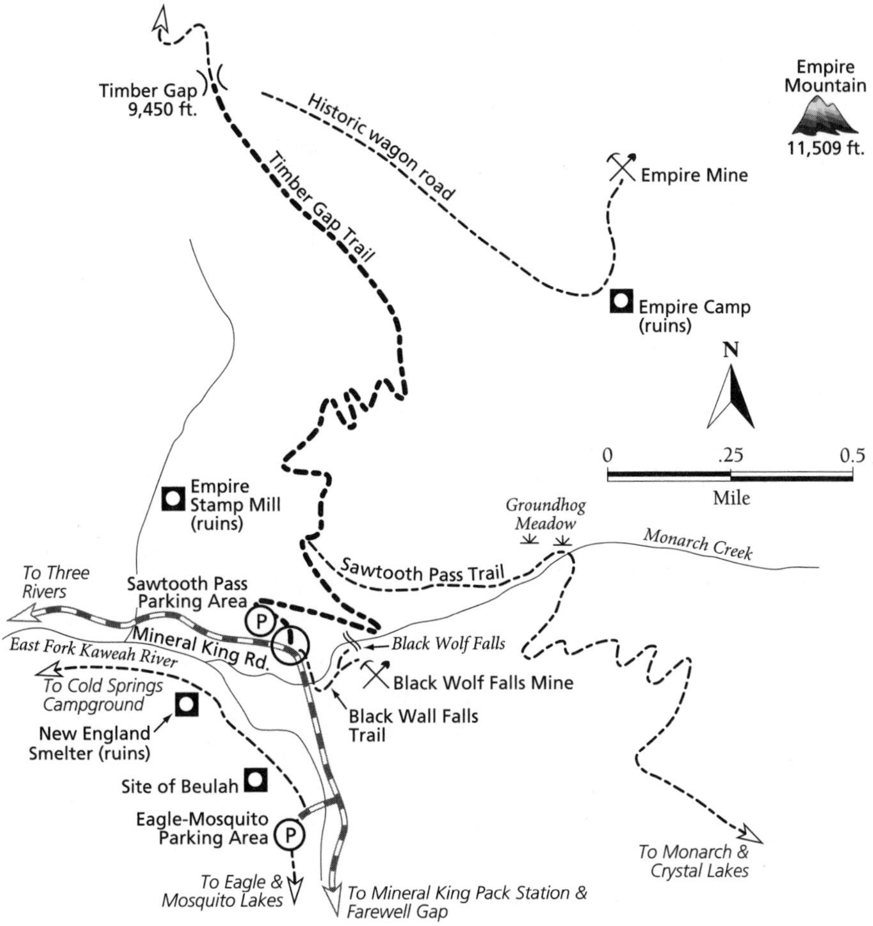

Timber Gap

Timber Gap
9,450 ft.

Historic wagon road

Timber Gap Trail

Empire
Mountain

11,509 ft.

Empire Mine

Empire Camp
(ruins)

N

| 0 | .25 | 0.5 |

Mile

Empire
Stamp Mill
(ruins)

Groundhog
Meadow

Monarch Creek

To Three
Rivers

Sawtooth Pass Trail

Sawtooth Pass
Parking Area

Mineral King Rd.

East Fork Kaweah River

Black Wolf Falls

Black Wolf Falls Mine

To Cold Springs
Campground

New England
Smelter (ruins)

Black Wall Falls
Trail

Site of Beulah

Eagle-Mosquito
Parking Area

To Monarch &
Crystal Lakes

To Eagle &
Mosquito Lakes

To Mineral King Pack Station &
Farewell Gap

seasonal drainage. Looking to the south you can see Farewell Gap, Vandever Mountain, White Chief Peak, and Eagle Crest, with the Mineral King Pack Station far below.

The trail then begins ascending several switchbacks above the site of the Empire Stamp Mill, the first through manzanita and chinquapin, and the rest through a shady fir forest. About halfway up the series of switchbacks, Timber Gap comes back into view.

After the last steep rise, the path exits the treeline and traverses an open, grassy, and more gently graded slope, working toward the woods of the gap. High above on the right (east) is the location of the Empire Mine and Empire Camp, now in ruins.

The trail climbs again, entering the shade of fir trees, and arrives at Timber Gap at 2.1 miles. Panther and Alta Peaks and Alta Meadow are visible across the Middle Fork Canyon to the north. The trail you have been traveling continues steeply down to Cliff Creek and Redwood Meadow, eventually meeting the High Sierra Trail.

After you have enjoyed the cool breezes of the gap, return the way you came (4.2 miles).

Option: Experienced hikers may want to explore the historic wagon road leading to the Empire Camp ruins (destroyed by an avalanche in 1880) and the Empire Mine. Be sure to bring a compass because the old road can be tricky to find.

To locate the roadbed, you must strike out cross-country, heading slightly uphill and through the trees to the right (east) of Timber Gap. This side trip will add about 1.6 miles and 515 feet of elevation gain to your hike.

62 Crystal Lakes

Highlights:	This jaunt takes you to lofty views from the Chihuahua Bowl and the Chihuahua Mine, then on to the peaceful lakes along Crystal Creek.
Type of hike:	Out-and-back, day hike or backpack.
Total distance:	8.8 miles.
Difficulty:	Difficult (day hike); moderate (backpack).
Best months:	July through October.
Maps:	USGS Mineral King; Sequoia National Park Mineral King; or TOPO! Sequoia Kings Canyon CD-ROM.
Permits:	Obtain a permit at the Mineral King Ranger Station if camping overnight.
Parking and facilities:	Parking is available on both sides of Mineral King Road. Restrooms are located in the southern parking area, and there is a "Charge A Call" phone (which only accepts calling cards or collect calls) in the northern parking area. No water is available.

Finding the trailhead: From central Three Rivers, drive north on California Highway 198 approximately 3.9 miles to Mineral King Road and turn right (east). Follow the narrow road for 10.1 miles to the Lookout Point entrance station. Continue east, losing and regaining the pavement before passing Atwell Mill Campground. Lose and regain the pavement again before Cabin Cove and the Silver City Store and Resort at approximately 20.5 miles. The road loses pavement once more, then becomes paved again, and reaches the Mineral King Ranger Station at 23.2 miles. The Sawtooth Pass parking area is 0.8 mile farther up the road.

Key points:
- 0.0   Trailhead.
- 0.6   Pass the Timber Gap Trail junction.
- 1.2   Make the Monarch Creek crossing.
- 3.0   Reach the trail fork.
- 4.4   Arrive at the lower Crystal Lake campsites.

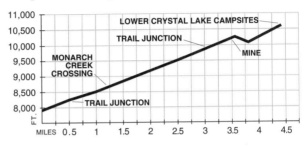

The hike: Follow the trail to Timber Gap (Hike 61), to the first junction at 0.6 mile, and make a right, heading east toward Sawtooth Pass. The trail climbs one more long switchback, then rises on a sunny slope above pretty cascades and a hillside meadow along Monarch Creek. The route winds up the lower flanks of Empire Mountain, and as you round a curve, a spring gushes forth on the opposite (south) side of the creek below.

Meet the abandoned Glacier Pass Trail at Groundhog Meadow; you can trace its steep route up the side of Empire Mountain, through brush and rock-slides, high above the creek. Continuing on the Sawtooth Pass Trail, you dip to a rock-hop crossing of Monarch Creek at 1.2 miles. On the other side of the creek, you can rest in a shady area before climbing several switchbacks that lead up through flowers and forest. The first few switchbacks offer views of the Mineral King Valley and the lower portion of the trail you have just traveled.

Upon reaching the last switchback, an unmaintained spur trail branches north to the abandoned Glacier Pass Trail. Traveling a short distance up this path gives you a grand view up the Monarch Creek Canyon to Sawtooth Peak. After taking in the view, resume traveling on the main trail, and crest the ridge separating Monarch Creek from the Chihuahua Bowl.

On the other side of the ridge, the route ascends slightly on a long, straight track, then climbs another switchback to the junction with the Monarch Lakes Trail at 3 miles. Turn right (southeast), and head up the obscure trail leading to Crystal Lakes.

Wind through rocky terrain and stunted trees as you enter the Chihuahua Bowl. Here, you will have views over Farewell Canyon to the White Chief Bowl, White Chief Peak, Eagle Crest, and Miner's Ridge. Pass the mineshafts and tailings of the old Chihuahua Mine, located to your right (west). The narrow path continues its steep, zigzagging ascent, with Mineral Peak towering above in the east. After cresting a breezy second ridge, the trail drops sharply and the Cobalt Lakes come into view below.

The narrow route descends to a trail fork, with the right footpath leading south across Crystal Creek, through willows and meadows, then across granite slabs to the Cobalt Lakes. Proceed on the left (east) fork up the valley, and climb a few more rocky switchbacks to campsites on a narrow ledge

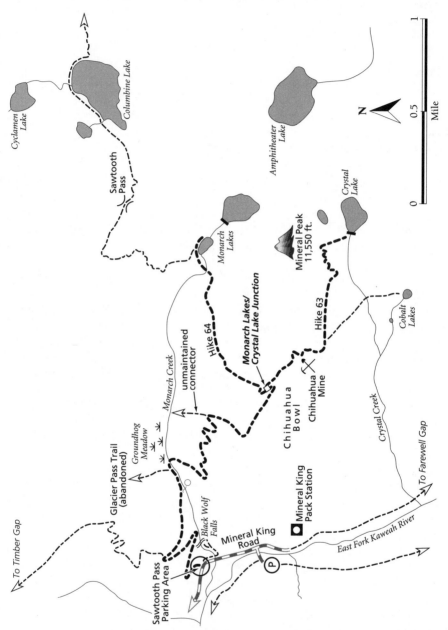

below the lower Crystal Lake (4.4 miles). This camping area is near the base of a dam built by the Mount Whitney Power Company around the turn of the last century. An unmaintained footpath leads up from this area, past the pretty lower lake to the smaller upper lake, and to more campsites.

To return, retrace your steps to the parking area (8.8 miles).

63 Monarch Lakes

Highlights: This hike takes you through the multicolored Monarch Canyon to serene lakes below Sawtooth Peak and Sawtooth Pass.

See Map on Page 208

Type of hike: Out-and-back, day hike or backpack.
Total distance: 8.2 miles.
Difficulty: Difficult (day hike); moderate (backpack).
Best months: July through October.
Maps: USGS Mineral King; Sequoia National Park Mineral King; or TOPO! Sequoia Kings Canyon CD-ROM.
Permits: Obtain a permit at the Mineral King Ranger Station if camping overnight.
Parking and facilities: Parking is available on both sides of Mineral King Road. Restrooms are located in the southern parking area and a "Charge A Call" phone (which only accepts calling cards or collect calls) is located in the northern parking area. No water is available.

Finding the trailhead: From central Three Rivers, drive north on California Highway 198 for approximately 3.9 miles to Mineral King Road, and turn right (east). Follow the narrow road for 10.1 miles to the Lookout Point entrance station. Continue east, losing and regaining pavement before passing Atwell Mill Campground. You will lose and regain the pavement again before Cabin Cove and the Silver City Store and Resort at approximately 20.5 miles. The road loses pavement once more, then becomes paved again, and reaches the Mineral King Ranger Station at 23.2 miles. The Sawtooth Pass parking area is 0.8 mile farther up the road.

Key points:
0.0   Trailhead.
0.6   Reach the Timber Gap Trail junction.
1.2   Make the Monarch Creek crossing.
3.0   Reach the trail fork.
4.1   Arrive at lower Monarch Lake.

The hike: Follow the trail to Timber Gap (Hike 61) to the junction at 0.6 mile, then follow the trail to Crystal Lakes (Hike 62) to the junction at 3 miles. Take the left (northeast) trail fork, and rise up switchbacks in a thinly forested area.

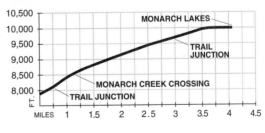

After rounding a curve, the path begins a long traverse over crushed rock on a wide shelf high above Monarch Creek. The abandoned Glacier Pass Trail can barely be seen across the canyon, with Timber Gap and Empire Mountain to the northwest. To the east you can spot the intimidating switchbacks of Sawtooth Pass, and possibly other hikers slowly ascending to or descending from the pass.

The path nears Monarch Creek's cascades, and you may see pikas, small relatives of the rabbit, scampering to hide as you pass an area of talus. After rock hopping two branches of the creek and climbing over a rocky hill, you arrive at the lower Monarch Lake at 4.1 miles. A pretty waterfall splashes down at the far end of the lake, while Sawtooth Peak appears as a nub to the east and Mineral Peak rises to the south. Campsites and bear boxes are just a little farther up the trail, on the northwest side of the lake, and an unmaintained trail travels along the north shore of this lake, leading to an arduous climb to the upper lake.

After enjoying your destination, return the way you came (8.2 miles).

Option: If you wish, you can continue another mile to Sawtooth Pass, adding on nearly another 1,000 feet of elevation gain. The trail passes spur trails to the old Glacier Pass Trail, then switchbacks through loose scree and broken granite, which is very slippery. The strenuous climb rewards you with views of Mount Eisen and Blackrock Pass to the north; the Kaweahs and the Sierra Crest from Mount Whitney to Cirque Peak to the northeast and east; and sparkling Columbine Lake below and Needham Mountain and Sawtooth Peak to the south.

64 Black Wolf Falls

Highlights:	This unmaintained footpath leads to the base of a beautiful waterfall, as well as to the entrance to an abandoned copper mine.
Type of hike:	Out-and-back, day hike.
Total distance:	0.25 mile.
Difficulty:	Very easy.
Best months:	June through October.
Maps:	USGS Mineral King; Sequoia National Park Mineral King; or TOPO! Sequoia Kings Canyon CD-ROM. (This trail does not actually appear on maps.)
Permits:	None.
Parking and facilities:	Parking is available on both sides of the road. There are restrooms in the southern parking area. A "Charge A Call" phone is in the northern parking area; you must use a calling card or call collect, as this phone won't accept change. No water is available.

Finding the trailhead: From central Three Rivers, drive north on California Highway 198 for approximately 3.9 miles to Mineral King Road, and turn right (east). Follow the road for 10.1 miles to the Lookout Point entrance station. Continue east, losing and regaining pavement before passing Atwell Mill Campground. You will lose and regain the pavement again before Cabin Cove and the Silver City Store and Resort at approximately 20.5 miles. The road loses pavement once more, then becomes paved again, and reaches the Mineral King Ranger Station at 23.2 miles. The Sawtooth Pass parking area is 0.8 mile farther up the road.

Key points:

    0.0   Trailhead.
    0.25   Reach Black Wolf Falls.

The hike: Follow Mineral King Road south from the parking area to a usually dry wash, just beyond the small bridges spanning Monarch Creek. The falls are already visible to your left (east). If the wash has swift moving water flowing in it, save this hike for another day.

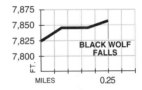

The cooling spill of Black Wolf Falls lies at the end of a very short hike.

Black Wolf Falls

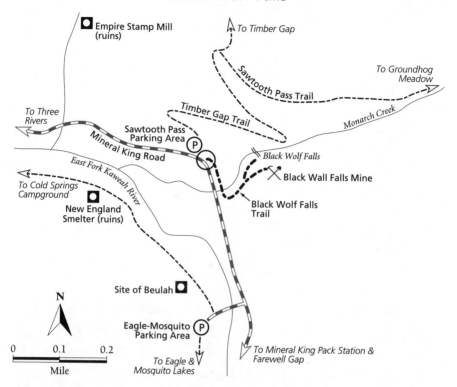

The unmaintained footpath begins on the north side of the wash, and may be tricky to find. If this is the case, walk in the wash until you see traces of foot traffic to your left (north). Then follow the rocky and sometimes dusty path a few hundred feet through the sagebrush and cross the wash. The peak to the northeast, above the falls, is Empire Mountain. Looking to the south you will be able to see (from left/east to right/west) Farewell Gap, Vandever Mountain, White Chief Peak, and Eagle Crest.

The path turns left (northeast) and becomes narrow and overgrown with foliage, but is easy to follow. A few hundred feet more, and you reach a fork in the trail. Caution should be exercised beyond this point. To the right, a steep descent leads to a large boulder near the base of Black Wolf Falls at 0.25 mile. In summer, wildflowers rim the tumbling water splashing over the golden-colored rock. Straight ahead is a rock ledge that leads through the overgrowth to the Black Wall Falls Mine, which is just to the right (south) of the falls. Differences in the names of the falls and the mine are thought to be a misinterpretation that stuck. Do not enter the mineshaft—there is always the danger of it caving in.

After you have enjoyed the falls, retrace your steps to the parking area.

Option: This hike is good for a lazy day, or can be combined with another hike in the area.

65 Franklin Lakes

Highlights: This trip brings you to the beautiful lower Franklin Lake, passing mines and meadows along the way.

Type of hike: Out-and-back, day hike or backpack.

Total distance: 10.8 miles.

Difficulty: Difficult.

Best months: July through October.

Maps: USGS Mineral King; Sequoia National Park Mineral King; USFS John Muir Wilderness and Sequoia–Kings Canyon Wilderness; or TOPO! Sequoia Kings Canyon CD-ROM.

Permits: Obtain a permit at the Mineral King Ranger Station if camping overnight.

Special considerations: This trail is used by horseback riders. Please remember proper trail etiquette by stepping off the trail on the downhill side and waiting quietly until the horses have passed. Stay in plain view of the horses; they may think you are a wild animal and bolt if you are hidden behind a rock or tree.

Parking and facilities: No restrooms or water are available at the trailhead. The nearest restrooms are located at the Sawtooth Pass Trailhead or across the road from the Mineral King Ranger Station. A "Charge A Call" phone (which only accepts calling cards or collect calls) is available. To reach the trailhead, walk back to the road fork and go right (south), toward the pack station. The trail begins just south of the corral.

Finding the trailhead: From central Three Rivers, drive north on California Highway 198 for approximately 3.9 miles to Mineral King Road and turn right (east). Follow the road for 10.1 miles to the Lookout Point entrance station. Continue east, losing and regaining the pavement before passing Atwell Mill Campground. Lose and regain the pavement again before Cabin Cove and the Silver City Store and Resort at approximately 20.5 miles. The road loses pavement once more, then becomes paved again, and reaches the Mineral King Ranger Station at 23.2 miles. The Eagle-Mosquito parking area is 1.3 miles farther down the Mineral King Road. At the junction with the dirt road to the pack station, turn right (southwest) and cross a wooden bridge to the parking area. Trailhead parking is not available at the pack station.

Key points:
- 0.0 Trailhead.
- 0.7 Cross Crystal Creek.
- 1.4 Cross Franklin Creek.
- 2.8 Reach the Franklin Lakes Trail.
- 5.4 Arrive at lower Franklin Lake.

The hike: The wide trail begins by traveling over a sage-covered low rise with Farewell Gap in view. The East Fork of the Kaweah River meanders through flowered meadows and willows to your right (west). A horse trail branches west to join the Eagle Crest Trail across the canyon. After passing

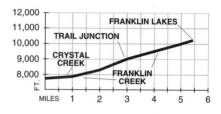

through stunted groves of quaking aspen, the path crosses shallow Crystal Creek at 0.7 mile. Located to your left (east), the creek tumbles down lacy cascades to the right (south) of Mineral Peak.

The path stays mostly level for about a mile, where it meets a side trail to Aspen Flat. Then the route climbs, rock-hopping Franklin Creek at 1.4 miles. After the creek crossing, the trail ascends several switchbacks, first with views of the many falls on the creek, then through a garden of colorful wildflowers. The path straightens its course and leaves the trees, entering a beautiful alpine zone. Farewell Gap comes back into view. Wildflowers, grasses, and sometimes patches of snow cover the steep hillsides as the East Fork cuts a deep canyon below. Marmots whistle and scamper about as you approach.

The trail swings toward the river, avoiding a closed section of trail, and mounts a hill before reaching the Franklin Lakes Trail at 2.8 miles. Turn left; the route heads north toward Franklin Creek, traversing high on the canyon wall, then enters the shade and contours into Franklin Canyon. Passing through multi-colored rock, the trail ascends a couple of switchbacks below the old Lady Franklin Mine. After traveling through a vivid rocky zone, the route dips into a willow-filled meadow below Rainbow Mountain and crosses Franklin Creek on stones, then switchbacks up past another mineshaft.

A dam holds back the waters of lower Franklin Lake.

Franklin Lakes • Farewell Gap

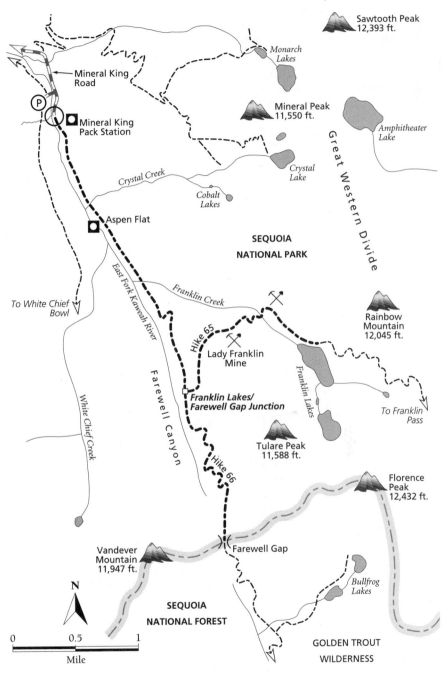

Sawtooth Peak
12,393 ft.

Monarch Lakes

Mineral King Road

P

Mineral King Pack Station

Crystal Creek

Mineral Peak
11,550 ft.

Amphitheater Lake

Great Western Divide

Crystal Lake

Cobalt Lakes

Aspen Flat

SEQUOIA
NATIONAL PARK

East Fork Kaweah River

Franklin Creek

Rainbow Mountain
12,045 ft.

To White Chief Bowl

Hike 65

Lady Franklin Mine

Franklin Lakes

**Franklin Lakes/
Farewell Gap Junction**

To Franklin Pass

Farewell Canyon

White Chief Creek

Tulare Peak
11,588 ft.

Hike 66

Florence Peak
12,432 ft.

Vandever Mountain
11,947 ft.

Farewell Gap

Bullfrog Lakes

N

SEQUOIA
NATIONAL FOREST

GOLDEN TROUT
WILDERNESS

0   0.5   1
Mile

A long section of trail leads through granite around another curve, and then up switchbacks past a small camping area with a bear box just below the lake. A rock-and-mortar dam, built by the Mount Whitney Power Company near the turn of the last century, still controls the flow of water here.

The path arrives at the north shore of lower Franklin Lake at 5.4 miles, with views of Florence and Tulare Peaks to the south, and more campsites equipped with bear boxes. An unmaintained footpath farther up the main trail leads south to the upper lake.

After your stay, return the way you came (10.8 miles).

Option: If you wish to continue to Franklin Pass, you will hike another 3 miles over scree-covered switchbacks, with more than 1,000 feet of elevation gain. Views to the northwest include the Castle Rocks and Paradise Peak. To the east, the Sierra Crest from Mount Whitney to Cirque Peak is visible. And to the south rise Florence and Tulare Peaks.

66 Farewell Gap

Highlights:	This excursion takes you to a windy gap, giving you a vista of the Mineral King Valley and a peek into the Golden Trout Wilderness.

See Map on Page 215

Type of hike:	Out-and-back, day hike.
Total distance:	11 miles.
Difficulty:	Difficult.
Best months:	July through September.
Maps:	USGS Mineral King; Sequoia National Park Mineral King; USFS John Muir Wilderness and Sequoia–Kings Canyon Wilderness; or TOPO! Sequoia Kings Canyon CD-ROM.
Permits:	None.
Special considerations:	This trail is used by horseback riders. Please remember proper trail etiquette by stepping off the trail on the downhill side and waiting quietly until the horses have passed. Stay in plain view of the horses; they may think you are a wild animal and bolt if you are hidden behind a rock or tree.
Parking and facilities:	No restrooms or water are available at the trailhead. The nearest restrooms are located at the Sawtooth Pass Trailhead or across the road from the Mineral King Ranger Station. A "Charge A Call" phone (which only accepts calling cards or collect calls) is available. To reach the trailhead, walk back to the road fork and go right (south), toward the pack station. The trail begins just south of the corral.

Finding the trailhead: From central Three Rivers, drive north on California Highway 198 for approximately 3.9 miles to Mineral King Road and turn right (east). Follow the road 10.1 miles to the Lookout Point entrance station. Continue east, losing and regaining the pavement before passing Atwell Mill Campground. Lose and regain the pavement again before Cabin Cove and the Silver City Store and Resort at approximately 20.5 miles. The road loses pavement once more, then becomes paved again, and reaches the Mineral King Ranger Station at 23.2 miles. The Eagle-Mosquito parking area is 1.3 miles farther down the Mineral King Road. At the junction with the dirt road to the pack station, turn right (southwest) and cross a wooden bridge to the parking area. Trailhead parking is not available at the pack station.

Key points:
- 0.0   Trailhead.
- 0.7   Cross Crystal Creek.
- 1.4   Cross Franklin Creek.
- 2.8   Pass the Franklin Lakes Trail.
- 5.5   Arrive at Farewell Gap.

The hike: Follow the trail to Franklin Lakes (Hike 65) to the junction with the Franklin Lakes Trail at 2.8 miles. Make a right (south) turn and begin switchbacking through stunted foxtail pines below Tulare Peak, crossing an abandoned segment of trail several times.

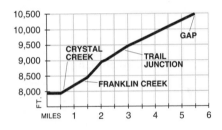

The route becomes more and more barren and rocky as you near the gap, though wildflowers add color to the grassy slopes below. After a traverse high on the canyon wall, you arrive at blustery Farewell Gap at 5.5 miles.

Views to the southeast include the Little Kern Drainage and the lower flanks of Hockett Peak in the Golden Trout Wilderness, as well as the back side of The Needles in the Sequoia National Forest. To the north are views over the Mineral King Valley to Timber Gap, Empire Mountain, and the tip of Mineral Peak.

Retrace your steps to the parking area after enjoying the view (11 miles).

67 White Chief Bowl

Highlights:	This trek to a magnificent alpine bowl passes the ruins of a cabin, an expansive meadow, mineshafts, and marble caverns.
Type of hike:	Out-and-back, backpack or day hike.
Total distance:	8.2 miles.
Difficulty:	Difficult.
Best months:	July through September.
Maps:	USGS Mineral King; Sequoia National Park Mineral King; USFS John Muir Wilderness and Sequoia–Kings Canyon Wilderness; or TOPO! Sequoia–Kings Canyon CD-ROM.
Permits:	Obtain a permit at the Mineral King Ranger Station if camping overnight.
Special considerations:	This trail is used by horseback riders. Please remember proper trail etiquette by stepping off the trail on the downhill side and waiting quietly until the horses have passed. Stay in plain view of the horses; they may think you are a wild animal and bolt if you are hidden behind a rock or tree.
Parking and facilities:	No restrooms or water are available at the trailhead. The nearest restrooms are located at the Sawtooth Pass Trailhead, or across the road from the Mineral King Ranger Station. A "Charge A Call" phone (which only accepts calling cards or collect calls) is available. The trail begins at the south end of the parking area.

Finding the trailhead: From central Three Rivers, drive north on California Highway 198 for approximately 3.9 miles to Mineral King Road and turn right (east). Follow the road for 10.1 miles to the Lookout Point entrance station. Continue east, losing and regaining the pavement before passing Atwell Mill Campground. Lose and regain the pavement again before Cabin Cove and the Silver City Store and Resort at approximately 20.5 miles. The road loses pavement once more, then becomes paved again, and reaches the Mineral King Ranger Station at 23.2 miles. The Eagle-Mosquito parking area is 1.3 miles farther down the Mineral King Road. At the junction with the dirt road to the pack station, turn right (southwest) and cross a wooden bridge to the parking area.

Key points:
0.0	Trailhead.
0.3	Cross Spring Creek.
0.9	Cross Eagle Creek.
1.0	Reach the trail junction.
2.0	Reach the cabin and White Chief Creek.
2.9	Pass the White Chief Mine.
4.1	Arrive at White Chief Bowl.

The hike: The trail immediately begins a slight ascent, passing the restored Honeymoon Cabin. Travel through sagebrush and avalanche-thinned firs and junipers; delicate wildflowers add a

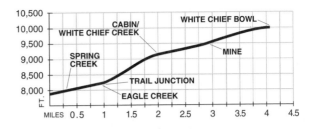

splash of color here and there. At 0.3 mile, cross Spring Creek on a wooden footbridge below Tufa Falls. The falls and the creek both originate from a spring high above you on the canyon wall. The Farewell Gap Trail (Hike 66) is across the canyon on the east bank of the East Fork of the Kaweah River.

After the creek crossing, a horse trail from the pack station across the river joins the trail to White Chief Bowl. Look east for a view up the cascades of Crystal Creek, tumbling down to the right (south) of Mineral Peak. Tulare Peak is to the southeast; the silver ribbon to its left (north) is Franklin Creek. Look north to see Timber Gap and Empire Mountain, high above the valley floor.

After stepping through the shallow waters of Eagle Creek at 0.9 mile, the climb steepens. Reach a trail fork at 1 mile, and continue straight (south) up the steep path. The route nears White Chief Creek, lined with blocks of metamorphic stone, and travels through more jagged rock before crossing the usually dry creek at 2 miles. Due to the porous nature of the marble in this area, White Chief Creek flows underground in some places. The meager ruins of Crabtree Cabin are to the right (west) of the trail, just before the creek crossing.

White Chief Meadow lies just below White Chief Bowl.

White Chief Bowl

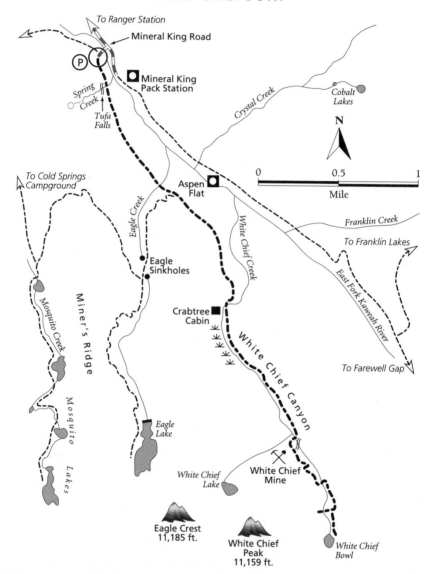

The path follows the edge of expansive White Chief Meadow, which is closed in by towering granite walls, then climbs up through a forested section, passing a primitive camping area on the right (west). The trail exits the trees and a pretty waterfall comes into view at the end of the lower portion of the canyon. As you near the waterfall, you can spot the creek trickling down from White Chief Lake, across the canyon to the right (west) of White Chief Peak. While a footpath continues to the base of the falls, a dim track splits off to the right (west), leading down to a rock-hop crossing of White Chief Creek and the continuation of the trail.

The route passes several mineshafts of the White Chief Mine at 2.9 miles, as switchbacks lead up through marble and metamorphic rock. Upon reaching the upper bench of the canyon, you pass sinkholes and marble caverns, then make another usually dry crossing of the creek. Do not attempt to enter any of the mineshafts or caverns—they are very dangerous!

Soon you reach a junction: The right fork leads to the ruins of a cavern-turned homestead, as well as a large sinkhole, and the left fork leads to White Chief Bowl. After passing through overgrown willows, you arrive at the canyon's end at 4.1 miles, where you will find steep rock walls, verdant meadows, and a small tarn. Hummingbirds flit about overhead, chattering as if you are there to challenge their food source, while Vandever Mountain towers above to the left (southeast) in dark and brooding colors.

Return the way you came (8.2 miles).

Options: This hike can be combined with Eagle Lake (Hike 68) or Mosquito Lakes (Hike 69) for an extended backpacking trip.

68 Eagle Lake

Highlights:	This trip brings you to a picturesque rockbound lake, and a large population of pikas.
Type of hike:	Out-and-back, backpack or day hike.
Total distance:	6.8 miles.
Difficulty:	Difficult.
Best months:	July through September.
Maps:	USGS Mineral King; Sequoia National Park Mineral King; USFS John Muir Wilderness and Sequoia–Kings Canyon Wilderness; or TOPO! Sequoia Kings Canyon CD-ROM.
Permits:	Obtain a permit at the Mineral King Ranger Station if camping overnight.
Parking and facilities:	No restrooms or water are available at the trailhead. The nearest restrooms are located at the Sawtooth Pass Trailhead or across the road from the Mineral King Ranger Station. A "Charge A Call" phone (which only accepts calling cards or collect calls) is available. The trail begins at the south end of the parking area.

Finding the trailhead: From central Three Rivers, drive north on California Highway 198 for 3.9 miles to Mineral King Road and turn right (east). Follow the road for 10.1 miles to the Lookout Point entrance station. Continue east, passing Atwell Mill Campground. Cabin Cove and the Silver City Store and Resort are at about 20.5 miles. Reach the Mineral King Ranger Station at 23.2 miles. To reach the Eagle-Mosquito parking area, continue for 1.3 miles down the Mineral King Road. At the junction with the dirt road to the pack station, turn right (southwest) and cross a wooden bridge to the parking area.

Key points:

- 0.0   Trailhead.
- 0.3   Cross Spring Creek.
- 1.0   Reach the Eagle/Mosquito Trail junction.
- 2.0   Pass the Mosquito Lakes Trail junction.
- 3.4   Reach Eagle Lake.

The hike: Follow the trail to White Chief Bowl (Hike 67) to the first trail junction at 1 mile, and make a right (west) turn on the trail to Eagle Lake and Mosquito Lakes. You then ascend the steep switchbacks; the pack station appears diminutive far below.

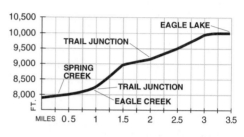

After climbing a bit more, you pass through a thick patch of woods, then come to a steeply sloped meadow and more switchbacks. The path levels and follows the dry canyon of Eagle Creek before arriving at the Eagle Sinkholes. Here, Eagle Creek disappears into a large, deep crater and flows underground (a result of the porous marble in this area), leaving its former streambed dry. Another sinkhole can be found farther down the onetime watercourse. Spring Creek may receive its water from a subterranean stream originating from this area.

After a few short switchbacks, you reach the Mosquito Lakes Trail junction at 2 miles. Continue straight (south) on the trail to Eagle Lake, passing an expansive meadow. Rise up more switchbacks to a smaller deep green meadow as the trail begins to climb an exposed talus slope. To the northeast, Mineral and Sawtooth Peaks are visible, as well as the Kaweah Group and the peaks north of the Middle Fork of the Kaweah River. You may see marmots, which live throughout the Mineral King area, but now you have entered the domain of the pika, a tiny relative of the rabbit with smaller, rounded ears. You will probably hear the pika's strange double-bark, sounding much like a rusty wagon wheel. To see the pika, you must sit still for a bit and look for movement among the talus blocks. They can be seen bounding from boulder to boulder, gathering their winter food supply of plants and grasses, as they do not hibernate.

As you near the lake, the trail levels slightly and enters a thin forest of foxtail pine. Reach Eagle Lake at 3.4 miles. A pit toilet is available, along with many tree-shaded campsites on the west side of the lake. Camping on the left side of the trail, along the shore of the lake, is prohibited, and campfires are not allowed.

Hundreds of pikas call to each other, sometimes nonstop, until dark. Eagle Crest walls in the lake to the east and patches of snow may linger among the rocks until late in the season. After you have enjoyed your stay at this rockbound lake, return to the trailhead (6.8 miles).

Options: This hike can be combined with White Chief Bowl (Hike 67) or Mosquito Lakes (Hike 69) for an extended backpacking trip.

Eagle Lake

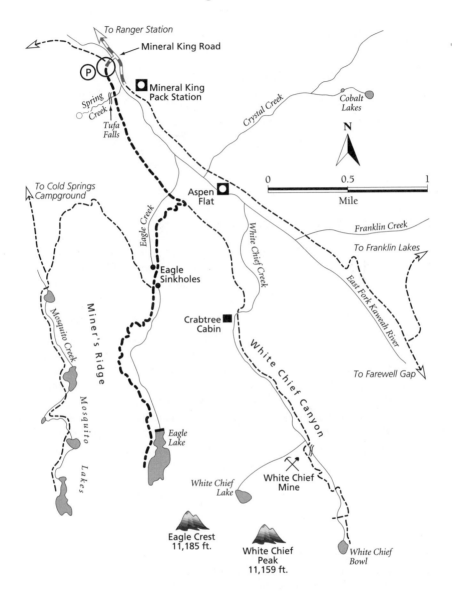

To Ranger Station
Mineral King Road
Mineral King Pack Station
P
Spring Creek
Tufa Falls
Crystal Creek
Cobalt Lakes
N
0   0.5   1
Mile
To Cold Springs Campground
Aspen Flat
Eagle Creek
White Chief Creek
Franklin Creek
To Franklin Lakes
East Fork Kaweah River
Eagle Sinkholes
Mosquito Creek
Miner's Ridge
Crabtree Cabin
White Chief Canyon
To Farewell Gap
Mosquito Lakes
Eagle Lake
White Chief Lake
White Chief Mine
Eagle Crest 11,185 ft.
White Chief Peak 11,159 ft.
White Chief Bowl

69 Mosquito Lakes

Highlights: This hike takes you on a nice trip to a pretty lake, perfect for a picnic lunch with time to relax on the shore.

Type of hike: Out-and-back, day hike.

Total distance: 7.2 miles.

Difficulty: Moderate.

Best months: July through September.

Maps: USGS Mineral King; Sequoia National Park Mineral King; USFS John Muir Wilderness and Sequoia–Kings Canyon Wilderness; or TOPO! Sequoia Kings Canyon CD-ROM.

Permits: Obtain a permit at the Mineral King Ranger Station if camping overnight.

Parking and facilities: No restrooms or water are available at the trailhead. The nearest restrooms are located at the Sawtooth Pass Trailhead or across the road from the Mineral King Ranger Station. A "Charge A Call" phone (which accepts only calling cards or collect calls) is available. The trail begins at the south end of the parking area.

Finding the trailhead: From central Three Rivers, drive north on California Highway 198 for approximately 3.9 miles to Mineral King Road and turn right (east). Follow the road 10.1 miles to the Lookout Point entrance station. Continue east, losing and regaining pavement before passing Atwell Mill Campground. Lose and regain the pavement again before Cabin Cove and the Silver City Store and Resort at approximately 20.5 miles. The road loses pavement once more, then becomes paved again, and reaches the Mineral King Ranger Station at 23.2 miles. To reach the Eagle-Mosquito parking area, continue for 1.3 miles down the Mineral King Road. At the junction with the dirt road to the pack station, turn right (southwest) and cross a wooden bridge to the parking area.

Key points:

0.0 Trailhead.
0.3 Cross Spring Creek.
1.0 Reach the Eagle/Mosquito Trail junction.
2.0 Reach the Mosquito Lakes Trail junction.
3.6 Arrive at the first Mosquito Lake.

The hike: Begin by following the trail to White Chief Bowl (Hike 67) to the junction with the trail to Eagle and Mosquito Lakes at 1 mile. Turn right (west) and follow the route to Eagle Lake (Hike 68), to the Mosquito

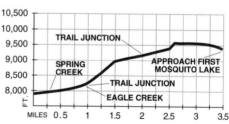

Mosquito Lakes

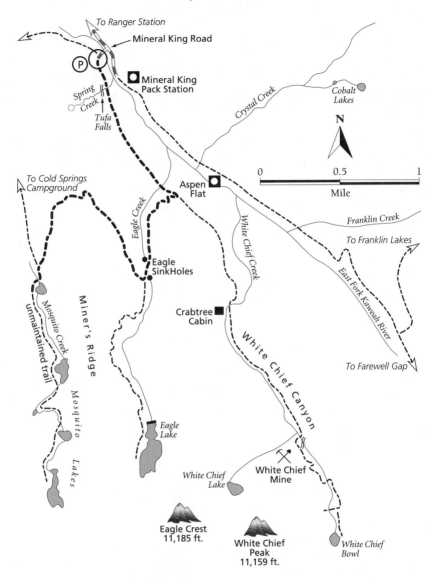

Lakes junction at 2 miles. Make another right (northwest) turn. The trail passes through a grassy meadow before winding up the slope and by an area of talus and tiny pikas. Views east across the Mineral King Valley to Sawtooth and Mineral Peaks are breathtaking. Behind you and to the south is dark and craggy Vandever Mountain.

The path steadily ascends Miner's Ridge through a shady fir forest, rounds a switchback, then descends short switchbacks through purple lupine to the first Mosquito Lake at 3.6 miles. Camping is not allowed at this lake, but it makes a good place to take a lunch break. An unmaintained trail crosses the outlet, passing another unmaintained route that leads down Mosquito Creek to Cold Springs Campground. This alternate path is much steeper than the main trail.

You can travel up the canyon on the easy unmaintained trail to the south side of the lake; then the path becomes more rugged and harder to follow. After you have finished exploring, return to the parking area (7.2 miles).

Options: Camping is available at Mosquito Lakes 2, 3, 4, and 5, which can be reached by following the unmaintained footpath that is sometimes marked with ducks, or by cross-country travel. To tour the upper lakes, stay west of the second lake, east of the third lake, and west of the fourth and fifth lakes. The best campsites are located at the fourth lake, while the fifth lake is the most scenic.

This hike can also be combined with White Chief Bowl (Hike 67) or Eagle Lake (Hike 68) for an extended backpacking trip.

70 Ladybug Camp and Whisky Log Camp

Highlights:	This trip follows the first portion of the historic Hockett Trail, a trans-Sierra route built in the 1860s, then leads to secluded campsites along the South Fork of the Kaweah River.
Type of hike:	Out-and-back, day hike or backpack.
Total distance:	8.4 miles.
Difficulty:	Moderate.
Best months:	Mid-March through May, October through mid-November.
Maps:	USGS Dennison Peak and Moses Mountain; USFS John Muir Wilderness and Sequoia–Kings Canyon Wilderness; or TOPO! Sequoia Kings Canyon CD-ROM.
Permits:	Obtain a permit at the South Fork Ranger Station if camping overnight.
Special considerations:	Mountain lions frequent this area; you are advised not to hike solo.
Parking and facilities:	Restrooms are located in the South Fork Campground. Day use parking is west of the campground; overnight parking is located east of the campground at the trailhead. The trail begins at the east end of the overnight parking area.

Finding the trailhead: From central Three Rivers, follow South Fork Drive southeast, then east, to the Sequoia National Park boundary. The pavement ends at the park boundary. Continue on the dirt road to South Fork Campground, which is approximately 13 miles from Three Rivers.

Key points:
- 0.0 Trailhead.
- 0.3 Pass the Clough Cave side trail.
- 0.5 Meet Pigeon Creek.
- 1.0 Cross Squaw Creek.
- 1.9 Reach Ladybug Camp and the trail junction.
- 3.2 Cross Cedar Creek.
- 4.2 Reach Whisky Log Camp.

The hike: The trail begins by following the south bluff of the South Fork of the Kaweah, then crosses the river on a long wooden footbridge. Upon reaching the other side and after a short climb, pass a dim path to the left (north) at 0.3 mile. This side trail rises uphill to Clough Cave, home to a colony of endangered bats. The path becomes narrow and washed out before arriving at the cave's entrance, which has been barred to prevent vandalism.

Beyond the cave, head east along the rocky main trail through the shade of oaks and cedars and abundant poison oak. Side trails branch off toward the river, and you pass a long-abandoned trail that climbs to Salt Creek Ridge. Meet the rarely flowing Pigeon Creek at 0.5 mile. The

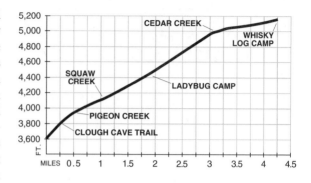

trail continues east, traversing high above the river on rocky shelves, with a view of a waterfall on Putnam Creek across the canyon.

The trail then curves into the Squaw Creek canyon and crosses the watercourse on a small log at 1 mile. The path swings back to the southeast, with views across the South Fork of the Kaweah to Dennison Ridge. Flat areas appear along the river below and you reach a signed trail junction, as well as Ladybug Camp, at 1.9 miles.

Follow a footpath down to Ladybug Camp, which is just below the trail to the right (south), along the banks of the river. Here, you can find wintering ladybugs on the undersides of fallen leaves during the cooler months of the hiking season. Be careful not to harm them as you explore.

Return to the trail junction and follow the east-trending path to its demise at the river. Metal stakes stick up through the granite, ruins of a bridge

The distinctive hump of Homer's Nose rises above the trail to Ladybug and Whisky Log Camps.

228

Ladybug and Whisky Log Camps • Garfield Grove

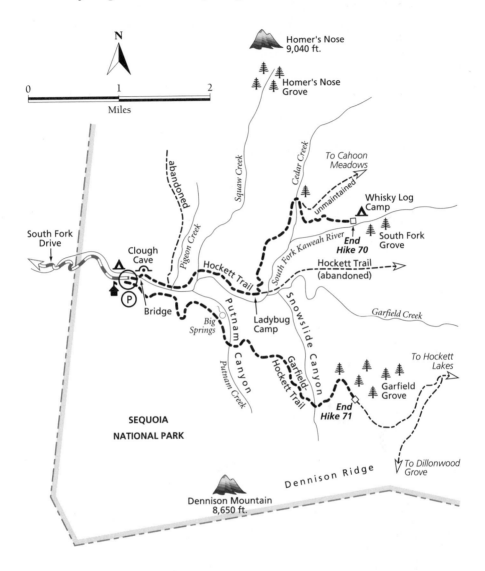

that collapsed in 1969 under an exceptionally heavy snowpack. The historic Hockett Trail continues on the other side of the river. This trail was constructed to transport supplies to the silver mines on the east side of the Sierra Nevada. It is now quite overgrown up to the point where it joins the Garfield-Hockett Trail, which also leads into the backcountry. Across the river, near the confluence of Garfield Creek, stands a single sequoia growing at one of the lowest elevations in the world. It is thought that, as a seedling, this tree was washed down the slope from the Garfield Grove in an 1876 landslide.

Return to the trail junction and make a right (north) turn, climbing switch-backs, then traveling high above the river along an open, grassy hillside. You have a nice view of Homer's Nose and Cahoon Rock to the north. After reentering the forest, reach Cedar Creek at 3.2 miles, and cross on a large log. Sequoias line the banks of the creek; trek uphill on an increasingly brushy trail, passing a dim but still signed trail to Cahoon Meadow.

The path becomes more narrow and eroded as it contours around the steep hillsides. Dip down to Whisky Log Camp at 4.2 miles, which has campsites among large logs and the sequoias of the South Fork Grove, most of which are across the river. Beyond the campsites, the trail continues on to a bluff along the river, but is covered with blowdowns and is very hard to follow.

After a peaceful rest or overnight stay, return the way you came (8.4 miles).

71 Garfield Grove

Highlights:	This hike takes you from the flora of the foothills to a shady sequoia grove.
Type of hike:	Out-and-back, day hike.
Total distance:	8.6 miles.
Difficulty:	Difficult.
Best months:	July through November.
Maps:	USGS Dennison Peak and Moses Mountain; USFS John Muir Wilderness and Sequoia–Kings Canyon Wilderness; or TOPO! Sequoia Kings Canyon CD-ROM.
Permits:	None.
Special considerations:	Mountain lions frequent this area; you are advised not to hike solo.
Parking and facilities:	Restrooms are located in the South Fork Campground. Day use parking is west of the campground; restrooms are available here, too. The trail begins in the campground, east of the overnight parking area.

See Map on Page 229

Finding the trailhead: From central Three Rivers, follow South Fork Drive southeast, then east, to the Sequoia National Park boundary. The pavement ends at the park boundary. Continue on the dirt road to South Fork Campground, which is approximately 13 miles from Three Rivers.

Key points:

- 0.0   Trailhead.
- 1.3   Pass Big Springs.
- 2.0   Enter Putnam Canyon.
- 3.5   Cross Snowslide Canyon.
- 3.8   Pass a campsite.
- 4.3   Arrive at Garfield Grove.

The hike: The trail begins by rising steeply under the shade of oaks, with baby-blue-eyes as a ground cover in the spring. You have a view north of bulbous Homer's Nose as the path bends into tiny side canyons to cross seasonal creeks.

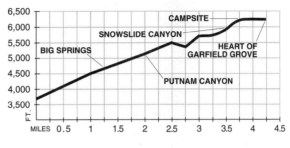

At about 1.3 miles you pass above Big Springs, which flows year-round. At 2 miles, you'll reach avalanche-sheared Putnam Canyon. The trail continues its ascent, traversing the South Fork Canyon's wall below Dennison Mountain.

After about a mile you begin to see sequoias. At 3.5 miles, you arrive at Snowslide Canyon. During years of heavy snowfall, this canyon can be snowbound into midsummer. The route passes above a campsite at 3.8 miles. And you will reach the heart of shady Garfield Grove at 4.3 miles.

It is possible to travel farther if you wish—at 5.5 miles you will intersect the abandoned Summit Trail, which leads up and over Dennison Ridge to the Dillonwood Grove (recently purchased by the Save the Redwoods League and soon to be added to Sequoia National Park), and then eventually to Summit Meadow and Lake. Otherwise, return as you came.

Option: If you would like to make this a backpacking trip, this trail can be followed past the abandoned section of the historic Hockett Trail all the way to the Hockett Lakes and the Hockett Plateau. The elevation gain is frightful, though—nearly 5,000 feet in less than 10 miles.

Hikes in and near the Jennie Lakes Wilderness

All hikes in this chapter leave from trailheads located off of Big Meadows Road, and are listed from west to east.

72 Weaver Lake

Highlights:	This enjoyable hike takes you by a pretty meadow, past superior views, and on to a striking lake—warm enough for swimming—at the base of Shell Mountain.
Type of hike:	Out-and-back, day hike.
Total distance:	6.4 miles.
Difficulty:	Easy.
Best months:	June through October.
Maps:	USGS Muir Grove; USFS Monarch and Jennie Lakes Wilderness; USFS John Muir Wilderness and Sequoia–Kings Canyon Wilderness; or TOPO! Sequoia Kings Canyon CD-ROM.
Permits:	None.
Parking and facilities:	A restroom is located at this trailhead, and campsites are available at its south end, but there is no water. The old trail began at the pay phone on Big Meadows Road, climbed over the hill, and passed through the campground to a sometimes wet crossing of Big Meadows Creek. The new trail starts at the northeast end of the parking area.

Finding the trailhead: Drive 9 miles south from Grant Grove on the Generals Highway to the signed Big Meadows Road (Forest Road 14S11), which is just past the Big Baldy Trailhead. Turn left (northeast), and follow the road past the ranger station and the former trailhead at the pay phone, to the new Big Meadows Trailhead parking area, which is on the right (south) at 12.9 miles, before the campgrounds.

Key points:
- 0.0   Trailhead.
- 0.6   Make the creek crossing.
- 1.4   Cross an unmapped trail at Fox Meadow.
- 1.8   Pass the Jennie Lake Trail junction.
- 3.0   Meet the Weaver Lake Trail.
- 3.2   Arrive at Weaver Lake.

The hike: The new portion of Forest Trail 29E05 leads downhill through an area where several good campsites in Big Meadows Campground were removed, unfortunately, to accommodate it. Cross Big Meadows Creek on a new wooden footbridge to a four-way junction. An anglers' trail

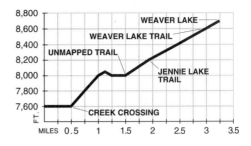

heads south along the creek, and a footpath/cow trail leads uphill straight ahead, then over to Big Meadows. Your route is the well-worn path to the left (east), which leads to a trail register.

The trail travels uphill, around a granite ridge, and follows an unnamed creek before crossing the watercourse at 0.6 mile. Climb into an open, sunny area where a side trail branches off to the left (northeast), heading toward a barren ridgetop before rejoining the rocky main route. The path reenters the forest and rises to cross a ridge, where you have views to the north of Spanish Mountain, Obelisk, and the Monarch Divide.

Another side trail, this time branching to the right (south), leads uphill and back to rejoin the main route. The trail to Weaver Lake descends to an unmapped pathway at beautiful Fox Meadow at 1.4 miles. (The unmapped path leads up from Forest Road 14S16.)

Wind around this patch of green in a dense woodland, then ascend through the thinning trees to the junction with the trail to Jennie Lake (Hike 73) at 1.8 miles. Make a left (northeast) turn onto Forest Trail 30E06 and step across a creek tumbling down from a small, unnamed lake near the base of Shell Mountain, then pass into the Jennie Lakes Wilderness.

The climb lessens a bit as the trail becomes stonier, and you may see the top of Shell Mountain peeking over the trees. The route spans a seasonal creek as well as the sometimes dry Weaver Creek, then arrives at trail signs and the short path forking to Weaver Lake on the right (south) at 3 miles.

A brief clamber through a rocky obstacle course deposits you at the shore of Weaver Lake below the rugged face of Shell Mountain at 3.2 miles. Campsites are along the grassy shores and a large camp is just north of the lake; this site is visible from the trail, on the right (west) side of the short path leading to the lake from the main route.

After relishing the scenery, take the same route back to the trailhead at 6.4 miles.

Option: This hike can also be done as an easy overnighter.

Weaver Lake • Jennie Lake

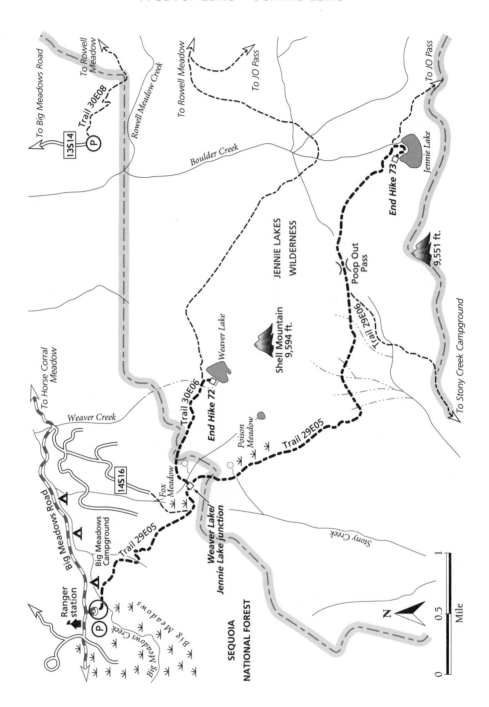

73 Jennie Lake

Highlights:	This trip takes you past a couple of attractive meadows, offers superb views, and ends at the exquisite namesake of the Jennie Lakes Wilderness.
Type of hike:	Out-and-back, backpack.
Total distance:	12.4 miles.
Difficulty:	Moderate.
Best months:	Mid-June through October.
Maps:	USGS Muir Grove; USFS Monarch and Jennie Lakes Wilderness; USFS John Muir Wilderness and Sequoia–Kings Canyon Wilderness; or TOPO! Sequoia Kings Canyon CD-ROM.
Permits:	None.
Parking and facilities:	A restroom is located at this trailhead, and campsites are available at its south end, but there is no water. The old trail began at the pay phone, climbed over the hill, and passed through the campground to a sometimes wet crossing of Big Meadows Creek. The new trail starts at the northeast end of the parking area.

> See Map on Page 234

Finding the trailhead: Drive 9 miles south from Grant Grove on the Generals Highway to the signed Big Meadows Road (Forest Road 14S11), which is beyond the Big Baldy Trailhead. Turn left (northeast), and follow the road past the ranger station and former trailhead at the pay phone to the new Big Meadows Trailhead parking area, which is on the right (south) before the campgrounds at 12.9 miles.

Key points:
- 0.0 Trailhead.
- 0.6 Make the creek crossing.
- 1.4 Pass the unmapped trail.
- 1.8 Reach the Weaver Lake Trail junction.
- 2.0 Pass the wilderness boundary.
- 4.4 Reach the Stony Creek Trail junction.
- 4.8 Cross Poop Out Pass.
- 6.2 Arrive at Jennie Lake.

The hike: Begin by following Forest Trail 29E05, also the route to Weaver Lake (Hike 72), to the junction with the trail to Weaver Lake at 1.8 miles. Make a right (south) turn and follow the Jennie Lake Trail uphill; it eventually levels out in a thick fir forest.

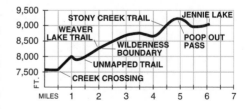

Enter the Jennie Lakes Wilderness at 2 miles, and continue to the lower end of long and peaceful Poison Meadow, rock hopping its small brook. The path skirts the edge of the expansive meadow in the woods, then climbs again as the trees become sparser. A view opens on the right (southwest) of Big Baldy Ridge and Chimney Rock before you round a ridge of Shell Mountain.

The trail rises and dips to cross several seasonal tributaries of Stony Creek, with vistas of the hazy San Joaquin Valley along the way. The timbered gap ahead is Poop Out Pass. At 4.4 miles, after another ascent, you meet Forest Trail 29E06, which leads up from Stony Creek Campground. Another taxing climb brings you to the vast expanse of Poop Out Pass at 4.8 miles.

After crossing the nearly level area of the pass, the route descends, first gently, then steeply switchbacking through talus. Dip across a seasonal creek, then climb through more granite for a view to the north of the Monarch Divide, Mount Maddox, and Mitchell Peak.

The trail descends and rises again, this time to meet the short spur trail to Jennie Lake. Take the spur trail right (south) to the lakeshore at 6.2 miles. There are many pleasant campsites all along the north shore of the lake.

After your stay, follow the trail back to the parking area at 12.4 miles.

Option: This hike can also be done as a long, ambitious day hike for a more challenging trip.

Lovely Jennie Lake lends its name to a wilderness area bordering Sequoia and Kings Canyon National Parks.

74 Deer Meadow

Highlights:	This lightly traveled path leads to excellent views and an old, collapsed cabin on the edge of a peaceful meadow.
Type of hike:	Out-and-back, day hike.
Total distance:	3 miles.
Difficulty:	Moderate.
Best months:	June through October.
Maps:	USGS Wren Peak; USFS Monarch and Jennie Lakes Wilderness; USFS John Muir Wilderness and Sequoia–Kings Canyon Wilderness; or TOPO! Sequoia Kings Canyon CD-ROM.
Permits:	None.
Parking and facilities:	There are no facilities at this trailhead. The trail begins at the north end of the parking area between two large rocks.

Finding the trailhead: Drive 9 miles south from Grant Grove on the Generals Highway to Big Meadows Road (Forest Road 14S11), which is just beyond the Big Baldy Trailhead. Turn left (northeast) and follow the road past the ranger station, Big Meadows Trailhead, and the campgrounds. The road narrows, crosses Big Meadows Creek, and passes a few spur roads before entering a deep canyon and crossing Boulder Creek at a large curve. Pass Forest Road 13S14 on the right (south), which is signed for the pack station and Sunset Meadow, then cross Horse Corral Creek. Continue to the next dirt road on the left (north)—Forest Road 13S11—at 18 miles. Turn left and follow the dirt road to the trailhead parking area at 18.8 miles.

Key points:
- 0.0 Trailhead.
- 0.8 Take the cross-country route to Peak 8,644.
- 0.9 Reach Peak 8,644.
- 1.5 Arrive at Deer Meadow.

The hike: Forest Trail 30E05 immediately begins a steady climb, passing through snowbrush and purple thistle. The narrow path leads past a flat metal stake with the word "trail" printed vertically on it, and passes through thimbleberries and pines as it follows a small stringer meadow. Cur-

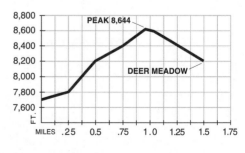

rants and willows line the route in a logged clearing. You then climb up through the forest before switchbacking through manzanita and granite outcroppings on the southwestern ridge of Peak 8,644.

Deer Meadow

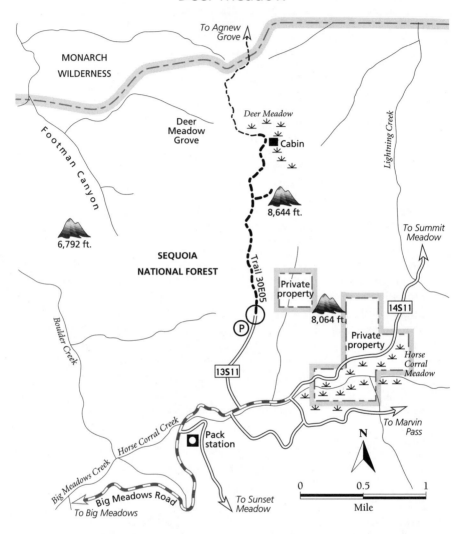

The path reaches its highest point at 0.8 mile, giving you a nice view to the west, through gaps in the trees, of Buck Rock, Burton Pass, the Kennedy Grove, and the Boulder Creek Canyon, and to the northwest of Marble Mountain, Spanish Mountain, and Obelisk. To your right (east), an easy cross-country side trip leads to the top of Peak 8,644 at 0.9 mile, and gives you fine views to the northeast and east of the Monarch Divide, the Sierra Crest, and Kings Canyon, with Lookout Peak (Hike 76) in the foreground. Mitchell Peak, Mount Maddox, Mount Silliman, and Shell Mountain are visible to the southeast.

Return to the main trail, which becomes a bit steep as you begin a descent under the shade of firs. The path passes a small meadow before entering a deeply forested area. You then proceed by another small meadow, reenter the forest, and cross the creek that waters Deer Meadow, which you reach at 1.5 miles. A collapsed cabin is located between some trees and fallen logs on the edge of the long, pretty meadow.

When you are ready to return, retrace your journey to the parking area (3 miles).

Options: If you wish to continue, you can follow this route into the Monarch Wilderness to the old Kanawyer Trail (Forest Trail 30E04) at 1.9 miles, which connects Camp Seven and Evans Grove with Cedar Grove. Agnew Grove is another 0.7 mile to the west. An excursion to Agnew Grove would add 5.2 miles and 1,180 feet of elevation gain to your trip.

The dilapidated cabin in Deer Meadow is an interesting relic of history, but offers dubious shelter in the case of a rainstorm.

75 Mitchell Peak

Highlights:	This trip takes you to a spectacular 360-degree vista on top of a windblown 10,365-foot peak.
Type of hike:	Out-and-back, day hike.
Total distance:	6.4 miles.
Difficulty:	Difficult.
Best months:	Mid-June through October.
Maps:	USGS Muir Grove and Mount Silliman; USFS Monarch and Jennie Lakes Wilderness; USFS John Muir Wilderness and Sequoia–Kings Canyon Wilderness; or TOPO! Sequoia Kings Canyon CD-ROM.
Permits:	None.
Special considerations:	A risk of being struck by lightning exists on the summit of Mitchell Peak. If dark clouds are nearby, or if hail, rain, thunder, or static electricity are in the air, descend immediately. Because the trail is used heavily by horseback riders and can be very dusty, the best times to hike are early in the season, when lingering moisture from snowmelt keeps the dust down, or later in the season, when rain showers settle the dust. If you meet horses on the trail, remember proper trail etiquette by stepping off the trail on the downhill side and waiting quietly until the horses have passed. Stay in plain view of the horses; they may think you are a wild animal and bolt if you are hidden behind a rock or tree.
Parking and facilities:	There are no facilities at this trailhead. Bring your own water. A small campsite is at the north end of the parking area. Restrooms are available 7.8 miles back down the road at the Big Meadows Trailhead. The trail begins at the southeast end of the parking area, behind the bulletin boards.

Finding the trailhead: Drive 9 miles south from Grant Grove on the Generals Highway to the signed Big Meadows Road (Forest Road 14S11), which is just beyond the Big Baldy Trailhead. Turn left (northeast) and follow the road past the ranger station, Big Meadows Trailhead, and the campgrounds. The road narrows, crosses Big Meadows Creek, and passes a few spur roads before entering a deep canyon and crossing Boulder Creek at a large curve. Pass the side road to the pack station, Sunset Meadow, and the Rowell Meadow Trailhead. Cross Horse Corral Creek, and continue to Forest Road 14S12, the second dirt road on the right (south) at 18.3 miles. This road is signed for the Marvin Pass Trailhead. Make a right (south) turn and follow the rough dirt road, passing several unsigned spur roads. It is easy to distinguish the main road until you reach the last unsigned spur road. It continues straight (east); make a right (south) turn on FR 14S12, following the smoother, well-used route to its end at the trailhead parking area at 20.6 miles.

Key points:
- 0.0   Trailhead.
- 0.2   Reach the trail to private property.
- 1.0   Cross Marvin Pass.
- 1.7   Reach the Mitchell Peak Trail.
- 3.2   Arrive on Mitchell Peak.

The hike: The trail, Forest Trail 30E43, follows an abandoned logging road for just a few feet and abruptly turns south at a wooden trail sign. The dusty path climbs to cross a ridge, then turns east and levels in a logged area, passing through currants, manzanita, and snowbrush. You can see Marvin Pass, the low wooded gap to the right (south). A trail that leads north to private property is reached at 0.2 mile. The footpath turns south again, rock hops a small brook and skirts a meadow clipped short by grazing cattle, then ascends several switchbacks. You may notice a horse trail to your right (west) along the way, which comes up from one of the spur roads passed on the drive to the trailhead. The trail crests timbered Marvin Pass at 1 mile and enters the Jennie Lakes Wilderness. This is a good place to rest and refuel.

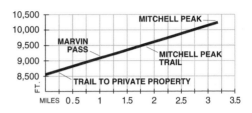

The Marvin Pass Trail continues straight (south), heading downhill to Rowell Meadow. Make a left (east) turn, and follow Forest Trail 30E07 between two large boulders and toward Mitchell Peak. The route rises and dips, passing through shady forest and dry, sunny slopes dotted with red skyrockets and lupine. Meadows are visible below you on the right (south). At 1.7 miles you reach the Mitchell Peak Trail (Forest Trail 30E07A), and again turn left (northeast). The route climbs gradually at first, and comes to a clearing from which you can see your destination—the rocky mountaintop on the right (east).

The path ascends more steeply and crosses the western ridge emanating from the peak. The grade lessens, and views of Horse Corral Meadow, where

The top of Mitchell Peak offers views of Sugarloaf Valley and the Great Western Divide.

Mitchell Peak

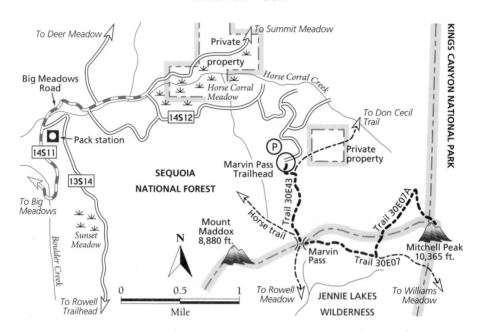

the last grizzly bear in California was shot in 1922, can be seen through the trees, downhill to the left (northwest). As the slope becomes steeper, the trail turns south and winds up through a thinning forest of foxtail pines and an undergrowth of lupines and phlox. Reach granite blocks, and follow ducks up through the talus that caps the peak. Some maneuvering through the blocks is necessary to attain the summit; go slowly and carefully.

Upon reaching a mostly flat area, you will see the pinnacle—the high point a few feet ahead of you at 3.2 miles. If you don't wish to climb to this small roost, you can see the view from the west and east sides of the mountaintop. A concrete slab on the west side of the summit is all that is left of the Mitchell Peak Lookout, but it provides a good spot to take in the views to the south, west, north, and northeast. A granite balcony on the east side of the pinnacle makes a great place to take in the views to the east and southeast.

To the northwest, in front of the John Muir Wilderness, is the Kings River Canyon, Spanish Mountain, and Obelisk; on a clear day, you can see Dogtooth Peak in the Dinkey Lakes Wilderness. To the north are the Monarch Divide, Mount Goddard, and northern Kings Canyon National Park. To the northeast is the country surrounding the headwaters of the Kings River, along with Middle Palisade on the Sierra Crest. The Great Western Divide is to the east, with Sugarloaf Valley below. The Kaweahs tower above all else to the southeast, and the Tablelands, Mount Silliman, Twin Peaks, and Kettle Peak rise to the south. Looking from the southwest to the west, you can see Poop Out Pass, Shell Mountain, Rowell Meadow, Mount Maddox, and Buck Rock Lookout.

After you have delighted in the vista, return to the trailhead at 6.4 miles.

76 Lookout Peak

Highlights:	This short hike to a small, rocky peak offers outstanding views down the Kings River Canyon, but it is not for acrophobics.
Type of hike:	Out-and-back, day hike.
Total distance:	1 mile.
Difficulty:	Difficult.
Best months:	June through October.
Maps:	USGS Cedar Grove; USFS Monarch and Jennie Lakes Wilderness; or TOPO! Sequoia Kings Canyon CD-ROM.
Permits:	None.
Special considerations:	A risk of being struck by lightning exists on the summit of Lookout Peak. If dark clouds are nearby, or if hail, rain, thunder, or static electricity are in the air, descend immediately.
Parking and facilities:	There are no facilities available at this trailhead. The trail begins on the northwest side of the parking area. A campsite is located near the beginning of the trail.

Finding the trailhead: Drive 9 miles south from Grant Grove on the Generals Highway to the signed Big Meadows Road (Forest Road 14S11), which is just beyond the Big Baldy Trailhead. Turn left (northeast), and follow the road past the ranger station, the Big Meadows Trailhead, and the campgrounds. The road narrows, crosses Big Meadows Creek, and passes a few spur roads before entering a deep canyon and crossing Boulder Creek at a large curve. Pass Forest Road 13S14, which leads to the pack station, Sunset Meadow, and the Rowell Meadow Trailhead, then cross Horse Corral Creek and pass Forest Road 14S12, which leads to the Marvin Pass Trailhead. Big Meadows Road loses pavement, skirts Horse Corral Meadow, passes many spur roads, and bisects Summit Meadow before ending at the trailhead parking area at 22.3 miles.

Key points:
- 0.0   Trailhead.
- 0.5   Reach the Lookout Peak summit.

The hike: The trail begins at a metal stake with "trail" printed vertically on it. Ascend gradually through manzanita and a thin forest, where you may hear chickadees and nuthatches calling from the trees above. The path switchbacks steeply up the slope, passing through boulders as you near the first and lowest microwave tower.

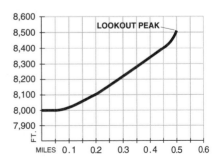

Lookout Peak

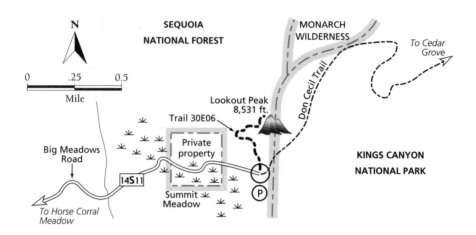

The route then leads very steeply up through manzanita and rock to a slot where some class 2 rock climbing skills are required. On the other side of this slot, you will reach a deep crevice; keep to the right and carefully lower yourself down the rocks to a thin ridge, where you will enjoy views up and down the Kings Canyon.

Directly across the canyon are Wren Peak, the Eagle Peaks, Mount Harrington, and the remainder of the Monarch Divide. As you look up the canyon to the east the most prominent spires are Mount Clarence King, Mount Gardiner, and Mount Rixford. To the southeast, Mount Farquhar, North Guard, Mount Brewer, and South Guard on the Great Western Divide are visible. After catching your breath and enjoying the views, return the way you came (1 mile).

Hikes in the Sugarloaf Valley and Mount Silliman Area

The hikes in this chapter begin from the Rowell Meadow Trailhead at the end of Forest Road 13S14. The hikes lead into the southern portion of Kings Canyon National Park.

77 Roaring River

Highlights:	This journey takes you past the spire of Sugarloaf, to the deafening Roaring River at the foot of Cloud and Deadman Canyons.
Type of hike:	Out-and-back, backpack.
Total distance:	26.2 miles.
Difficulty:	Difficult.
Best months:	Mid-June through October.
Maps:	USGS Muir Grove, Mount Silliman, and Sphinx Lakes; USFS John Muir Wilderness and Sequoia–Kings Canyon Wilderness; or TOPO! Sequoia Kings Canyon CD-ROM.
Permits:	Obtain a permit at the Grant Grove Visitor Center.
Special considerations:	Because the trail is used heavily by horseback riders and can be very dusty, the best times to hike are early in the season, when lingering moisture from snowmelt keeps the dust down, or later in the season, when rain showers settle the dust. If you meet horses on the trail, remember proper trail etiquette by stepping off the trail on the downhill side and waiting quietly until the horses have passed. Stay in plain view of the horses; they may think you are a wild animal and bolt if you are hidden behind a rock or tree.
Parking and facilities:	Both water and a large, new outhouse are available at the trailhead. The trail begins at the north end of the parking area, near the entrance.

Finding the trailhead: Drive 9 miles south from Grant Grove on the Generals Highway to the signed Big Meadows Road (Forest Road 14S11), which is just beyond the Big Baldy Trailhead. Turn left (northeast) and follow the road past the ranger station, Big Meadows Trailhead, and the campgrounds. The road narrows, crosses Big Meadows Creek, and passes a few spur roads before entering a deep canyon and crossing Boulder Creek at a large curve. At 17 miles you reach Forest Road 13S14, which is signed for the pack station and Rowell Meadow Trailhead. Turn right (east, then south) and follow the rough dirt road to its end at the trailhead parking area (20 miles).

Key points:

- 0.0   Trailhead.
- 1.1   Reach the Jennie Lakes Wilderness boundary.
- 2.0   Reach the JO Pass Trail junction.
- 2.4   Arrive at the four-way junction.
- 3.7   Reach the park boundary.
- 6.0   Pass the Seville Lake Trail junction.
- 7.6   Reach the side trail to the packers' campsite at Sugarloaf Meadow.
- 9.2   Make the Sugarloaf Creek crossing.
- 10.5 Cross Ferguson Creek.
- 13.1 Reach the Roaring River.

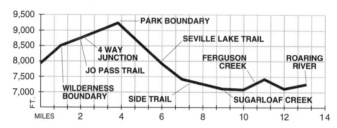

The hike: As you start up Forest Trail 30E08, you will pass a trail register. Head uphill, meeting a track from the pack station as you turn south. After passing through an open, rocky area, the trail switchbacks. A large, salmon-colored outcrop is above you on the top of the ridge. The trail becomes more exposed, crossing large rocks and slabs, and you can hear the rushing of Rowell Meadow Creek below. At 1.1 miles, reach a wooden sign denoting the Jennie Lakes Wilderness boundary.

The trail follows Rowell Meadow Creek, then one of its tributaries, which is lined with mountain bluebells in summer. The route continues uphill, and eventually crosses the tributary just before the junction with the JO Pass Trail at 2 miles. Beyond, you reach a snow survey cabin and expansive Rowell Meadow. When this meadow is not grazed, it is filled with lavender-colored asters in the summer. A family of marmots may be living under the cabin.

From the cabin, the level trail travels through an area thick with purple

Sugarloaf rises above Sugarloaf Meadow along the Roaring River route.

penstemons and crosses Rowell Meadow Creek on a wooden bridge. Large campsites are located to the right (south) of the path among the lodgepole pines. At the signed four-way junction at 2.4 miles, take the trail straight (east) to the Roaring River.

The route climbs steeply, crosses a small ridge, then dips and rises, crossing seasonal brooks before reaching the park boundary at 3.7 miles. The path begins a sharp descent, passing a seasonal creek and Pond Meadow. A picture-perfect view of the Great Western Divide opens to the east, where you feel you can almost reach out and touch the peaks.

After crossing a tiny tributary of Sugarloaf Creek and the meadow it irrigates, the trail meanders through the woods and down the steep slope. You will pass a north-trending path to Williams Meadow, and arrive at the Seville Lake Trail at 6 miles. A few more steps bring you to Comanche Meadow; campsites and a bear box are located on the south side of the trail. A step-across ford of the tiny brook emerging from the meadow, and the wider crossing of the shallow stream flowing down from Williams Meadow follows.

The path winds down another steep slope, thinly forested with Jeffrey pine. You may notice a vanilla scent as you walk by the first few trees. The route parallels aspen and cottonwood-lined Sugarloaf Creek, then veers away through a previously burned area toward Sugarloaf, a pointed granite turret rising from the western edge of Sugarloaf Valley that you may be able to see through the trees. Pink pussypaws cover the ground in summer.

At 7.6 miles, a path leads north to a packers' campsite on the edge of Sugarloaf Meadow. Your route crosses a trickling creeklet issuing from the meadow and passes below the monolith, entering the sparsely forested Sugarloaf Valley. The trail reaches a wide and shallow ford of Sugarloaf Creek at 9.2 miles.

After crossing the creek, you will cross the brook flowing down from Ellis Meadow. Rise over a ridge and step over a seasonal creek before arriving at Ferguson Creek at 10.5 miles—this crossing can be a bit swift in early season.

After the crossing, the trail follows the creek upstream, then clambers over a dry, manzanita-covered ridge, following the course of a waterless snowmelt creek. The path then drops down through rocky zones interspersed with meadows and nears the Roaring River, which sounds very much like its name. Pass just above the rushing water before the route swings away to a gate in a drift fence. Passing over a rocky moraine you near the river once more, then arrive at Scaffold Meadows. Pass through another gate just before you reach the Roaring River Ranger Station and a trail junction (13.1 miles).

One campsite, an open-air pit toilet, and a bear box are just up the trail to your left (east), next to the Roaring River Bridge; a couple more sites are across the river and to the north. A few more campsites are up the trail leading into Deadman Canyon.

After your stay, return the way you came (26.2 miles).

Options: Roaring River makes a perfect base camp for the exploration of Deadman Canyon, which contains the grave of a Portuguese shepherd, and Cloud Canyon, with its gorgeous Big Wet Meadow and unparalleled views of the Whaleback.

Roaring River

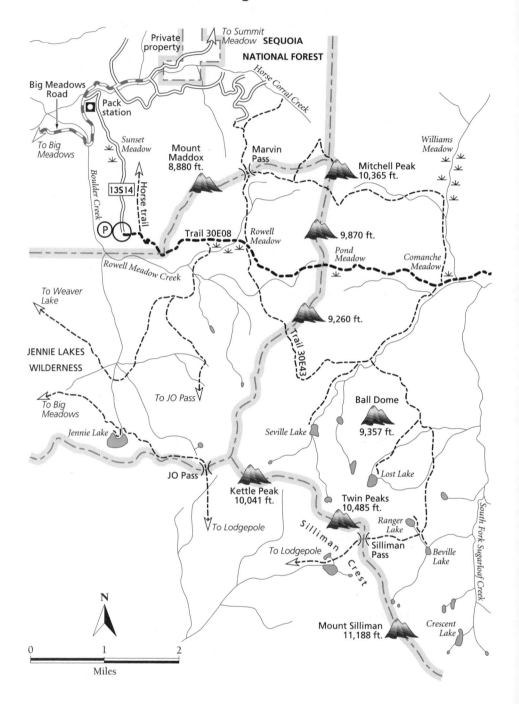

Private property

To Summit Meadow

SEQUOIA

NATIONAL FOREST

Horse Corral Creek

Big Meadows Road

Pack station

To Big Meadows

Sunset Meadow

Boulder Creek

13S14

Horse trail

Mount Maddox 8,880 ft.

Marvin Pass

Mitchell Peak 10,365 ft.

Williams Meadow

Trail 30E08

Rowell Meadow

9,870 ft.

Pond Meadow

Comanche Meadow

Rowell Meadow Creek

To Weaver Lake

JENNIE LAKES WILDERNESS

9,260 ft.

Trail 30E43

To JO Pass

To Big Meadows

Ball Dome 9,357 ft.

Jennie Lake

Seville Lake

Lost Lake

JO Pass

Kettle Peak 10,041 ft.

To Lodgepole

Twin Peaks 10,485 ft.

Silliman Crest

Ranger Lake

Silliman Pass

Beville Lake

To Lodgepole

South Fork Sugarloaf Creek

N

Mount Silliman 11,188 ft.

Crescent Lake

0   1   2

Miles

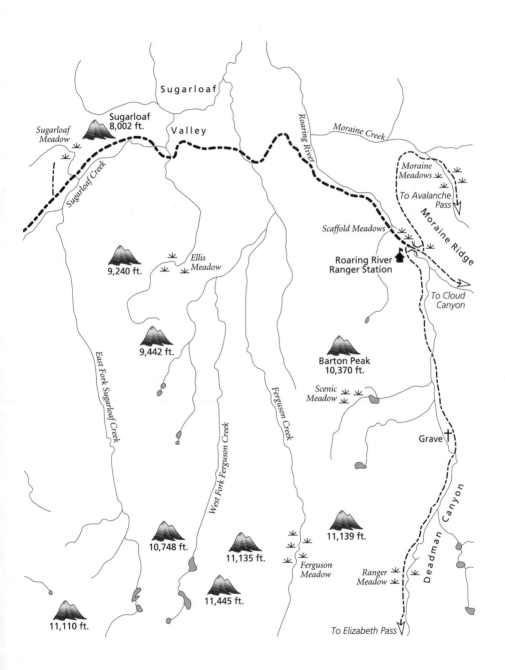

78 Seville Lake

Highlights:	This trip takes you through the Jennie Lakes Wilderness and into Kings Canyon National Park, to a beautiful lake at the base of the Silliman Crest.
Type of hike:	Out-and-back, backpack.
Total distance:	13.2 miles.
Difficulty:	Moderate.
Best months:	Mid-June through October.
Maps:	USGS Muir Grove and Mount Silliman; USFS Monarch and Jennie Lakes Wilderness; USFS John Muir Wilderness and Sequoia–Kings Canyon Wilderness; or TOPO! Sequoia Kings Canyon CD-ROM.
Permits:	Obtain a permit at the Grant Grove Visitor Center.
Special considerations:	Because the trail is used heavily by horseback riders and can be very dusty, the best times to hike are early in the season, when lingering moisture from snowmelt keeps the dust down, or later in the season, when rain showers settle the dust. If you meet horses on the trail, remember proper trail etiquette by stepping off the trail on the downhill side and waiting quietly until the horses have passed. Stay in plain view of the horses; they may think you are a wild animal and bolt if you are hidden behind a rock or tree.
Parking and facilities:	Water and a large, new outhouse are available at the trailhead. The trail begins at the north end of the parking area, near its entrance.

Finding the trailhead: Drive 9 miles south from Grant Grove on the Generals Highway to the signed Big Meadows Road (Forest Road 14S11), which is just beyond the Big Baldy Trailhead. Turn left (northeast) and follow the road past the ranger station, Big Meadows Trailhead, and the campgrounds. The road narrows, crosses Big Meadows Creek, and passes a few spur roads before entering a deep canyon and crossing Boulder Creek at a large curve. Take the next side road, Forest Road 13S14, which branches off to the right (east, then south) at 17 miles. This road is signed for the pack station and Rowell Meadow Trailhead. Follow the rough dirt road to its end at the trailhead parking area at 20 miles.

Key points:
0.0	Trailhead.
1.1	Reach the Jennie Lakes Wilderness boundary.
2.0	Pass the JO Pass Trail junction.
2.4	Reach the four-way junction at Rowell Meadow.
3.9	Reach the Kings Canyon National Park boundary.
5.4	Arrive at the Seville Lake Trail junction.
6.6	Reach Seville Lake.

The hike: Follow Forest Trail 30E08 for 2.4 miles to the signed, four-way junction beyond Rowell Meadow, as outlined in the trail description for Roaring River (Hike 77). Turn right (southeast) and take Forest Trail 30E43 toward Seville Lake.

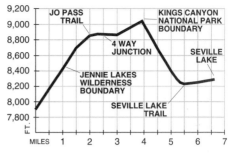

The course dips across a small brook, then ascends through a sunny, sparsely forested zone. Reentering the forest, the trail passes through meadows full of shooting stars in early summer. Step across another creeklet and resume climbing, reaching the park boundary and fir trees at 3.9 miles.

A steep downhill awaits you on the other side of the boundary, with areas of bright red skyrockets along the trail. A supposed shortcut follows a wash to the right (southeast), but becomes hard to follow when it enters a marsh about halfway to the lake. Your trail winds down the ridge, through thickets and open, flowered areas.

As the trail turns east and begins to level, you pass over raised trailbeds. At 5.4 miles, you attain the Seville Lake Trail junction in Belle Canyon. Turn right (southwest), cross a very shallow creek, and travel up a slight incline paralleling Sugarloaf Creek. Seville Lake is at 6.6 miles. The lake is rimmed with green grasses and tall firs to the north and surrounded by white granite cliffs to the south. Kettle Peak is the high point to the southwest. A bear box is available near the trail's end, and good campsites are located at various points on the north side of the lake.

Return the way you came (13.2 miles).

Option: Journeys to Lost Lake (Hike 79) and Ranger and Beville Lakes (Hike 80) can be combined with this hike for an extended backpacking trip.

Kettle Peak hovers above Seville Lake.

Seville Lake

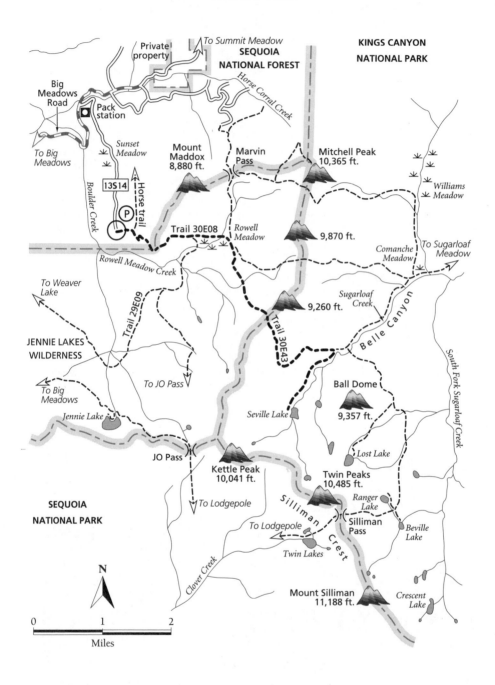

79 Lost Lake

Highlights:	This trek takes you through the Jennie Lakes Wilderness and Kings Canyon National Park to a high, forested lake at the base of Twin Peaks.
Type of hike:	Out-and-back, backpack.
Total distance:	15.6 miles.
Difficulty:	Difficult.
Best months:	Mid-June through October.
Maps:	USGS Muir Grove and Mount Silliman; USFS Monarch and Jennie Lakes Wilderness; USFS John Muir Wilderness and Sequoia–Kings Canyon Wilderness; or TOPO! Sequoia Kings Canyon CD-ROM.
Permits:	Obtain a permit at the Grant Grove Visitor Center if you plan to spend the night.
Special considerations:	Because the trail is used heavily by horseback riders and can be very dusty, the best times to hike are early in the season, when lingering moisture from snowmelt keeps the dust down, or later in the season, when rain showers settle the dust. If you meet horses on the trail, remember proper trail etiquette by stepping off the trail on the downhill side and waiting quietly until the horses have passed. Stay in plain view of the horses; they may think you are a wild animal and bolt if you are hidden behind a rock or tree.
Parking and facilities:	Water and a large, new outhouse are available at the trailhead. The trail begins at the north end of the parking area, near its entrance.

Finding the trailhead: Drive 9 miles south from Grant Grove on the Generals Highway to the signed Big Meadows Road (Forest Road 14S11), which is just beyond the Big Baldy Trailhead. Turn left (northeast) and follow the road past the ranger station, Big Meadows Trailhead, and the campgrounds. The road narrows, crosses Big Meadows Creek, and passes a few spur roads before entering a deep canyon and crossing Boulder Creek at a large curve. At 17 miles, go right (east, then south) on Forest Road 13S14, which is signed for the pack station and Rowell Meadow Trailhead. Follow the rough dirt road to its end at the trailhead parking area at 20 miles.

Key points:
0.0	Trailhead.
1.1	Pass the Jennie Lakes Wilderness boundary.
2.0	Reach the JO Pass Trail junction.
2.4	Reach the four-way junction at Rowell Meadow.
3.9	Pass the Kings Canyon National Park boundary.
5.4	Arrive at the Seville Lake Trail junction.
5.5	Pass the Comanche Meadow Trail junction.
6.8	Arrive at the Lost Lake Trail junction.
7.8	Reach Lost Lake.

The hike: Follow the Roaring River trail (Hike 77) to the four-way junction near Rowell Meadow at 2.4 miles. Next, follow the trail to Seville Lake (Hike 78) to the trail junction in Belle Canyon at 5.4 miles. From this junction turn left (east), crossing

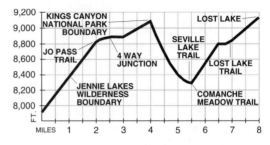

a very shallow creek and passing the trail leading left (northeast) to Comanche Meadow at 5.5 miles.

Wade the wide but shallow Sugarloaf Creek, then begin an ascent through a dense forest. After a small switchback the trail follows a stringer meadow uphill before entering an area of boulders at the ridgecrest. A view of Mitchell Peak can be had through the trees to the north.

The path levels on a thinly wooded plateau, then descends to cross a few small brooks above a grand meadow. Meet the signed Lost Lake Trail at 6.8 miles and make a right (southwest) turn. The route winds up through the woods, skirts a meadow, and reenters the timber. Cross another meadow and the small creek flowing through it; the trail then steepens and arrives at Lost Lake at 7.8 miles.

Red heather lines the shores of the lake, with white- and buff-colored granite cliffs serving as a backdrop. A bear box is available near the trail's end, and good campsites can be found on the north and northeast sides of the lake. The east and southeastern areas of the lake are closed for restoration.

When you are ready for the trek back, retrace your steps to the trailhead at 15.6 miles.

Option: The trails to Seville Lake (Hike 78) and Ranger and Beville Lakes (Hike 80) can be combined with this hike for an extended backpacking trip.

Lost Lake • Ranger and Beville Lakes

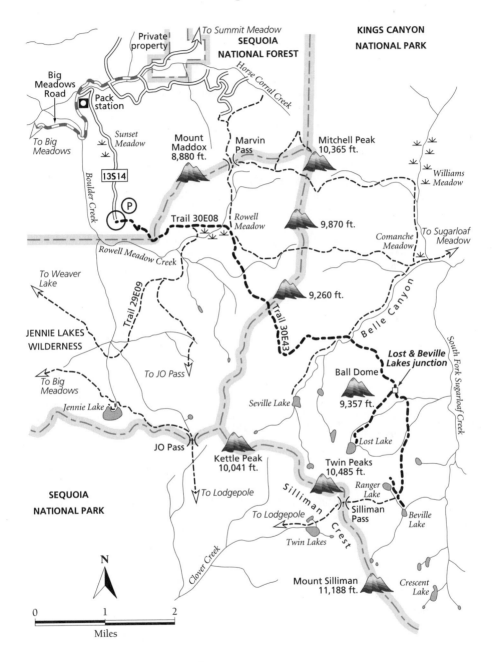

Private property

To Summit Meadow

SEQUOIA NATIONAL FOREST

KINGS CANYON NATIONAL PARK

Horse Corral Creek

Big Meadows Road

Pack station

To Big Meadows

Sunset Meadow

Mount Maddox 8,880 ft.

Marvin Pass

Mitchell Peak 10,365 ft.

Williams Meadow

Boulder Creek

13S14

P

Trail 30E08

Rowell Meadow

9,870 ft.

Comanche Meadow

To Sugarloaf Meadow

Rowell Meadow Creek

To Weaver Lake

Trail 29E09

9,260 ft.

Trail 30E43

Belle Canyon

South Fork Sugarloaf Creek

JENNIE LAKES WILDERNESS

To Big Meadows

To JO Pass

Lost & Beville Lakes junction

Ball Dome 9,357 ft.

Jennie Lake

Seville Lake

Lost Lake

JO Pass

Kettle Peak 10,041 ft.

To Lodgepole

Twin Peaks 10,485 ft.

Ranger Lake

Beville Lake

SEQUOIA NATIONAL PARK

Silliman Crest

To Lodgepole

Silliman Pass

Clover Creek

Twin Lakes

Mount Silliman 11,188 ft.

Crescent Lake

N

0   1   2

Miles

80 Ranger and Beville Lakes

Highlights: This excursion takes you through the Jennie Lakes Wilderness and into Kings Canyon National Park to a couple of breathtaking alpine lakes at the base of Twin Peaks and Mount Silliman.

See Map on Page 255

Type of hike: Out-and-back, backpack.

Total distance: 18 miles.

Difficulty: Difficult.

Best months: Mid-June through October.

Maps: USGS Muir Grove and Mount Silliman; USFS Monarch and Jennie Lakes Wilderness; USFS John Muir Wilderness and Sequoia–Kings Canyon Wilderness; or TOPO! Sequoia Kings Canyon CD-ROM.

Permits: Obtain a permit at the Grant Grove Visitor Center.

Special considerations: Because the trail is used heavily by horseback riders and can be very dusty, the best times to hike are early in the season, when lingering moisture from snowmelt keeps the dust down, or later in the season, when rain showers settle the dust. If you meet horses on the trail, remember proper trail etiquette by stepping off the trail on the downhill side and waiting quietly until the horses have passed. Stay in plain view of the horses; they may think you are a wild animal and bolt if you are hidden behind a rock or tree.

Parking and facilities: Water and a large, new outhouse are available at the trailhead. The trail begins at the north end of the parking area, near its entrance.

Finding the trailhead: Drive 9 miles south from Grant Grove on the Generals Highway to the signed Big Meadows Road (Forest Road 14S11), which is just beyond the Big Baldy Trailhead. Turn left (northeast), and follow the road past the ranger station, Big Meadows Trailhead, and the campgrounds. The road narrows, crosses Big Meadows Creek, and passes a few spur roads before entering a deep canyon and crossing Boulder Creek at a large curve. At 17 miles, turn right (east, then south) on Forest Road 13S14, which is signed for the pack station and Rowell Meadow Trailhead. Follow the rough dirt road to its end at the trailhead parking area at 20 miles.

Key points:

0.0   Trailhead.

1.1   Cross the Jennie Lakes Wilderness boundary.

2.0   Pass the JO Pass Trail junction.

2.4   Reach the four-way junction at Rowell Meadow.

3.9   Cross the Kings Canyon National Park boundary.

5.4   Pass the Seville Lake Trail junction.

5.5   Pass the Comanche Meadow Trail junction.

6.8   Reach the Lost Lake Trail junction.

8.7   Arrive at the Ranger Lake Trail junction.

8.8   Reach the Beville Lake Trail junction (the Ranger Lake campsites are at 8.9 miles).

9.0   Arrive at Beville Lake.

The hike: Begin by following the trail to Roaring River (Hike 77), arriving at the four-way junction near Rowell Meadow at 2.4 miles. Continue on the route to Seville Lake (Hike 78), reaching the trail junction in Belle Canyon at 5.4 miles.

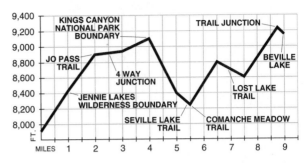

Then trace the trail to Lost Lake (Hike 79), arriving at the Lost Lake Trail junction at 6.8 miles.

From this junction, take the fork to the left (southeast) and continue downhill, crossing a few small creeks. Beyond the creeks, you will trek uphill through boulders and a thick and shady forest, then climb many short switchbacks, gradually entering a world of granite and increasing views. To the west, the Twin Peaks tower above you, and to the northwest Ball Dome and Mitchell Peak are visible. To the north, part of the Monarch Divide and Palmer Mountain can be seen. To the east is the Great Western Divide, and to the south rise the majestic Tablelands.

After crossing the area of slabs, you reenter the woods as the trail dips to the Ranger Lake Trail at 8.7 miles. Turn right (north) and follow the short trail up to the lake. Red heather rims this lake, and one of the Twin Peaks' turrets stands guard. Campsites and a bear box are along the east side of the lake, and a small island is at the north end.

To reach Beville Lake, continue downhill (southwest) at the junction with the Ranger Lake Trail, and meet the Beville Lake Trail at 8.8 miles. Turn left (south); in a few yards the trail forks, leading to campsites on the east and west sides of the lake at 9 miles. No bear box is available. Mount Silliman is the picturesque backdrop for this grass-rimmed lake, which is completed by a small tumbling waterfall and an island frequented by ducks. Deer and marmots can be sighted in the vicinity as well.

After a good night's sleep, backtrack to the trailhead at 18 miles.

Options: A strenuous hike up to Silliman Pass can be done from the lakes, with an elevation gain of 1,100 feet in 1.5 miles. Another option is to combine this hike with treks to Seville Lake (Hike 78) and Lost Lake (Hike 79), for an extended backpacking trip.

Hikes in Northern and Eastern Kings Canyon and Eastern Sequoia

The first two hikes in this chapter begin at the Florence Lake Trailhead, which is in northwest Kings Canyon National Park in the Sierra National Forest. The Dusy Basin hike begins at the South Lake Trailhead, which is southwest of Bishop. The hikes from Onion Valley to Kearsarge Lakes and Charlotte Lake begin at the Onion Valley Trailhead west of Independence. And the Mount Whitney hike begins at the Whitney Portal Trailhead, west of Lone Pine.

81 Goddard Canyon

Highlights:	A ferry trip is just one of the highlights of this excursion–which takes you by the Muir Trail Ranch and up the roaring South Fork of the San Joaquin River to the flower gardens of Goddard Canyon.
Type of hike:	Out-and-back, backpack.
Total distance:	35.4 miles.
Difficulty:	Difficult.
Best months:	July through mid-October.
Maps:	USGS Florence Lake, Ward Mountain, Mount Henry, Blackcap Mountain, and Mount Goddard; USFS John Muir Wilderness and Sequoia–Kings Canyon Wilderness; or TOPO! Sequoia Kings Canyon CD-ROM.
Permits:	Get a permit at Pine Ridge Ranger Station in Prather.
Special considerations:	If you are using the ferry to get across Florence Lake, be sure to check with the Forest Service and confirm the schedule before your departure.
Parking and facilities:	Restrooms are available at the parking area. The trail proper begins farther down the road, beyond the picnic area, but this hike utilizes the ferry, cutting off about 3 miles of hiking. Tickets are available at the store just south of the parking area. When this guide was researched, the fares were $8 one-way, $14 round-trip, per person.

Finding the trailhead: From Fresno, follow California Highway 168 for approximately 70 miles to its end at the east end of Huntington Lake. Go right (northeast) toward Kaiser Pass. The road narrows to one lane and passes the High Sierra Ranger Station (permits can be picked up here when the station is open). Reach a road fork at about 87 miles. Go right (east) and follow Forest Road 80 for 6 miles to the overnight parking area at Florence Lake.

Key points:
- 0.0 Trailhead.
- 0.5 Pass the trail junction.
- 1.6 Pass Double Meadow.
- 2.4 Cross Alder Creek.
- 3.2 Pass Blayney Meadows.
- 3.8 Cross Sallie Keyes Creek.
- 4.0 Cross Senger Creek.
- 4.2 Reach the Muir Trail Ranch.
- 4.5 Pass the cutoff trail.
- 4.7 Pass Shooting Star Meadow.
- 5.8 Reach the John Muir Trail/Pacific Crest Trail junction.
- 8.3 Reach the Piute Pass junction and the park boundary.
- 9.6 Pass Aspen Meadow.
- 11.1 Cross the bridge.
- 12.1 Reach the Goddard Canyon Trail junction.
- 12.7 Pass Franklin Meadow.
- 14.3 Pass Pig Chute.
- 15.7 Reach The Falls.
- 17.7 Reach the Hell For Sure Pass Trail junction and the campsite.

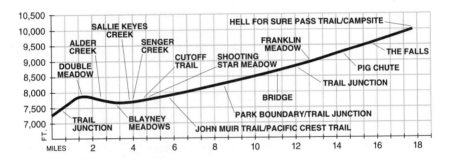

The hike: The journey begins at the ferry dock on the north end of Florence Lake. After boarding the ferry, an exhilarating ride to the south end of the lake deposits you at the trailhead.

The trail follows the jeep road leading to the Muir Trail Ranch, climbing over large slabs of granite. After mounting the ridge, the jeep trail swings away; continue over the ridge and join the trail that leads around the west shore of Florence Lake at 0.5 mile. The view across the South Fork of the San Joaquin is of pointed Mount Shinn, with Ward Mountain to its left (east).

The course dips and crosses a tiny seasonal creek, then climbs through a hot and sunny zone, crossing paths with the jeep road again. High above you to the north is a small granite dome known as The Tombstone. The trail passes through pretty Double Meadow at 1.6 miles, crossing its seasonal creek. Descend across Alder Creek at 2.4 miles, pass Blayney Meadows at 3.2 miles, and reach the boundary of the Muir Trail Ranch. Pass through its gate, and remember to stay on the trail while passing through the private property.

The route continues above the ranch, intersecting the jeep road near the trail to Blayney Hot Springs and the public campground. Cross Sallie Keyes

The Falls in Goddard Canyon are a refreshing sight on this wonderful backpacking trip.

Creek at 3.8 miles, and wade or rock-hop Senger Creek at 4 miles. After climbing a short switchback, the trail rounds a granite ridge and meets the steep unnamed trail connecting to the northbound John Muir/Pacific Crest Trail (JMT/PCT) and Sallie Keyes Lakes, along with a trail leading back to the ranch and hot springs at 4.5 miles.

At 4.7 miles, pass the east end of Shooting Star Meadow, then a small pond, before dropping to shaded campsites along the river. The path rises again to join the JMT/PCT at 5.8 miles, and undulates through sun and a bit of shade with views of Pavilion Dome to the east.

At 8.3 miles, you reach the junction of the Piute Pass Trail. Turn right to cross the bridge spanning Piute Creek and enter Kings Canyon National Park. Several campsites are located on the east side above Piute Creek, and just over the small hill a side trail leads to more campsites along the South Fork of the San Joaquin. The Goddard Canyon route travels above the river, passing deep chasms of crystal clear, aquamarine water.

At 9.6 miles step across a small creek in Aspen Meadow (more like a stunted aspen grove), then climb again above the rushing water. At 11.1 miles, cross the river on a large bridge. A side trail to your right (north) leads to campsites, while the JMT/PCT continues south. After passing more campsites and crossing a small brook, you arrive at the junction with the Goddard Canyon Trail at 12.1 miles.

Leaving the JMT/PCT, head south up Goddard Canyon, reaching the grassy expanse of Franklin Meadow at 12.7 miles. Rock-hop another small creek; after yet another creek crossing, the trail climbs higher on the canyon wall, traversing above rapids and cascades. The Pig Chute is east of you at about 14.3 miles, where a tributary glides down a very narrow hanging valley to join the river.

The path rises over a rocky area and crosses tumbling creeks lined with colorful Indian paintbrush, yellow cinquefoil, and other wildflowers in summer. The watercourse below is lined with precipitous, rectangular blocks of granite. The path draws near the river, and at 15.7 miles you gain a view of The Falls, a billowy waterfall that drops into a sky-blue pool of water.

The trail curves toward the river past the waterfall, just above a campsite, then continues up the canyon. Rock-hop a creek with its own cascading waterfall, lined with greenery and flowers. After passing more campsites, you arrive at the Hell For Sure Pass Trail junction at 17.7 miles. A campsite is located here, and another is a bit farther up the trail. Beyond the trail junction, the path begins to fade out, but Martha Lake can be reached by traveling cross-country to the southeast.

Return the way you came, reaching the trailhead at 35.4 miles.

Option: This hike can be combined with the route into Evolution Valley (Hike 82) for an extended backpacking trip.

Goddard Canyon • Evolution Valley

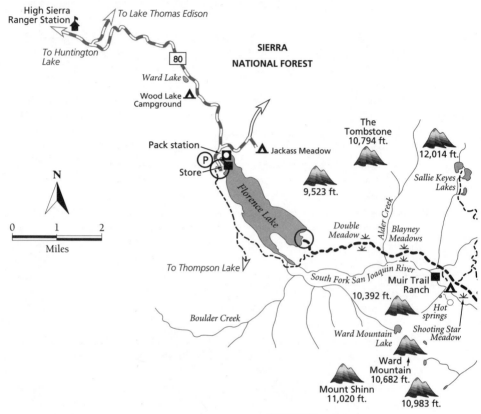

High Sierra Ranger Station

To Lake Thomas Edison

To Huntington Lake

SIERRA NATIONAL FOREST

80

Ward Lake

Wood Lake Campground

Pack station

Store

Jackass Meadow

N

0   1   2
Miles

The Tombstone 10,794 ft.

12,014 ft.

Sallie Keyes Lakes

9,523 ft.

Florence Lake

Double Meadow

Alder Creek

Blayney Meadows

To Thompson Lake

South Fork San Joaquin River

Muir Trail Ranch

10,392 ft.

Hot springs

Boulder Creek

Ward Mountain Lake

Shooting Star Meadow

Ward Mountain 10,682 ft.

Mount Shinn 11,020 ft.

10,983 ft.

JOHN MUIR WILDERNESS

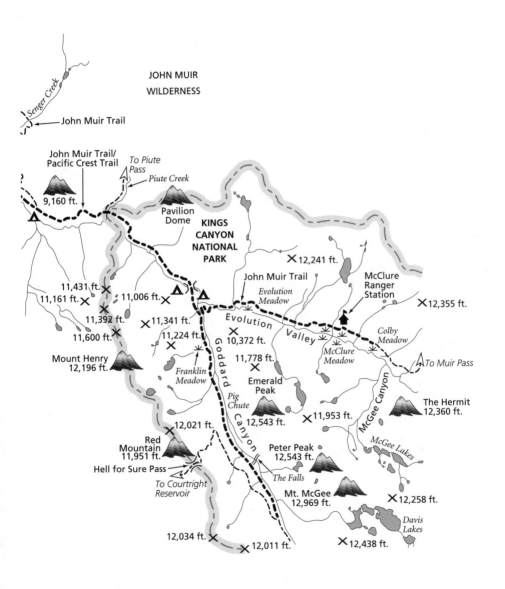

JOHN MUIR
WILDERNESS

Senger Creek

← John Muir Trail

John Muir Trail/
Pacific Crest Trail

*To Piute
Pass*

Piute Creek

9,160 ft.

Pavilion
Dome

**KINGS
CANYON
NATIONAL
PARK**

×12,241 ft.

John Muir Trail

*Evolution
Meadow*

McClure
Ranger
Station

11,431 ft.×

11,161 ft.×   ×11,006 ft.

11,392 ft.×

11,600 ft.×   ×11,341 ft.

×11,224 ft.

Evolution   Valley

×
10,372 ft.

*McClure
Meadow*

*Colby
Meadow*

×12,355 ft.

To Muir Pass

Mount Henry
12,196 ft.

*Franklin
Meadow*

11,778 ft.
×

Emerald
Peak

*Pig
Chute*

12,543 ft.

×11,953 ft.

McGee Canyon

The Hermit
12,360 ft.

McGee Lakes

12,021 ft.×

Red
Mountain
11,951 ft.

Hell for Sure Pass

*To Courtright
Reservoir*

Peter Peak
12,543 ft.

The Falls

Mt. McGee
12,969 ft.

×12,258 ft.

*Davis
Lakes*

12,034 ft.×   ×12,011 ft.   ×12,438 ft.

82 Evolution Valley

Highlights:	This hike takes you to one of the most beautiful areas along the John Muir and Pacific Crest Trails.
Type of hike:	Out-and-back, backpack.
Total distance:	34 miles.
Difficulty:	Difficult.
Best months:	July through mid-October.
Maps:	USGS Florence Lake, Ward Mountain, Mount Henry, Blackcap Mountain, and Mount Darwin; USFS John Muir Wilderness and Sequoia–Kings Canyon Wilderness; or TOPO! Sequoia Kings Canyon CD-ROM.
Permits:	Get a permit at Pine Ridge Ranger Station in Prather.
Special considerations:	If you are using the ferry to get across Florence Lake, be sure to check with the Forest Service and confirm the schedule before your departure.
Parking and facilities:	Restrooms are available at the parking area. The trail proper begins farther down the road, beyond the picnic area, but this hike utilizes the ferry, cutting off about 3 miles of hiking. Tickets are available at the store, just south of the parking area. When this guide was researched, the fares were $8 one-way, $14 round-trip, per person.

See Map on Page 262

Finding the trailhead: From Fresno, follow California Highway 168 for approximately 70 miles to its termination at the east end of Huntington Lake and go right (northeast), toward Kaiser Pass. Continue up this winding road as it narrows to one lane and passes the High Sierra Ranger Station (permits can be picked up here when the station is open; check with the Forest Service), to a road fork at about 87 miles. Go right (east) and follow Forest Road 80 for another 6 miles to the overnight parking area at Florence Lake.

Key points:
- 0.0 Trailhead.
- 0.5 Pass the trail junction.
- 1.6 Pass Double Meadow.
- 2.4 Cross Alder Creek.
- 3.2 Pass Blayney Meadows.
- 3.8 Cross Sallie Keyes Creek.
- 4.0 Cross Senger Creek.
- 4.2 Reach the Muir Trail Ranch.
- 4.5 Pass the cutoff trail.
- 4.7 Pass Shooting Star Meadow.
- 5.8 Reach the John Muir Trail/Pacific Crest Trail junction.
- 8.3 Reach the Piute Pass junction and the park boundary.
- 9.6 Pass Aspen Meadow.
- 11.1 Cross the bridge.

12.1	Reach the Goddard Canyon Trail junction.
13.2	Cross Evolution Creek.
13.6	Pass Evolution Meadow.
16.0	Reach McClure Meadow.
17.0	Arrive at Colby Meadow.

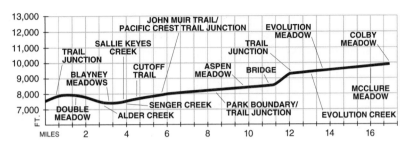

The hike: Begin by hiking the trail to Goddard Canyon (Hike 81) to the Goddard Canyon Trail junction at 12.1 miles. Make a left (east) turn on the John Muir Trail/Pacific Crest Trail (JMT/PCT), cross the South Fork of the San Joaquin on a large bridge, and switchback up a very steep slope, enjoying occasional views of the pretty cascades on Evolution Creek.

At 13.2 miles you come to a wide ford of Evolution Creek—be prepared for a wade! Enter the enchanting and peaceful Evolution Valley, which is walled in by 12,000-foot-plus peaks on both sides. You will reach lovely Evolution Meadow and campsites at 13.6 miles.

After reentering the forest and crossing a couple of brooks, the flower-lined trail leads slightly uphill to scenic McClure Meadow, with Emerald Peak towering above, at 16 miles. A backcountry ranger station is located here. A few more wooded creek crossings and another slight ascent bring you to pleasant Colby Meadow at 17 miles, which is near the head of the valley and guarded by The Hermit. At sunset, alpenglow lights the surrounding peaks in an exquisite display.

At the end of your journey, retrace your steps to the ferry landing and return to the parking area at 34 miles.

Option: This hike can be combined with the route to Goddard Canyon (Hike 81) for an extended backpacking trip.

83 Dusy Basin

Finding the trailhead: From Bishop, head southwest on California Highway 168 for approximately 15.5 miles to the South Lake turnoff, and make a left (south) turn. Follow South Lake Road south for about 7 more miles to the trailhead parking area. Overnight parking is in the upper lot.

Key points:

0.0	Trailhead.
0.7	Reach the wilderness boundary.
0.8	Meet the Treasure Lakes Trail.
1.4	Pass the Marie Louise Lakes Trail.
1.8	Pass the Bull and Chocolate Lakes Trail.
2.0	Reach Long Lake.
2.6	Pass the Ruwau Lake Trail.
3.4	Reach the Timberline Tarns.
3.6	Pass Saddlerock Lake.
4.2	Make the creek crossing.
5.6	Cross Bishop Pass.
7.7	Reach Dusy Basin.

The hike: The trek begins by crossing two small footbridges, then joins a trail from the pack station. Make a slight descent before climbing through lodgepole pines, firs,

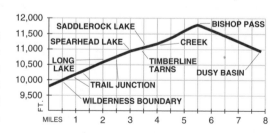

Dusy Basin

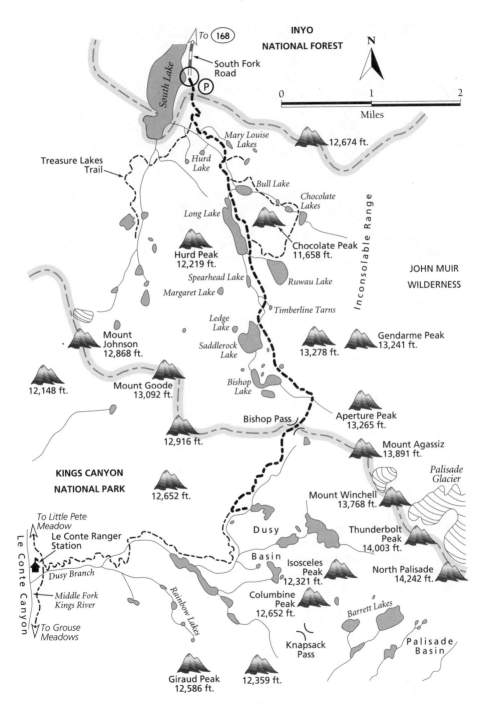

To (168)

South Fork Road

South Lake

P

INYO NATIONAL FOREST

N

0   1   2
Miles

12,674 ft.

Mary Louise Lakes

Hurd Lake

Treasure Lakes Trail

Bull Lake

Chocolate Lakes

Long Lake

Chocolate Peak 11,658 ft.

Hurd Peak 12,219 ft.

Spearhead Lake

Ruwau Lake

Margaret Lake

Timberline Tarns

Ledge Lake

Saddlerock Lake

Bishop Lake

Mount Johnson 12,868 ft.

12,148 ft.

Mount Goode 13,092 ft.

12,916 ft.

Bishop Pass

13,278 ft.

Gendarme Peak 13,241 ft.

Aperture Peak 13,265 ft.

Mount Agassiz 13,891 ft.

Inconsolable Range

JOHN MUIR WILDERNESS

Palisade Glacier

Mount Winchell 13,768 ft.

12,652 ft.

KINGS CANYON NATIONAL PARK

To Little Pete Meadow

Le Conte Ranger Station

Dusy Branch

Middle Fork Kings River

To Grouse Meadows

Le Conte Canyon

Dusy

Basin

Rainbow Lakes

Thunderbolt Peak 14,003 ft.

North Palisade 14,242 ft.

Isosceles Peak 12,321 ft.

Columbine Peak 12,652 ft.

Barrett Lakes

Palisade Basin

Knapsack Pass

Giraud Peak 12,586 ft.

12,359 ft.

Dusy Basin and the high peaks that frame it spread before Bishop Pass.

and quaking aspens on a rocky trailbed. The route climbs above South Lake, with magnificent views of Hurd Peak and other crags to the south, and enters the John Muir Wilderness at 0.7 mile.

The path meets the Treasure Lakes Trail at 0.8 mile, where you stay to the left (southeast). Cross the outlet of the Marie Louise Lakes on a small footbridge in a flowery meadow. After a jaunt through the shady forest and another creek crossing, the route passes the dim trail to the Marie Louise Lakes at 1.4 miles.

Switchbacks lead up a rocky slope as Hurd Lake appears below, to the north. A little more climbing brings you to the junction with the Bull/Chocolate Lakes Trail at 1.8 miles. After crossing the outlet of these lakes, you arrive at sapphire-hued Long Lake at 2 miles. The trail follows its east shore. Side trails lead to campsites on the right (west) here and there as you pass below chestnut-colored Chocolate Peak.

The Ruwau Lake Trail is at 2.6 miles. Rock-hop the outlet of Ruwau Lake and rise above aquamarine Spearhead Lake. Below, you may notice an abandoned section of trail that leads down to the shore of this lake. The route becomes increasingly rocky, ascends switchbacks, and rock-hops the outlet of the blue-green Timberline Tarns at 3.4 miles. Beyond the tarns, the trail climbs along a splashy waterfall. You will cross the stream on a footbridge upon reaching expansive Saddlerock Lake at 3.6 miles.

The path rises above the lake, with side trails branching off to campsites once more. Another short climb leads above Bishop Lake, where a side trail leads toward the lake and campsites among its stunted foxtail pines. At 4.2 miles, rock-hop a small creek flowing through an alpine meadow studded with snow survey poles, and switchback above small tarns into an area of talus. The route ascends several switchbacks up a nearly vertical wall, with views east of the Inconsolable Range, as well as of Gendarme and Aperture Peaks, and west of Mount Goode. To the north are Bishop Lake, Saddlerock Lake (with Ledge Lake now visible above it), and Hurd Peak.

The path then winds through rocks and boulders to Bishop Pass, climbing slightly and intersecting side trails to viewpoints. At 5.6 miles you reach Bishop Pass, with views east of Mount Agassiz and Mount Winchell, and south of Thunderbolt Peak, North Palisade, Isosceles Peak, Columbine Peak, and Giraud Peak. To the southwest is the Black Divide.

The sandy trail gently switchbacks its way down toward the Dusy Basin. As you near the inlet to its northernmost lake, leave the main trail and head east over granite and tundra to campsites along the lake's west shore at 7.7 miles. Please camp at least 100 feet from the water.

When you are ready to return, retrace your steps to the parking area at 15.4 miles.

84 Onion Valley to Kearsarge Lakes

Highlights:	This journey travels up the Onion Valley, passing several beautiful lakes, then climbs over windswept Kearsarge Pass and down to the dazzling Kearsarge Lakes.
Type of hike:	Out-and-back, backpack.
Total distance:	9.8 miles.
Difficulty:	Difficult.
Best months:	July through October.
Maps:	USGS Kearsarge Peak and Mount Clarence King; USFS John Muir Wilderness and Sequoia–Kings Canyon Wilderness; or TOPO! Sequoia Kings Canyon CD-ROM.
Permits:	Obtain a permit through Inyo National Forest Wilderness Reservations (see Appendix A) or at the Mount Whitney Ranger Station in Lone Pine.
Special considerations:	Bear-proof food storage canisters are required.
Parking and facilities:	Restrooms are available just west of the parking area. The trail begins just beyond the restrooms.

Finding the trailhead: From U.S. Highway 395 in central Independence, take West Market Street, which turns into Onion Valley Road, for 15 miles to the road's end at a large parking lot below the Onion Valley Campground.

Key points:

0.0   Trailhead.
1.4   Pass Little Pothole Lake.
1.9   Pass Gilbert Lake.
2.2   Reach the trail junction at Flower Lake.
4.0   Cross Kearsarge Pass.
4.4   Reach the Charlotte Lake Trail junction.
4.7   Pass the trail junction.
4.9   Reach the second highest Kearsarge Lake.

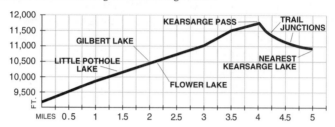

The hike: The rocky trail begins by switchbacking up a sunny slope through sage and scattered pines. After climbing a few of the switchbacks, you can see the trail leading to Golden Trout Lake to the north. Within a mile you enter the John Muir Wilderness, continuing to switchback with views back down to the trailhead and across the Owens Valley to the Inyo Mountains.

Clamber through rock and talus to a side trail to Little Pothole Lake at 1.4 miles. This tranquil lake has a few campsites and two waterfalls cascading into its still waters.

The path resumes switchbacking and reaches the ripples of Gilbert Lake at 1.9 miles. You will find large campsites at this lake. Traveling first along the lake's north shore, then its west, you pass a side trail to more campsites on its south shore. At 2.2 miles, beyond a couple of switchbacks, you reach the path leading to Matlock Lake and campsites across Independence Creek on the east end of azure Flower Lake. The main route switchbacks again, climbing above campsites on the north shore of this lake, then looping around a small pond.

Switchbacks lead up granite ledges, high above the royal blue waters of Heart Lake. Upon cresting the ridge, the barren landscape of Kearsarge Pass comes into view. The path gently climbs long, easy switchbacks, then ascends in earnest above cobalt-hued Big Pothole Lake. As you climb you may notice a spur trail leading steeply downhill from near the pass to below your route. This footpath has been created by hikers cutting the switchbacks; please stay on the main trail.

At 4 miles you reach Kearsarge Pass and the Kings Canyon National Park boundary, with University Peak your companion to the south. To the west of this peak, the Kearsarge Pinnacles rise above the sparkling Kearsarge Lakes, and in the far west is Mount Bago. North of the pass is Mount Gould, and to the east, Independence Peak towers above the Owens Valley, the town of Independence, and US 395. The Inyo Mountains hem in the valley on its east side.

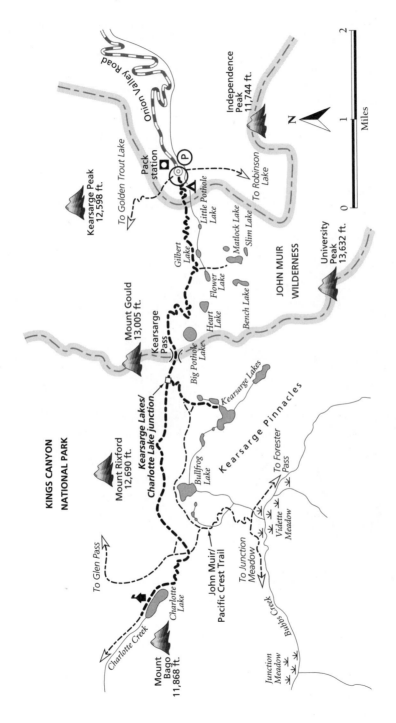

Descending the steep trail on the other side is a rocky and slippery experience—watch your footing! At 4.4 miles you come to the junction with the route to Charlotte Lake and turn left. The path swings to the south, dropping steadily. At 4.7 miles, you reach an unsigned track leading south to the second highest Kearsarge Lake, which is at 4.9 miles.

A large camping area is located on a bluff overlooking the lake, with the crags of the Kearsarge Pinnacles towering above. A footpath leads along the lakeshore to more campsites at the largest of the Kearsarge Lakes. Due to overuse, there is a two-night camping limit at these lakes.

When it is time to return, retrace your steps to the parking area at 9.8 miles total.

Option: A semi-loop backpack can be accomplished by continuing west down the main trail, past Bullfrog Lake (closed to camping), to the John Muir/Pacific Crest Trail at 6.6 miles. Make a right (north) turn, and travel up the switchbacks and over a small rise to the Charlotte Lake/Kearsarge Pass Trail at 6.9 miles. Go left (west) to visit Charlotte Lake (Hike 85) at 8 miles. Return by following Hike 85 in reverse, for a grand total of 15.5 miles.

The Kearsarge Pinnacles tower over one of the Kearsarge Lakes.

85 Charlotte Lake

Highlights: This excursion travels up the Onion Valley, passing several beautiful lakes, then climbs

See Map on Page 271

over windswept Kearsarge Pass. The trail passes high above the Kearsarge Lakes, and leads to pleasant Charlotte Lake.

Type of hike: Out-and-back, backpack.

Total distance: 15 miles.

Difficulty: Difficult.

Best months: July through October.

Maps: USGS Kearsarge Peak and Mount Clarence King; USFS John Muir Wilderness and Sequoia–Kings Canyon Wilderness; or TOPO! Sequoia Kings Canyon CD-ROM.

Permits: Obtain a permit through Inyo National Forest Wilderness Reservations (see Appendix A) or at the Mount Whitney Ranger Station in Lone Pine.

Special considerations: Bear-proof food storage canisters are required.

Parking and facilities: Restrooms are available just west of the parking area. The trail begins just beyond the restrooms.

Finding the trailhead: From U.S. Highway 395 in central Independence, take West Market Street, which turns into Onion Valley Road, for 15 miles to the road's end at the large parking lot below the Onion Valley Campground.

Key points:

0.0	Trailhead.
1.4	Pass Little Pothole Lake.
1.9	Pass Gilbert Lake.
2.2	Reach the trail junction at Flower Lake.
4.0	Cross Kearsarge Pass.
4.4	Reach the Kearsarge Lakes Trail junction.
6.4	Pass a trail junction.
6.6	Reach the John Muir Trail/Pacific Crest Trail junction.
7.5	Arrive at the Charlotte Lake campsites.

The hike: Begin by following the Kearsarge Lakes trail from Onion Valley (Hike 84) to the Kearsarge Lakes Trail junction at 4.4 miles. Continue straight (west), undulating above the beautiful Kearsarge Lakes. The path traverses high on a ledge as you pass

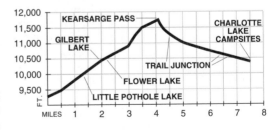

above the deep, blue water of Bullfrog Lake, affording you a view of Deerhorn Mountain, flanked by East and West Vidette.

Lovely Charlotte Lake features campsites with bear boxes for overnight camping.

Drop to a junction with a spur trail to the John Muir/Pacific Crest Trail (JMT/PCT) at 6.4 miles and stay left (west). The route dips through a large, barren area, and you meet the JMT/PCT and the Charlotte Lake Trail at a four-way junction at 6.6 miles (not shown on some maps).

Continue straight (west) toward Charlotte Lake, and descend numerous switchbacks on a forested hillside. Upon reaching the shoreline, side trails lead to primitive campsites. The main trail leads on, past a signed trail leading to the backcountry ranger station. Larger campsites with a bear box lie ahead, where this hike concludes at 7.5 miles.

If you have time to explore, this path continues to the abandoned Gardiner Pass Trail, which leads to Gardiner Basin, as well as the climber's trail to Charlotte Dome.

Return the way you came, returning to the trailhead at 15 miles total.

Option: A semi-loop backpacking trip can be accomplished by returning to the JMT/PCT and turning right (south). Travel over a small rise and down several switchbacks to the Bullfrog/Kearsarge Lakes Trail at 8.9 miles. Make a left (east) turn and climb steadily up the trail, past Bullfrog Lake (closed to camping) and on to the Kearsarge Lakes (Hike 84) at 10.6 miles. Return by following Hike 84 in reverse, for a grand total of 15.5 miles.

86 Mount Whitney

Highlights:	This expedition takes you to the top of the highest peak in the contiguous United States, and to unparalleled views.
Type of hike:	Out-and-back, day hike or backpack.
Total distance:	22 miles.
Difficulty:	Difficult.
Best months:	Mid-July through September.
Maps:	USGS Mount Whitney and Mount Langley; USFS John Muir Wilderness and Sequoia–Kings Canyon Wilderness; or TOPO! Sequoia Kings Canyon CD-ROM.
Permits:	Obtain a permit through Inyo National Forest Wilderness Reservations (see Appendix A).
Special considerations:	A special Whitney Zone Permit is required for both day hikes and backpacking trips to the peak (see the Introduction for more information). Bear-proof food storage canisters are required. A risk of being struck by lightning exists on the summit of Mount Whitney. Get an early start to avoid afternoon thunderstorms. If dark clouds are nearby, or if you notice hail, rain, thunder, or static electricity in the air, descend immediately.
Parking and facilities:	A small store, water, and restrooms are located just west of the trailhead. The trail begins across the road, at the large trailhead display, north of the overnight parking area.

Finding the trailhead: At the signal light in central Lone Pine, head west on Whitney Portal Road for 13 miles to the parking area at Whitney Portal. Use the appropriate parking areas for day hiking or backpacking.

Key points:
- 0.0   Trailhead.
- 0.5   Make the spring crossing.
- 0.8   Cross the North Fork Lone Pine Creek.
- 0.9   Reach the wilderness boundary.
- 2.7   Reach Lone Pine Creek.
- 2.8   Pass the Lone Pine Lake Trail.
- 3.5   Reach Bighorn Park.
- 3.8   Arrive at Outpost Camp.
- 4.3   Reach Mirror Lake.
- 5.3   Pass Trailside Meadow.
- 6.3   Reach Trail Camp.
- 8.5   Arrive at Trail Crest.
- 9.0   Meet the John Muir Trail.
- 11.0   Arrive on the Mount Whitney summit.

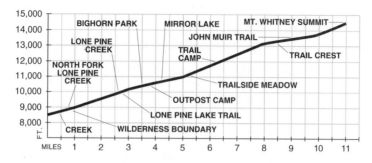

The hike: The trek begins by ascending small switchbacks through sage, manzanita, and pinyon pine. The path then straightens a bit, giving you a view of falls on Lone Pine Creek, before crossing a group of small springs at 0.5 mile. Just before the crossing of Lone Pine Creek at 0.8 mile (requiring some rock-hopping), a footpath branches off to the right (west). This is the mountaineers' route, used by climbers who scale the steep eastern face of Mount Whitney.

The main trail reaches the John Muir Wilderness boundary at 0.9 mile, and rises up a number of sunny switchbacks lined with sage, chinquapin, mountain mahogany, and a few pines. As you near Lone Pine Lake, the forest cover becomes thicker, and at 2.7 miles, several hewn logs aid in crossing Lone Pine Creek. Another tenth of a mile brings you to the signed junction with the side trail to Lone Pine Lake, which is visible from the main trail.

The path swings west, through a canyon of talus on a sandy trail, before climbing a few more switchbacks and crossing a ridge. You then dip down to Bighorn Park—a long, verdant meadow filled with willows—at 3.5 miles.

Viewed from the infamous switchbacks that lead to its summit, Mount Whitney (in the distance) is the highest point in the contiguous United States. Mount Muir rises in the foreground.

Mount Whitney

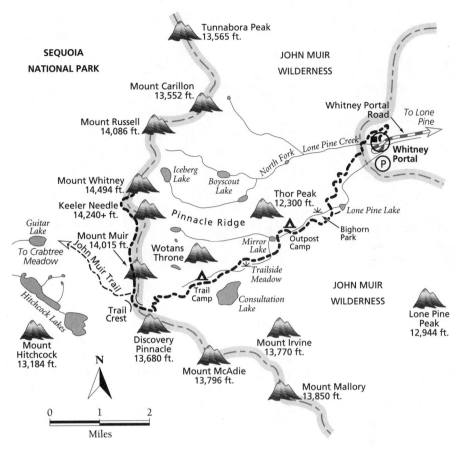

The trail skirts the south side of the meadow, first closely following Lone Pine Creek, with Thor Peak towering in the north. A wide rock hop downstream from the misty waterfall of a tributary stream leads across Lone Pine Creek. Outpost Camp, the first of two camping areas on the Mount Whitney Trail, is at 3.8 miles. After an easy rock hop of a tributary, a side trail splits to the right, leading north to the solar toilets.

The route leads up more switchbacks to arrive at pretty Mirror Lake, which is closed to camping, at 4.3 miles. Beyond the lake, the trail switchbacks up through granite, then levels off on the ridge above. Passing through a few stunted whitebark pines, you climb above the treeline. The route crosses Lone Pine Creek on a small rock bridge, and comes to Trailside Meadow at 5.3 miles. Wildflowers, the bubbling creek, and a waterfall at its far end make this a charming rest stop. Tiny pikas, which are related to rabbits, also inhabit this area.

Switchbacks lead up through the granite, crossing muddy seeps. Consultation Lake comes into view below Mount Irvine, Arc Pass, and Mount

The convoluted face of Mount Hitchcock comes into view at Trail Crest as you ascend the trail to the summit of Mount Whitney.

McAdie. After passing through an overflow camping area, you reach Trail Camp at 6.3 miles. This camp is equipped with solar toilets and is the last camping area along the trail. Whether you are camping or just resting, watch your pack! Yellow-bellied marmots, golden mantled ground squirrels, and tiny chipmunks are ready and waiting to raid any unattended item. The gray-crowned rosy finches are a little more polite—they just search for crumbs. The last reliable water source along the trail is located at the small lake here, which is easily reached from the trail.

Now the climb of the infamous 96 switchbacks begins. With long stretches at first, the lower switchbacks are sometimes riddled with seeps. About halfway to Trail Crest, you encounter a section of trail outfitted with a handrail, which offers a measure of safety against snow and ice that accumulate here. If it is icy, watch your footing!

Short switchbacks then lead up, passing a signed rock marker at 8 miles. A few longer switchbacks lead past a good rest area below Discovery Pinnacle, then on to Trail Crest at the boundary of Sequoia National Park at 8.5 miles.

Trail Camp appears miniature below to the east, while in the west, from left (south) to right (north) are Sawtooth Peak and the Kaweah group, with Mount Hitchcock in the foreground and the Hitchcock Lakes below. From the crest, the trail drops to the John Muir Trail at 9 miles.

Stay north on the route, which traverses a rocky ledge below craggy spires, with occasional "windows" offering views down to the Owens Valley. Steep drop-offs to the left (west) may rattle those who suffer from acrophobia a bit, but the trail remains wide. The route becomes increasingly rocky and a slower pace is needed to travel safely, especially at this high elevation.

Arc Pass and Consultation Lake lie along the trail to Mount Whitney's lofty summit.

At about 10 miles, after rounding a curve, the summit of Mount Whitney comes into view, as well as Keeler, Day, and the Third Needles. The path is easy to follow until you reach the southwest side of the summit. Here, the trail splits into several steep paths, some marked with ducks, and you must decide which is the best for you to follow. Steep drop-offs are no longer a problem, but watch your footing—no need for a sprained ankle or a scraped knee this far from the trailhead. Winding up through the sand and talus, you soon strike a more traveled route and spot the summit hut.

At 11 miles, you attain the summit of the highest peak in the lower 48 states. A register is located on the south side of the hut, and the highest point is just to the east. An open-air pit toilet is located to the northwest of the structure.

Views to the east include the Inyo Mountains, the Owens Valley, the Alabama Hills, and Lone Pine Peak. To the south, Mount Irvine, Mount Langley, Arc Pass, Mount McAdie, Olancha Peak (in the distance), Mount Muir, Keeler, Day, and the Third Needles, and Mount Hitchcock are all visible. In the west, from the south to the north, are Sawtooth Peak, the Kaweah Peaks—Mount Kaweah, Second Kaweah, Red Kaweah, and Black Kaweah—then the northern section of the Great Western Divide: Centennial Peak, Milestone Mountain, Midway Mountain, Table Mountain, Thunder Mountain, South Guard, and Mount Brewer. To the north you can see Junction Peak, Mount Tyndall, Mount Williamson (the second-highest peak in the lower 48), Mount Russell, and Mount Carillon.

After you have enjoyed the view and your accomplishment, begin the grueling descent, either back to camp or to your car at 22 miles.

Appendix A: For More Information

Sequoia and Kings Canyon
National Parks
Three Rivers, CA 93271

**Wilderness Permits, Road and
Weather Conditions, and General
Information**
(559) 565-3341 (24 hours)

Sequoia Natural History
Association
HCR 89 Box 10
Three Rivers, CA 93271
(559) 565-3759
Fax: (559) 565-3728
e-mail: seqnha@inreach.com

Inyo National Forest

Mount Whitney Ranger Station
640 S. Main St.
Lone Pine, CA 93545
(760) 876-6200

White Mountain Ranger Station
798 N. Main St.
Bishop, CA 93514
(760) 873-2500

Wilderness Permit Office
Reservations and Changes Only (open
Monday-Friday from 1 P.M. to 5 P.M.):
(760) 873-2483
Fax: (760) 873-2484
Wilderness Information:
(760) 873-2485

General Recreation Information
(760) 873-2408
website: www.r5.fs.fed.us/inyo

Sequoia National Forest

Hume Lake Ranger District
35860 E. Kings Canyon Rd.
Dunlap, CA 93621
(559) 338-2251
Fax: (559) 338-2131

Sierra National Forest

Pine Ridge Ranger District
P.O. Box 559
Prather, CA 93651
(559) 855-5360

For Road and Weather Conditions:

**California Department of Trans-
portation**
Highway Conditions: (559) 445-5647
or (800) 427-7623

For Maps

Global Map Store
5091 N. Fresno St.
Fresno, CA 93710
(559) 224-9831

U.S. Geological Survey
Information Services
P.O. Box 25286
Denver, CO 80225-9916
(800) USA-MAPS or (800) HELP-MAP
Fax: (303) 202-4693

Garcia Machine, Backpacking Canister
14097 Ave. 272
Visalia, CA 93292
(559) 732-3785
Cost: Approximately $65 and up for purchase. $3 and up per night rental fee.
Specifications: 8-inch diameter by 12-inch length cylindrical canister.
Weight: 2.7 pounds of molded plastic.
Model: 812-C.
This canister is also available through the Sequoia Natural History Association and outdoor retail outlets. It features two large screw latches on the lid that can be opened by using a coin, key, or screwdriver, then pushing a button to easily pop up the canister's lid.

Wild Ideas
P.O. Box 60813
Santa Barbara, CA 93160
(805) 693-0550
www.wild-ideas.net
Cost: Approximately $5 per night rental fee.
Specifications: 9-inch diameter by 15 1/4-inch length cylindrical canister.
Weight: More than 1 pound.
This canister features three large screw latches that can be twisted open with a coin, key, or screwdriver. The lid is flush and requires some manipulation to open.

Bear Kan, Backpacking Canister
P.O. Box 4507
Oceanside, CA 92052
(760) 938-3277
Cost: Approximately $66.
Specifications: 8-inch diameter by 12-inch length cylindrical canister.
Weight: 2 pounds 3 ounces.
This canister is made of aircraft aluminum and has openings on either end. The four screw latches on each end require the use of a screwdriver. Lids are flush, requiring some manipulation to lift open; they can be rather cumbersome to open and close properly. The two lids are handy for separating garbage from food.

Appendix B: Sources and Further Reading

Browning, Peter. *Place Names of the Sierra Nevada—From Abbot to Zumwalt.* Berkeley: Wilderness Press, 1986.

Farrand, John Jr. *National Audubon Society Pocket Guide—Familiar Mammals of North America.* New York: Alfred A. Knopf, 1988.

Grater, Russell K. *Discovering Sierra Mammals.* Yosemite Association and Sequoia Natural History Association, Inc., 1978.

Hartesveldt, R. J., Harvey, H. T., Shellhammer, H. S., Stecker, R. E. *Giant Sequoias.* Three Rivers: Sequoia Natural History Association, Inc., 1981.

Johnston, Hank. *They Felled the Redwoods.* Fish Camp: Stauffer Publishing, 1996.

Little, Elbert L. *The Audubon Society Field Guide to North American Trees—Western Region.* New York: Alfred A. Knopf, 1980.

Palmer, John J. *Sequoia–Kings Canyon—The Continuing Story.* Las Vegas: K. C. Publications, Inc., 1990.

Reader's Digest. *North American Wildlife.* Reader's Digest Association, 1982.

Sequoia and Kings Canyon. Handbook 145. Washington, D.C.: Division of Publications National Park Service. U.S. Government Printing Office, 1993.

Spellenberg, Richard. *The Audubon Society Field Guide to North American Wildflowers—Western Region.* New York: Alfred A. Knopf, 1979.

Stocking, Stephen K. and Rockwell, Jack A. *Wildflowers of Sequoia and Kings Canyon National Parks.* Three Rivers: Sequoia Natural History Association, Inc., 1989.

Storer, Tracy I. and Usinger, Robert L. *Sierra Nevada Natural History.* Berkeley: University of California Press, 1963.

Tweed, William C. *Sequoia–Kings Canyon—The Story Behind the Scenery.* Las Vegas: K. C. Publications, Inc., 1980.

Tweed, William C. *Kaweah Remembered—The Story of the Kaweah Colony and the Founding of Sequoia National Park.* Three Rivers: Sequoia Natural History Association, Inc., 1986.

Tweed, William C. and Dilsaver, Lary M. *Sequoia Yesterdays—Centennial Photo History.* Three Rivers: Sequoia Natural History Association, Inc., 1990.

Udvardy, Miklos D. F. *The Audubon Society Field Guide to North American Birds—Western Region.* New York: Alfred A. Knopf, 1977.

Appendix C: Hiker's Checklist

Hiking equipment does not have to be new or fancy (or expensive), but make sure you test everything before you leave home. The list that follows includes items you should have for a day hike.

- ☐ Day pack or fanny pack
- ☐ Drinking water
- ☐ Insect repellent
- ☐ Tissue
- ☐ Toilet paper
- ☐ Toilet trowel
- ☐ Small flashlight or headlamp
- ☐ Extra batteries for flashlight
- ☐ Maps and field guides
- ☐ Compass
- ☐ Watch
- ☐ Sunscreen and lip balm
- ☐ Sunglasses
- ☐ Cap or hat with brim
- ☐ Fleece jacket or woolen sweater
- ☐ Long-sleeve shirt
- ☐ Sturdy hiking boots (waterproof is best)

- ☐ Light, natural-fiber socks
- ☐ Lightweight windproof coat
- ☐ Lightweight hiking shorts or long pants
- ☐ Mittens or gloves
- ☐ Rain gear
- ☐ Small first-aid kit, with bandages and antibacterial ointment for cuts, moleskin for blisters, and aspirin or anti-inflammatory for aches and pains
- ☐ Small scissors or Swiss Army knife with scissors
- ☐ Camera and film
- ☐ Notebook and pencils
- ☐ Binoculars
- ☐ Food: Bring high-energy snacks for lunching along the way. Don't overburden yourself with too much food.

Equipment recommended for overnight trips follows:

- ☐ Tent and waterproof fly
- ☐ Garbage sacks
- ☐ Sleeping bag (20 degrees F or warmer) and stuff sack
- ☐ Zip-locked bags
- ☐ Stuff sacks
- ☐ Sleeping pad
- ☐ Paper towels
- ☐ Cooking pots and pot holder
- ☐ Bear canister
- ☐ More water bottles
- ☐ Full-size pack
- ☐ Cup, bowl, and eating utensils
- ☐ Personal toilet kit
- ☐ Lightweight camp stove and adequate fuel
- ☐ Clothing: In general, strive for natural fibers such as wool, and "earth tones" instead of bright colors. Dig around in the closet for something "dull." Your wilderness partners will appreciate it. Try out clothing before leaving home to make sure everything fits loosely with no chafing. In particular, make sure your boots are broken in, lest they break you on the first day of the hike.
- ☐ Warm hat (e.g. stocking cap)
- ☐ One pair of socks for each day, plus one extra pair
- ☐ A change of underwear for each day
- ☐ Long underwear
- ☐ Water-resistant, windproof coat
- ☐ Extra shirts
- ☐ A sweater and/or insulated vest
- ☐ Sandals or lightweight shoes for wearing in camp
- ☐ Long pants
- ☐ Food: Plan your meals carefully, bringing just enough food, plus some emergency rations. Freeze-dried foods are the lightest and safest in bear country, but expensive and not really necessary. Don't forget hot and cold drinks.

Glossary

Bear boxes: Heavy, metal bear-proof boxes located at many campsites in Sequoia and Kings Canyon National Parks, provided for food storage.

Blaze: A mark carved on or an object nailed to a tree to mark the trail.

Blowdown: A tree toppled by the wind.

Bushwhack: To travel through a brushy area where a trail is overgrown or non-existent.

Cable: A wire strung between two trees on which food bags can be hung out of a bear's reach.

Cross-country: Traveling without a trail.

Duck: A low stack of rocks (usually three) used to mark a trail. Also called a cairn.

Moraine: Rocks and sand carried by a glacier and deposited upon its recession.

Packers' campsite: A campsite used by groups traveling on horseback, usually littered with horse droppings.

Pass: A passage between two mountains.

Prospect: A mineral deposit or mineshaft.

Scree: Coarse, loose, decomposed rock that can be very slippery.

Seasonal creek: A watercourse that runs in spring and early summer but is generally dry by late summer or autumn.

Stringer meadow: A long, thin meadow that follows a seasonal creek or a moist depression in the earth.

Switchback: A sharp-angled turn that reverses the direction of a trail on a steep slope.

Talus: An assemblage of large boulders and blocks of rock.

Tarn: A small glacially carved lake.

Use trail: An informal and unmaintained trail developed by repeated use. Also called a "social" trail.

About the Author

Laurel Scheidt, born and raised in the central San Joaquin Valley, considers the Sierra Nevada her home away from home. She has trekked through the Sequoia and Kings Canyon region for several years, and can name nearly every peak, animal, bird, plant, or wildflower in the area. She also possesses a conviction to protect the environment, and a love of animals and nature. She is well studied in the fields of wildlife and forestry conservation, and is a member of the Audubon Society, the Nature Conservancy, the Sierra Club, and the Cornell Laboratory of Ornithology.

After living most of her 33 years in Fresno, she now resides in Modesto, California, with her husband, Scott. She works as an apprentice ATM technician and as a freelance writer.

—Scott Scheidt